DAUGHTERS OF THE GODDESS

DAUGHTERS OF THE GODDESS
Studies of Healing, Identity, and Empowerment

Wendy Griffin
Editor

ALTAMIRA
PRESS
A Division of
ROWMAN & LITTLEFIELD PUBLISHERS, INC.
Walnut Creek• Lanham • New York • Oxford

ALTAMIRA PRESS
A Division of ROWMAN & LITTLEFIELD PUBLISHERS, INC.

Published in the United States of America
by Rowman & Littlefield Publishers, Inc.
4720 Boston Way, Lanham, Maryland 20706

12 Hid's Copse Road
Cumnor Hill, Oxford OX2 9JJ, England

AltaMira Press
A Division of Rowman & Littlefield Publishers, Inc.
1630 North Main Street, Suite 367
Walnut Creek, CA 94596
http://www.altamirapress.com

Copyright © 2000 by AltaMira Press

British Library Cataloguing in Publication Information Available

Library of Congress Cataloging-in-Publication Data

Daughters of the goddess : studies of healing, identity, and
   empowerment / [edited] by Wendy Griffin.
      p. cm.
   Includes bibliographical references and index.
   ISBN 0-7425-0347-X (cloth : alk. paper)
   ISBN 0-7425-0348-8 (paper : alk. paper)
   1. Women—Religious life. 2. Feminism—Religious aspects.
  3. Goddess religion. I. Griffin, Wendy, 1941–
BL625.7.D37 1999
200'.82—dc21
                                               99-635
                                                 CIP

Typesetting: ibid, northwest
Cover design: Kim Ericsson
Cover Painting: *MedusaTondo* by Gay Griffin Riseborough
               Oil on panel 36" diameter

Printed in the United States of America
The paper used in this publication meets the minimum requirements of American National
Standard for Information Sciences—Permanence of Paper for Printed Library Materials,
ANSI/NISO Z39.48–1992.

ᴆ Contents ᴆ

๑ Acknowledgments ๑

I would like to take this opportunity to thank all the people who contributed to the formation of this book: the chapter authors who received my detailed and sometimes demanding editing comments positively, the outside anonymous reviewer who returned the manuscript in under two weeks with suggestions that showed me how to do what I wanted to do better, the enthusiastic staff at AltaMira Press, and the many Goddess women whose voices and rituals are in these pages. Special thanks gó to Eileen Barker and the Sociology Department at the London School of Economics and Political Science for the invitation to spend my sabbatical there. Without that time for reflection and exploration, the valuable contacts I made, and the data available to me there, this book would not have been possible.

ஐ About the Contributors ஐ

Ruth Rhiannon Barrett is a seasoned Dianic elder priestess, ritualist, educator, musician, and award-winning recording artist of original Goddess-oriented songs. She has been teaching Feminist Craft and ritual-making internationally since her ordination by Zsuzsanna Budapest in 1980 and is religious director of Circle of Aradia in Los Angeles, a local chapter of Re-formed Congregation of the Goddess. In 1997, Ruth was recipient of the L.A.C.E. award for outstanding contributions in the area of Spirituality from the Gay and Lesbian Center in Los Angeles. Ruth teaches and gives concerts internationally, and is currently writing a book on ritual-making for women.

Helen A. Berger is an Associate Professor of Sociology at West Chester University of Pennsylvania. She is the author of A Community of Witches: Contemporary Neo-Paganism and Witchcraft in the United States, *part of the religious studies series from the University of South Carolina, in addition to several articles on Wicca. She became interested in this topic when preparing a series of talks on Witchcraft in New England for the Boston Public Library and initially thought she would do six months of research for the last lecture. Eleven years later, she is still intrigued and learning about this new religious movement.*

Janice Crosby is an Assistant Professor of English at Southern University in Baton Rouge, Louisiana. She was nominated for the 1998 Kathleen Gregory Klein Award for excellence in feminism and popular culture, awarded by the Women's Caucus of the Popular Culture Association/American Culture Association. Her publications include "Spirituality" in Feminist Literary Theory: a Dictionary *(Garland, 1997), and "Difference and Dialogue: Identity in the College Classroom" in the* Louisiana English Journal. *She received her doctorate at LSU, where she held the Alumni Federation Fellowship.*

Vivianne Crowley is a chartered psychologist, a U.K.-registered spiritual healer, and a Lecturer in the psychology of religion at the Department of

Theology and Religious Studies, King's College, University of London. She is the author of seven books and various chapters in edited collections. She has been a Wiccan priestess for 25 years and, with her husband Chris, is the founder of the Wicca Study Group which provides teaching on the Wiccan path. Past Honorary Secretary of Europe's Pagan Federation, she has been active in promoting interfaith dialogue, setting up prison chaplaincy, and organizing annual gatherings for European Wicca.

Cynthia Eller *is an Affiliate Fellow at the Center for the Study of American Religion at Princeton University. Trained in religious studies, she is the author of* Living in the Lap of the Goddess: the Feminist Spirituality Movement in America, *published in 1993 by Crossroad, and is currently writing a book titled* The Myth of Matriarchal Prehistory, *scheduled for publication in 1999 by Beacon Press.*

Tanice Foltz *is an Associate Professor of Sociology at Indiana University Northwest, where she teaches Women's Studies, the Sociology of Women's Spirituality, and Deviance/Criminology. Her interest in alternative healing within new religious movements led her to research a Hawaiian Kahuna's group (*Kahuna Healer, *1994), and then, somewhat hesitantly, a Dianic Witch's coven with co-researcher Wendy Griffin. Later she interviewed feminist spirituality practitioners in the U.S., and more recently spent a sabbatical with Witches and pagans in Australia. Celebrating eleven years since she first participated in a Spring Equinox ritual, she is using the results of these research adventures to provide the context for her new book on Goddess Spirituality and healing.*

Ann-Marie Gallagher *is Subject and Course Leader in Women's Studies at the University of Central Lancashire in Preston, U.K., where she has taught history and women's studies for seven years. An historian by training, she researches and publishes in the areas of cultural history, feminist pedagogy, and women and spirituality. In addition, she guests on national and regional radio, speaking on Witchcraft, paganism, and women's issues, and provides free workshops for women on magic and spirituality at national events. A feminist Witch and mainly solo-worker, Ann-Marie works occasionally with other women engaged in developing their own spiritual paths. She currently lives in Lancashire with her three children and five cats.*

Marilyn Gottschall received her Ph.D. from the Social Ethics Program, School of Religion at the University of Southern California in 1998. She is currently Visiting Assistant Professor in the Religion Department at Whittier College, in Whittier, California. Her research interests include feminist ethics and postmodern culture, and New Religious Movements. She has been a participant and observer within the Goddess Movement for more than ten years.

Susan Greenwood is a Research Fellow at Goldsmiths College, University of London, and lectures in anthropology, shamanism, and women's studies. She is in the process of completing a book on British paganism and is also engaged in research on paganism and environmentalism.

Wendy Griffin's training is in the interdisciplinary social sciences, with an emphasis on the sociology of sex and gender. She is an Associate Professor of Women's Studies at California State University, in Long Beach, California. In 1988, she and Tanice Foltz began to do team research in Goddess Spirituality and were among the first to publish scholarly field research in this area. In addition to her traditional academic work, she is also a published novelist, a long-time community activist, a drummer, koi keeper, and founding member of a women's performance group.

Vajra Ma is a Priestess of the Goddess. Designing and facilitating women's ritual for over a decade, she has integrated Goddess knowledge, feminist consciousness, and experiential body wisdom to forge a new women's mystery tradition. She holds ministerial credentials through the Reformed Congregation of the Goddess and Circle of Aradia. Her background includes Continuum, Tantric, Middle Eastern and Sufi dance; BA and graduate work in Theatre Arts; and professional work as an actor, bodyworker, and teacher. She is author of The Tantric Dance of Feminine Power: Sacred Sensual Moving Meditation for Women and her one-woman show "The Autobiography of a Yoni."

Melissa Raphael considers herself a thea/theologian. She is Senior Lecturer in Religious Studies at Cheltenham and Gloucester College of Higher Education, U.K., teaching in the field of religion and gender. Her research interests include thealogy and Jewish feminist theology. She is the author of Thealogy and Embodiment: The Post-Patriarchal Reconstruction of Female Sacrality *(1996)*, Rudolf Otto and the Concept of Holiness *(1997), and* Introducing Thealogy: Discourse on the Goddess *(1998). She is currently working on a Jewish feminist theo/alogy of the Holocaust. Melissa Raphael is married and has a young daughter.*

Layne Redmond *studied the frame drum with master drummer Glen Velez, performing and recording with him for eight years and playing a primary role in his first five recordings. She has lectured, taught, and performed at universities and music festivals in the United States, Canada, Europe, and Brazil, as well as the Percussive Arts Society International Convention, the meetings of the National Association of Music Therapy, and the annual Healing Sound Colloquium. Her recordings include* Since the Beginning, Being in Rhythm *and an instructional video,* A Sense of Time. *She is the author of* When the Drummers Were Women: A Spiritual History of Rhythm, *Three Rivers Press, 1997.*

❧ Introduction ❧

by Wendy Griffin

When American feminist magazines ran articles on the budding Goddess spirituality movement in the mid- to late '70s and early '80s, the information was largely limited to those feminists who either subscribed to or borrowed copies of these magazines. When newspapers in California began to carry feature stories on Witches and Goddess groups in the late '80s, people attributed it to the reputation California has for attracting eccentrics. In 1992, *Elle*, an upscale American women's magazine, ran a feature titled "Goddesses, Gaia and the Witch Next Door," and more people began to take notice. Even more took note when the extremely popular newsmagazine *Time* ran an article on Witches in the heartland of Wisconsin and reported a possible 100,000 adherents nationwide. Public attention increased dramatically when famed television evangelist Pat Robertson denounced a proposed equal rights amendment to the Iowa state constitution by saying it was part of a "feminist agenda . . . a socialist, anti-family political movement that encourages women to leave their husbands, kill their children, practice witchcraft, destroy capitalism and become lesbians" (Goodman 1992). And during the American visit of Pope John Paul II, when he censured women's involvement in the worship of an earth goddess and the celebration of her myths and symbols, something that conservative American clerics had already identified with Witchcraft (Cowell 1993), Goddess spirituality made newspapers all over the country.

The problem was that few outside the community of Goddess celebrants really knew what Goddess spirituality was. Although thealogical explorations (the*a* meaning *female* divinity) had been published and a considerable number of books and journals by practitioners had appeared that dealt with everything from revisionist history to spell-casting, academic *research* on the practice itself was extremely limited. It still is. In Britain, the story is not that different. Even though some aspects of the movement are older in

13

the United Kingdom, only a few British academics have published in this field.

This is true in spite of clear evidence that the movement has grown and continues to grow at a rapid rate. *Gnosis*, an American journal of mystery traditions, recently reported a population of up to 500,000 in the U.S. Goddess community (Smoley 1998). Academic scholar Ronald Hutton (1998) suggests that the United Kingdom has between 110,000 and 120,000.[1] In some cases, research in this area has been actively discouraged. One colleague was advised not to put an article she had published on Goddess spirituality into her tenure review file because the topic was "questionable." Fundamentalist Christians picketed a presentation she gave on her research. Another was told to take the word "Goddess" out of the title of a book she was working on, as "the Goddess was passe." Funding for doing research into religious and spiritual groups in general is typically hard to come by, unless, of course, these groups are suspected of being dangerous cults threatening to kidnap children or kill themselves and others. Funding for research into Goddess spirituality is especially difficult to obtain. This may be particularly ironic, as most practitioners of Goddess spirituality believe it *is* a serious threat to traditional religions and customs, not in the way that most people expect, but in its insistence on using very different frameworks of meaning and its reconstruction of gender and identity.

Who are the *Daughters of the Goddess*?[2] They are women in the United States and Britain who may call themselves Witches,[3] neo-pagans, pagans, Goddesses, Goddess women, spiritual feminists, Gaians, members of the Fellowship of Isis, Druids, and none of these names. They practice Wicca, Witchcraft, the Craft, Women's Mysteries, and Earth Mysteries; they worship and celebrate in covens, large community rituals, and alone in front of their household or garden altars. They are housewives, students, teachers, secretaries, therapists, graphic designers, accountants, scholars, civil servants, travel agents, truck drivers, and some are even musicians performing in mainstream churches for a living. They are women who use female imagery in exploring and celebrating the Divine, and who see the Goddess as primary and immanent, encompassing all things, as the source and substance of being.[4] They are women involved in a new naming of reality.

In planning *Daughters of the Goddess,* I took into consideration the argument that the boundaries between many academic disciplines are artificial and a fuller understanding of the human experience can be achieved by refusing the limitations inherent in using just one perspective to study a particular cultural phenomenon. The academic researchers in this book come from the fields of anthropology, English, history, psychology, religious studies, sociology, and women's studies. In addition to multidisciplinary perspectives, I have included several academic authors from Britain.[5] Though variations in emphases of belief and practice exist on either side of the ocean, the contemporary story of what has become known as Goddess spirituality has one of its major tap roots in Britain, and to ignore that would be to lose the depth that gives perspective its vision.

Along with the rich offerings to be found in these ethnographies, in-depth interviews, surveys, conversations, written materials, and corresponding analyses, I felt it important to include the voices and visions of a small sample of women who are not academics, but who are actively engaged in teaching a variety of forms of Goddess spirituality. These women are among those who are creating the rituals, conducting the workshops, and authoring the books that practitioners devour and we academics refer to in our writing. They are giving birth to contemporary images of female divinity that resonate with growing numbers of women and men. These three women have been selected because, in very different ways, they teach women to "heal and be healed" and "become the Goddess." Although they are not among the most famous of Goddess teachers, through their workshops, community rituals and writings, these three authors have reached thousands of women.

The inclusion of their voices serves several purposes. In the debate about objective scholarship and privileged knowledge, this can be used as a device to compare epistemologies and raise questions about the nature of understanding. Clearly both their methodology and knowledge base differ dramatically from those of the academic authors, some of whom are also practitioners. In addition, it is important to understand the fluidity of practice that is permissible in Goddess spirituality because it lacks a sacred, authoritative text. In our culture, reverence for the written word, the Word, often leads us to ignore the physical, subjective side of religious or spiritual experience. But Goddess spirituality is radically embodied; to totally ignore experiential knowledge would be to dramatically and unnecessarily limit our understanding of the phenomenon. The voices of this second group of authors provide an alternative way to learn the kinds of things that practitioners learn and what they believe they are capable of experiencing.

The predominant theme weaving in and out of all the chapters is one of wholeness of self and the power to define exactly what that self is. Healing the split between mind and body, feminist and Pagan, sexuality and spirituality, nature and human, and ancient and contemporary understandings of the Numinous is seen as healing the wounds believed to be inflicted by patriarchy. It is this process in Goddess or Gaian spirituality that appears to allow the possibility of creating a post-Christian, post-patriarchal, multifaceted and integrated identity.

Coming from a background in religious studies, Cynthia Eller presents a thorough discussion of the American history of what she calls feminist spirituality in chapter one. She traces how this evolved out of a meeting of radical feminism, Jewish and Christian feminism, and contemporary Witchcraft. Although there were significant early conflicts between feminist and non-feminist Witches, today Witches in the United States practice a religion that has been shaped by feminism, at the same time that Eller maintains the Feminist Spirituality movement is beginning to move away from Witchcraft and create new visions and definitions.

In Britain, and in spite of the commonalties between these groups and communities, significant tensions still exist, in particular between Witchcraft and feminism, according to historian Ann-Marie Gallagher. These tensions arise from the Wiccan belief in gender bipolarity and from feminist Marxist materialism, which sees all spirituality as false consciousness. In her chapter, Gallagher argues that the feminist anti-spirituality stance denies women agency and assumes a dichotomous and masculinist separation of the spiritual and the material. Interviews with Pagan feminists in chapter two reveal a use of language that reflects a different understanding of the concepts of gender and political activism. Pagan feminists may not refer to themselves as political activists, but clearly the women interviewed are actively subversive. Gallagher concludes that thealogy, like feminism itself, is praxis-based and so it, too, is fertile ground for transformational politics.

In part, these kinds of tensions may also be due to the conceptual framework through which we understand Goddess spirituality. In chapter three, Marilyn Gottschall reminds us that examining a phenomenon through a particular lens allows us to see some things more clearly, but often obscures those things that fall outside the boundaries of the lens. Looking at Goddess spirituality as a religion, within its traditional framework of meaning, may limit what we can see. Coming from a background in religious studies, Gottschall suggests we shift our perspective to understand better how the Goddess community approaches the sacred. Rather than a New Religious Movement, her survey research indicates that it is an expression of popular religiosity, which is dynamic, syncretic, and more typical of this time in human history than our traditional understanding of religion can accommodate. And typical of its participants are increasingly idiosyncratic beliefs, practices, and spiritual identities.

Although the spiritual identities may appear idiosyncratic, the new understanding of female identity is not. In chapter four, which I have written, I use an interdisciplinary approach to show how women in Goddess spirituality are crafting a new narrative about what it means to be a woman. By subverting traditional representations of the female body to transgress traditional cultural boundaries and presenting these images in a spiritual or religious context, Gaians create "truth messages" about the nature of women, the nature of social relations in the modern world, and the nature of our relationship with the universe. This form of "writing the body" constructs a new cultural narrative that teaches a different way of experiencing and understanding the world. Through Goddess imagery and ritual, practitioners are attempting to create new integrated interpretations of female identity that are liberating in their wholeness. In the process, I suggest, ideas from Goddess spirituality have already begun to spread and take root in mainstream America.

Thea/theolgian Melissa Raphael warns that sometimes the representations created in Goddess spirituality only appear to be subversive. Chapter five takes a unique approach by examining reactions to the death of Princess Diana to explore the contemporary meaning of the Goddess. The "Cult of Diana" mourned an image of sanctity that was constructed and mediated by patriarchy, which creates an idea of female divinity that women can never hope to achieve. In this manner, it furthers women's sense of spiritual unworthiness. Raphael discusses what it means when women discover the Goddess/self and say that they are the Goddess. She concludes that the Goddess is indivisible from post-patriarchal female becoming, but cautions that there is a danger that women will be bought off by post-Christian, but still patriarchal, visions of female divinity.

The formally recognized role of female religious leadership and authority in Wicca is filled by women who have radically transformed the patriarchal role of mother, according to sociologist Helen Berger in chapter six. The High Priestess uses a reconstructed image of mothering in "ministering" to coven members, and is both nurturant and confrontational. She creates rituals, exercises, and tasks for coven members that facilitate change and growth and which are consistent with the feminist principles Berger found among the American women she interviewed. At the same time that this role serves to empower coven members, it also empowers the High Priestess herself, providing a better sense of who she is and what she values. Although the language used is maternal, this new Mother is seen and experienced as sexual, powerful, loving, and demanding. She is a whole, integrated adult.

The American women interviewed and surveyed by sociologist Tanice Foltz emphasize wholeness of self and the healing that this entails. Chapter seven focuses on women who are recovering alcoholics and who believe that Alcoholics Anonymous fails to meet their recovery needs in very specific areas that necessitate their denying parts of themselves. They have turned to Goddess spirituality to supplement, mediate, and sometimes replace the support they had hoped to find in AA. Through Goddess spirituality, they affirm the totality of their identities and claim their power to heal themselves rather than admit to their powerlessness.

This concept of healing implies that there is a self independent of cultural conditioning to heal. Anthropologist Susan Greenwood finds the claim of feminist Witchcraft to offer women the possibility of finding the true self—the authentic being they would have been had patriarchy not existed—a problematic one. She holds it is a response to the postmodern condition, because any meaning of "self" *must* be a cultural one. Her research on and experience in British Witchcraft in chapter eight illustrate a different approach to healing in the search for a "reclaimed" post-patriarchal identity.

Using demographic data from surveys conducted on Witches in the U.S. and the U.K., psychologist Vivianne Crowley demonstrates that Wicca is about more than "merely" healing participants. The Witch is also a healer. In chapter nine, she discusses the ethics, ideology, and methodology of healing. She points out that there are three components to healing—healing the self, healing the other, and healing the environment—and discusses how these components are thoroughly integrated into Witchcraft. She posits that, for some, Wicca may be primarily a form of therapeutic process, and that, once healed, these people will move on. For others, Witchcraft is a belief and place where ongoing, post-healing self-actualization needs are being met.

Janice Crosby's study of American bellydancers in chapter ten, the last academic chapter, explores a healing of that which separates the human from the Divine. Her on-line and in-class research portrays the dance as a form of spiritual expression grounded in Goddess imagery. In a culture where women are disconnected and alienated from their own bodies, the dancers report that bellydance has a healing power which provides the dancer with a sense of connection with the Numinous. Coming from a perspective that weaves together English and women's studies, Crosby proposes that when Goddess spirituality and bellydance interact, they create a space where the art form is transformed into spiritual expression, and sensuality and play are understood to be meaningful attributes of the Divine.

Ruth Rhiannon Barrett has been helping women to demystify patriarchal teachings and experiences through Goddess ritual for twenty-one years. In chapter eleven, she draws on these experiences to explain how and why she believes effective ritual works. She breaks ritual into its component parts to show how "conscious" ritual is constructed and then demonstrates her teachings with the example of a healing ritual for a rape survivor. She points out that Goddess ritual is an active experience rather than a passive one. It changes the consciousness of those involved by engaging both mind and body. In order for it to be successful, she argues, the whole self must be present and involved. It is this initial wholeness of focus that permits the development of a healed, transformed and empowered self.

Like Crosby, Vajra Ma believes that sacred dance is a tool for healing and empowerment. Witch, priestess, and founder of a Women's Mystery School, she combines Goddess studies, feminist spirituality, and Tantric Dance in her teachings. In chapter twelve, she describes how her students learn what she calls body energetics. This technique involves an attunement to subtle body sensations through breath, sound, and movement that she believes allows one to directly experience or know the Divine. She writes that, by focusing on body energetics and participating in a female shamanic group, students learn to break through patriarchal conditioning and change their consciousness. Like the women in Crosby's chapter, these women experience dance as prayer. In addition, Vajra Ma teaches them that it is a source of knowledge that holds the potential to integrate the self.

Layne Redmond has done considerable research on ancient priestesses who used the frame drum as a powerful sacred tool. An internationally known drummer herself, Redmond argues that women played this instrument for over three thousand years to transform, heal, and connect individuals and communities to the Divine. The thirteenth and last chapter delves into the significance and technology of rhythm and into women's role as transmitters of the sacred. Redmond also tells how she travels the Goddess path today, teaching women to drum, to reclaim their rhythms, and to reconnect with the natural world. She believes that this enables women to remember who we were and to see what we can become.

In 1994, Witches in Bristol, England, declared that patriarchy was dead. It may indeed be dying, and certainly these chapters suggest significant social revisioning is taking place in both the U.K. and U.S., an example of what New Religious Movements scholar Wade Clark Roof calls, "seethings of the spirit" (1998:12). Of course, even if the life and spirit have departed from patriarchal frameworks of meaning, the body has not finished thrashing about in its death throes. But as the old reality begins to lose its hold, a new reality is taking shape.

The process reminds me of a weekend I spent with Witches several years ago camping in the mountains outside Los Angeles. We hiked to a small spring that bubbled out at the foot of a granite boulder. The large rock was vaguely human-like in shape. One woman climbed to the top of it and placed there a wreath she had woven out of yellow wildflowers. Another spontaneously took red berries and tucked them into cracks and crevices in the stone. Over the weekend, individual women would follow the trail to the spring, many adding leaves, flowers, pine cones, and other offerings. With each addition, the shape in the rock became clearer, until it was no longer just a boulder. Pine needles outlined the curve of an arm, wild sage drew the eye to what could have been a pregnant belly, yellow flowers to flowing hair. With each visit, each offering, the Goddess of the Spring emerged from the rock and became more visible, more real.

With each woman, each ritual today, Goddess spirituality contributes to the new reality that is taking form. This book explores the shaping.

Notes

[1] Census figures for the U.S. suggest a current population of approximately 270,540,000 (http:www.census.gov/cgi-bin/popclock). For the U.K., the latest figures amount to 58,660,000 (http://www.statistics.gov.uk/stats/ukfigs/pop/htm/). Given both, these numbers reflect relatively equal percentages.

[2] Although male practitioners of Goddess spirituality also exist, female participants vastly outnumber male, especially in the U.S.

[3] Throughout this book, I have capitalized the word Witch as I would Christian, the word Witchcraft, Wicca, or Craft as I would Judaism, the word Gaian as I would Muslim.

[4] While some women and men also acknowledge a male divinity, the Goddess is always primary.

[5] British and American ranking systems for academia differ. In the United States, we have lecturers, assistant professors, associate professors and professors. In Britain, there are lecturers, senior lecturers, principal lecturers, and professors, often with only one professor to a department. To complicate things even further, British titles may vary according to the university or college system, making an accurate comparison problematic.

Works Cited

Clark, Wade Roof. 1998. Religious borderlands: challenges for future study. *Journal for the Scientific Study of Religion*. Vol. 37, No. 1, March. Pages 1–14.

Cowell, Alan. 1993. Pope issues censure of 'nature worship' by some feminists. *The New York Times*. July 5. Pages 1,4,6.

Goodman, Ellen. 1992. The ERA is back—older, wiser and playing to win. *The Los Angeles Times*. October 20.

Hutton, Ronald. 1998. Personal Communication, September 2.

Smoley, Richard. 1998. The old religion. *Gnosis*. No. 48, Summer. Pages 12–14.

PART ONE – THE RESEARCH

ᔑᘓ 1 ᔑᘓ

The Roots of Feminist Spirituality[1]

by Cynthia Eller

In only thirty years, mainly in the United States but increasingly in Europe and the broader English-speaking world, a vibrant religious subculture for women has been created virtually from scratch. Sharing ground with other alternative religions—especially neopaganism and New Age spiritualities—the feminist spirituality movement nevertheless breaks ground of its own, insistently privileging (rather than marginalizing or tokenizing) femaleness.

This feat of religious innovation can be credited to the intermingling of three social trends emerging in the late 1960s and early 1970s: radical (secular) feminism; Jewish and Christian feminism; and neopaganism. Radical feminism gave rise to concerns with religion and spirituality for some women whose experiences with feminism were particularly all-encompassing. Jewish and Christian feminism went so far beyond the bounds of orthodoxy in some quarters that a new spirituality became necessary. These two social trends came from outside the domain of alternative religions where feminist spirituality would eventually make its home. But fortuitously, there was already an alternative religious presence in America that seemed nearly tailor-made for spiritual feminists' needs: neopaganism. Recently imported from Britain (though there were parallel, independent occult movements in the United States), neopaganism was not at the outset an explicitly feminist religion. But neopaganism quickly attracted women who later became feminists, and it eventually attracted feminists outright. Though feminist spirituality is nothing if not syncretistic—borrowing elements from religions and spiritualities worldwide—its earliest and still most important base is American neopaganism.

SECULAR FEMINISM

For some women in the late 1970s, the journey from secular feminism to feminist spirituality was direct and simple: feminism precipitated such deep and comprehensive changes in consciousness that it already functioned as spirituality. A sufficient change in the quantity and scope of secular feminism became a qualitative change to religious feminism. This pattern of entry into spirituality through radical feminism was particularly marked in the lesbian community, where for many women religion came as an unexpected but natural outgrowth of their experiments in radical feminism. One of these experiments of the 1970s was *Womanspirit*, a magazine published by a small collective in Oregon from 1974 to 1984 that served as a weathervane for the early feminist spirituality movement. Though not limited to lesbian separatists, it was from the lesbian community that the greatest energy for *Womanspirit* came. That spirituality was for these women an acquired language rather than a mother tongue is perhaps evident in the fact that, according to Carol Christ, early contributors to *Womanspirit* hesitated to speak of Goddess (1987:49).

For other women of the same era, feminism was not tantamount to a religious conversion experience, and did not naturally present itself as having spiritual depths. But a feminist perspective that began by asking why little girls had to wear pink and big girls had to wear high heels segued naturally into one that asked why God was a man and women's religious experiences went unnoticed. Jean Mountaingrove, one of the founders of *Womanspirit*, describes the process in this way:

> Feminism tells us to trust ourselves. So feminists began experiencing something. We began to believe that, yes indeed, we were discriminated against on the job; we began to see that motherhood was not all it was advertised to be. We began to trust our own feelings, we began to believe in our own orgasms. These were the first things. Now we are beginning to have spiritual experiences and, for the first time in thousands of years, we trust it. (Adler 1979:178)

This belief that feminist spirituality is the natural outcome of feminist questioning has been reified into what might be called the movement's "myth of origins." For when spiritual feminists turn to the topic of the movement's beginnings, they are inclined to talk about consciousness-raising as the seedbed from which feminist spirituality sprang. Consciousness-raising (CR) groups were active in the late 1960s and early 1970s, and were a place where many women first began to think through what being a woman in American culture entailed. The intention, captured in the phrase "consciousness-raising," was to wake women up to an appreciation of their oppression as women and to recruit them for the feminist movement. Early CR groups came together spontaneously, and were first called "rap sessions" or "bitch sessions," only later (around 1970) defining themselves as consciousness-raising groups. By 1972, the National Organization for Women (NOW) along with CR's pioneers, the New York Radical Feminists, took a hand in CR, helping groups to organize, providing a prepared list of discussion topics, and introducing new groups to the CR format. In 1973, probably the height of CR, an estimated 100,000 women in the United States belonged to CR groups (Shreve 1989:5–6, 9–14).

The basic format of CR was to select a discussion topic for the evening, and with the five to fifteen women present sitting in a circle, each would take turns speaking about the topic. Each woman was to be allowed to talk without interruption, and without criticism or praise from the other women, in an effort to ensure that all felt free to say whatever was on their minds. Oftentimes women discovered that experiences they had believed to be unique to them were shared by many other women, and together they began to explore the reasons why. Some of the experiences women related were spiritual experiences, and one arena that came to be seen as male-defined was established religion.

It is surely true that some women began a process of questioning in CR whose end result was a denunciation of established religions and an attempt to create a religion for women. Yet the place of CR in feminist spirituality's self-understanding has become greater than the experiences of these few women (who do not make up the majority of women in the feminist spirituality movement). Now when spiritual feminists refer to CR, they see it not just as a type of discussion group, but as a ritual group, the natural predecessor of today's feminist spirituality groups. As Carol Christ puts it, "consciousness raising can be seen as a ritual in which stories are shared and sisterhood is affirmed" (1980:127). The tendency to enshrine CR as the birthplace of feminist spirituality reaches its apogee in a casual reference made by Jade, founder of the Re-formed Congregation of the Goddess. In a discussion of women's exploration of the history of medieval witchcraft, she remarks, "Back in the consciousness-raising groups, which by now had turned into spirituality groups . . ." (1991:11), seeming to indicate that the transition from CR to feminist spirituality was smooth, uncontested, and complete.

That spiritual feminists should hearken back to CR as their birthplace reveals much about how they perceive themselves and their movement. They could have seized upon a different homeland—for instance, feminist political demonstrations or the countercultural movements of the 1960s—but they did not, and their choice of CR is significant. CR was a place where women looked into themselves, into their personal lives, feelings, and reactions, to discover important truths about the status of women generally and the nature of a society that worked to exclude and belittle them. The move was inward, particularistic, but the discoveries were broad, even universal. In choosing CR to encapsulate a myth of their origins, spiritual feminists are seeing in CR a pattern that is essentially that of the religious quest: an inner journey, shared with other seekers, that reveals insights of cosmic importance reaching far beyond the bounds of any one individual's experience.

One final path secular feminists took into feminist religion was somewhat less direct, though it brought them to a similar place as those women who found feminism itself to be a religion, or at least a frame of reference that eventually led to matters of religious importance. This group of women took an excursion through political feminism that proved unsatisfying to them, and they turned to spiritual feminism in the hope of finding something better. Their primary disappointment with political feminism was that it did not seem to provide a position from which they could make broader criticisms of male-dominated society or from which they could create real alternatives. These women did not just want the freedom to do what men had always done (though they generally wanted that, too); they also wanted the freedom to do what women had always done, but to see it valued differently. Further, they wanted not just to use traditional political means for reaching these ends, but to utilize the full range of their capabilities to live in new, self-realized ways as women, and to offer other women the cultural space to do the same.

This branch of the women's movement is sometimes called "cultural feminism," and though the term has taken on pejorative meaning for many, it remains a useful term for distinguishing the quest for political equality and gender-blindness from the effort to incorporate traditionally female values into our common life (Kimball 1980:2–29). These two patterns of feminism are not mutually exclusive, but feminist spirituality encourages attention to the latter, and is frequently less interested in the former, even though it may share these goals as well.

JEWISH AND CHRISTIAN FEMINISM

Some women did not need to be led or driven to religious concerns by the strength of their feminism; their first language was religious, and they were already enmeshed in a religious world. These women were active in established religions when the feminist movement came along, and noticing and criticizing the male slant of these religions was an obvious focus for them. They were merely discovering the sexism in their own backyard—which is where secular feminism was encouraging them to look for it anyway. The first wave of feminism had provided important critiques of male-dominated religion, so religious feminists had foresisters to whom they could appeal. Elizabeth Cady Stanton and friends wrote a feminist exegesis of the Bible in the late 1890s under the title *The Woman's Bible*; in 1893, Matilda Joslyn Gage's *Woman, Church, and State* provided an analysis of how Judaism and Christianity worked to oppress women. Infused with the vitality of a growing women's movement, feminists in traditional religions updated and expanded on this work, and their attacks on sexism gradually gained force and momentum.

Initial feminist onslaughts against established religions demanded specific reforms: Women should be admitted into the rabbinate, priesthood, or ministry; hymns and prayer books should use language that included women. But increasingly, larger targets emerged: Biblical texts were found to be sexist, religious ethics were seen to fit men's experience and men's interests and not those of women. Eventually, feminists in established religions took on the Big Man himself, the God who was described and invoked in almost exclusively male terms, in spite of theological apologetics that insisted on his ultimate lack of gender. Many feminists felt a sufficiently deep attachment to established religions that they remained within them to work for change. But others came to believe that traditional religions were so laced with patriarchal ideology that the surgery necessary to remove it would end up killing the patient, and, as Mary Daly puts it, they "graduated" from Christianity and religious Judaism (King 1989).

Mary Daly, a brilliant Catholic theologian and an ardent feminist, led the way for many women to matriculate into feminist spirituality after long years as the perennial freshmen of the established religions. In 1971, Daly was invited to be the first woman preacher in Harvard Memorial Church. Her sermon topic was "The Women's Movement: An Exodus Community." She ended her sermon by walking out of the church in protest against it, and inviting the other women present to do likewise. She defended this exodus in her sermon, saying: "We cannot really belong to institutional religion as it exists. It isn't good enough to be token preachers. . . . Singing sexist hymns, praying to a male god breaks our spirit, makes us less than human. The crushing weight of this tradition, of this power structure, tells us that *we do not even exist*" (King 1989:70). In an article published in *Commonweal* that same year, Daly advised: "The women's movement will present a growing threat to patriarchal religion less by attacking it than by simply leaving it behind. Few of the leaders in the [women's] movement evince an interest in institutional religion, having recognized it as an instrument of their betrayal" (Daly 1979:57).

This feminist rejection of established religions saw women's oppression in patriarchal religion occurring along many axes—theological, biblical, institutional, and so on—and all of these came in for feminist criticism. But the entire interlocking system of oppressions was finally summed up in a single metaphor: the maleness of God. Mary Daly explains: "If God in 'his' heaven is a father ruling 'his' people, then it is in the 'nature' of things and according to divine plan and the order of the universe that society be male-dominated" (1973:13). It was a matter of some consensus among religious feminists that exclusively male language for God was not in the best interests of women. But those feminists who came to believe that the maleness of God mandated the subordination of women took this one step further. In pointing the finger back at the god of established religions, these feminists said that he was not *a* cause of women's oppression, but *the* cause: the "ultimate prop," the "underlying rationale" (Starhawk 1982:72; Stone 1976:xi). This is in part a social analysis of how the patriarchy operates, but for most of these women, it was also a larger comment on how the world operates. It was not only that a male god happens to be the linchpin of this patriarchal social system, but that religion is always and inevitably the distilled essence of what a culture holds valuable.

This being the case, what is a feminist to do? Well, if male gods support male power, women must stop worshipping male gods. If the patriarchy is built on the foundation of patriarchal religion, male dominance will not be eroded until the foundation is razed. But more than this, a nonpatriarchal society cannot exist until a foundation has been prepared for it, a foundation that must of necessity be religious. This is the true source of the surge of religious feminists into the feminist spirituality movement. Some feminists gave up on traditional religions when they decided they were too sexist to be tolerated or reformed, but were not inspired to sashay into the world of alternative religions. They were just tired of religion altogether. But for women who came to believe that religion is necessarily a culture's building blocks, the repertoire on which it can play variations but no new themes, religion could not be abandoned. It had to be transformed.

NEOPAGANISM AND FEMINISM

When feminists made their way toward an alternative religion for women, their initial point of contact was with neopaganism or Witchcraft. Feminist spirituality's contact with neopaganism has left its mark on every aspect of feminist spirituality: its thealogy, ritual, and social organization. Indeed, many spiritual feminists happily call themselves neopagans or Witches, though their particular feminist adaptations of neopaganism set them apart from the mainstream of that religion. Feminist spirituality and mainstream neopaganism coexist and overlap, usually (but not always) quite happily, but they are not the same thing.

Neopaganism in America is a movement organized (or not) in much the same way as feminist spirituality. Small groups of practitioners join together on a regular basis, though probably as many practice alone. There are large festivals and retreats, magazines and newsletters, bookstores and occult supply shops, and one effort at an umbrella organization (the Covenant of the Goddess) which serves as a clearinghouse of information and a badge of respectability (and tax-exempt status) for the neopagan community, particularly those who define themselves as Witches. As with feminist spirituality, variety is the order of the day, and there are numerous schools of thought and types of practice available for the interested seeker, and plenty of interaction between neopaganism and other types of alternative spirituality. The number of people who are affiliated with neopaganism is difficult to estimate, since there is nothing remotely like an official membership roll. However, in the early 1990s, in an attempt to quantify the movement, Aidan Kelly extrapolated from book sales, mailing lists, and festival attendance to come up with a figure of somewhere between 50,000 to 100,000 "serious adherents" of neopaganism (Kelly 1993; Denfeld 1995:299).

Neopagans believe they are reviving (and sometimes creating anew) ancient nature religions. They usually trace their genealogy to Europe, and sometimes even more narrowly to Britain. Many call their religion "Witchcraft" as well as paganism, since they believe that when paganism was forced underground by the Christian church, it was passed in secret from parent to child (or believer to believer) as Witchcraft.[2] In spite of its insistence that it dates to ancient times, neopaganism also has a more recent history, dating to 1954, when Gerald Gardner published *Witchcraft Today*. Gardner was a British folklorist, nudist, and occultist, who after his retirement in 1936 joined an occult society with connections to the Rosicrucians and Theosophists. He says that he was initiated into Wicca (or Witchcraft) by an old woman, Dorothy Clutterbuck, in 1939, she having herself been initiated by someone else in a line reaching back, presumably, to the Middle Ages if not further. Gardner wrote one book on Witchcraft under a pen name, and after the last of the Witchcraft Acts were repealed in Britain in 1951, he wrote two more books in his own name, *Witchcraft Today* and *The Meaning of Witchcraft*. The Witchcraft he described included the worship of a goddess and a god, the officiation of a priestess, and communal rituals involving dancing, nudity, chanting, and meditation that took place on the solstices, equinoxes, and the four cross-quarter days that fall between them (Adler 1979:60–66, 80–84; Purkiss 1996:37–88). All these forms are still common among neopagans today. Gardner himself initiated many individuals into a neopagan practice that came to be called "Gardnerian Witchcraft" after him. Some of Gardner's apprentices split from him to create different Witchcraft "traditions," and other sects of Witchcraft sprang up with little connection to Gardner, giving rise to the tremendous variety found in modern neopaganism.

Gardner is what many neopagans would call "a hereditary Witch," claiming to have fallen heir to a tradition of Witchcraft that existed prior to the twentieth century. Those who say they are hereditary Witches are rare; some practitioners note that their families passed along interesting bits of folklore, but nothing akin to the comprehensive religion that Gardnerian Witchcraft purports to be. But especially in its early years, hereditary Witchcraft was very important to neopagans as proof that the religion they practiced had a real tradition behind it. Wiccan lineages and ancient practices are of less and less importance nowadays, as neopagans feel more secure in the religions they have created (or maybe only more certain that their hereditary claims will be disproved). Modern Witches accept and sometimes even revel in the novelty of what they create. Still, the lure of the ancient calls to them. Gwydion Pendderwen does an excellent job of summing up how most neopagans feel about the newness of their religion:

> What has come down [from the Old Religion, or paganism] is so minimal, it could be thrown out without missing it. Many groups have received nothing through apostolic succession and do not miss it. Objectively, there's very little that has gone from ancient to modern in direct succession. But subjectively, an awful lot is ancient. It is drawn from ancient materials. It represents archetypal patterns. (Adler 1979:88)

Neopagans (who sometimes refer to themselves simply as pagans) agree on little, and count it as one of the advantages of their chosen religion that they do not have to agree. Still, many neopagans have tried to define just what holds them together, and the thing they mention most consistently is nature worship. Selena Fox, a priestess who heads up Circle Sanctuary, a pagan retreat center in rural Wisconsin, offers this description of Wicca:

> The Wiccan religion is a nature religion with roots that go back to pre-Christian Europe. It's a religion that focuses on communing with the divine through nature. . . . Wiccans worship the "life force" in all people and animals, revere nature and harm no one. We believe that all of life is sacred and we see ourselves as part of a community of life forms on the planet. (Lux 1988)

What Fox doesn't mention is that most neopagans also worship a goddess. This is often coupled with worship of a god, and their gender polarity is frequently seen as expressing an important truth about the cosmos. But following Gardner, the Goddess is usually given some kind of primacy,[3] and in some neopagan circles women's presence is required for rituals to occur.

The appeal of neopaganism to feminists searching for religious alternatives must have been tremendous: Here were people already worshipping a goddess, naming women as priestesses, and talking about "the feminine." There were no elaborate rites of entry, if one wished to avoid them; groups were small and intimate, leaving ample space for individual experience; and in a religion with no central headquarters, religious hierarchies were unlikely to get in the way. But well before feminists discovered neopaganism en masse, the word *witch* entered the feminist vocabulary in other, highly politicized terms. In New York on Halloween of 1968, a collective of women named themselves WITCH, an acronym standing for "Women's International Terrorist Conspiracy from Hell." This first group was followed by others across the United States, all of which used the same acronym, but different names to indicate the targets of their rage: "Women Infuriated at Taking Care of Hoodlums," "Women Incensed at Telephone Company Harassment," "Women Indentured to Traveler's [insurance company] Corporate Hell," and so on. These first feminist Witches did not gather to worship nature, but to crush the patriarchy, and to do so in witty, flamboyant, and theatrical ways. They engineered various political actions, drawing on the witch theme. Though never pretending to be a spiritual group, and probably unaware of the neopagan revival in America, WITCH anticipated several of the motifs of the feminist spirituality movement that was to follow upon the meeting of feminism and neopaganism. In its manifesto, WITCH justified its existence by citing its political mission ("witches and gypsies were the original guerrillas and resistance fighters against oppression"); it posited a long-dead golden age ("the oldest culture of all . . . a truly cooperative society"); named nature as one of the patriarchy's primary victims (along with human society); and rested its social analysis on the single cornerstone of male domination ("the Imperialist Phallic Society"). It advocated creativity and independence, and exulted in the innovative use of all manner of media to communicate personal and political views (Morgan 1970:538–39, 1977:77). But the most significant aspect of WITCH was its choice of central symbol: the witch. By choosing this symbol, feminists were identifying themselves with everything women were taught not to be: ugly, aggressive, independent, and malicious. Feminists took this symbol and molded it—not into the fairy tale "good witch," but into a symbol of female power, knowledge, independence, and martyrdom.

This latter association with Witchcraft, that of martyrdom, was particularly important to early feminists. Mary Daly in her 1973 book *Beyond God the Father*, and Andrea Dworkin in 1974 with *Woman Hating*, laid the groundwork for a feminist martyrology by researching the witch persecutions of the Middle Ages and labeling them "gynocide," the purposeful murder of women. This theme was further developed in Daly's 1978 work *Gyn/Ecology*, in which the witch burnings were portrayed as an instance of the patriarchal "Sado-Ritual Syndrome," a pattern of the abuse of women that Daly locates cross-culturally and trans-historically. This identification of women with witchcraft was not an explicitly religious one. Women were not named witches because they worshipped a goddess in circles in the woods or because they made herbal charms to encourage prophetic dreaming. Women were named witches because they refused to submit to demeaning and limiting roles, even knowing that this rebellion might literally cost them their lives.

Witchcraft was fast becoming a feminist symbol, even a religiously charged one, dealing as it did with ultimate commitment and ultimate value. But it was a symbol without a practice. It still remained for someone to lower the drawbridge and let religious neopaganism out and feminists in. The first to take on this task was Zsuzsanna Budapest, the closest thing feminist spirituality has to a founder. Budapest grew up in Hungary and took her city's name as her own when as a teenager she left for the West to escape the failing Hungarian revolution. Later, after immigrating to the United

States and leaving her marriage, she moved to Los Angeles and became very active in the women's movement: organizing protests, attending meetings, helping to form an anti-rape squad. But, like others, she came to believe that the women's movement needed a women's religion, and she proposed to give it one. In this, Budapest did not come without resources: She claimed to be the heir of a Witchcraft tradition at least eight hundred years old, inherited from her mother, Masika Szilagyi. According to Budapest, Masika was initiated into Witchcraft by Victoria, a household servant, who in addition to teaching Masika psychic skills, took her into the woods at night to meet with groups of Witches who invoked the Goddess, sang of ancient shamans, and spat into the fire. Masika communed with the dead in her dreams, and could speak ancient Egyptian while in a trance, a talent Budapest attributes to Masika's previous incarnation as a priestess of Hathor in ancient Egypt (Kimball 1980:238; Adler 1979:76–77). In her *Holy Book of Women's Mysteries*, Budapest includes materials she received from her mother, including her "book of superstitions," "book of dreams," "book of cures," and "book of sorrows." They are a treasure trove of Eastern European folk wisdom, including such gems as: "if a bird shits on you, you will have good luck all that day if you don't wipe it off until the following day"; "if you bang your elbow into a corner, an unexpected visitor will soon arrive"; and "if you are chased by wild animals in your dreams, it simply means you ate too much dinner" (1989:258–68).

If these provided the seeds for Budapest's women's religion, the sprouting and blossoming were strictly her doing, and that of her feminist sisters. Budapest's experiments in feminist Witchcraft began in 1971, when she and a few friends celebrated the winter solstice together. They named themselves the Susan B. Anthony Coven No. 1, to stress their commitment to feminism—and, it would seem, to express their hope that others would follow in their footsteps, adding covens numbers 2, 3, 4, et seq. And others did follow, though with names of their own: the Amelia Earhart Coven in New York, the Elizabeth Gould Davis Coven in Florida, the Sojourner Truth Coven in the Catskills, the Jane Addams Coven in Chicago, and the Elizabeth Cady Stanton Coven in Orange County, California (Adler 1979:119). The Susan B. Anthony Coven itself grew rapidly, by its founders' reports, from the six women who met at the 1971 winter solstice, to seven hundred initiated members just nine years later

(Budapest 1979:82). Women came and went, and there were never seven hundred women meeting at one time, but it is reported that Budapest led rituals in the 1970s where attendance was well over one hundred (Rhiannon 1983).

Though Zsuzsanna Budapest was a ground-breaking figure in the feminist move to neopaganism, she was not alone. In addition to the women working with her, there were other women across the country building bridges between feminism and paganism: some by reaching out to existing Wiccan groups in their areas, some by radicalizing the covens of which they were already members, some by creating new groups with new traditions. By the mid-1970s, resources were beginning to become available in the women's community, and feminists were able to invent their religion secure in the knowledge that there was a groundswell of feminist energy behind them. Interest in witchcraft as women's persecution history broadened into inquiry into ancient goddess worship. The publication of Merlin Stone's *When God Was a Woman* in 1976, a study of representations of prehistoric goddesses woven together with a story of their overthrow in historical times, gave the feminist Wicca movement credibility in new quarters, and inspired more women to search out the supposed surviving remnants of ancient goddess worship in neopaganism. Feminist imagery and politics was rapidly becoming feminist spirituality, as women went beyond talking about witches and goddesses as symbols of female power, and started to become them and worship them.

Yet the meeting of feminists and neopagans was not one big happy family reunion, with everyone rushing deliriously into each other's arms. The neopagan movement was small, and feminists entered in numbers large enough to make a real impact. Moreover, they did not usually enter humbly and meekly, asking if they might please be initiated into the wise ways of the Witches. Quite the contrary, they flung open the doors, squared their shoulders, and swaggered in, ready to rearrange the furniture. And in spite of substantial areas of shared interest, there were real differences between the newly anointed feminist Witches and neopagans of older vintage.

The first point of conflict was that feminists by and large had no interest in sharing their circles with men, and precious little interest in worshipping a god of any sort. With their palate not yet conditioned to savor the new tastes of "traditional" neopaganism, they often had little patience for the measured pageantry and role-playing that characterized some neopagan rituals or for the ency-clopedic lists of greater and lesser divinities and spirits. They wanted to worship a Goddess—a big one, bigger than the God of patriar-chy—and they wanted to worship themselves through her. For many neopagans, this was anathema. Polytheism and gender duality were considered essential parts of Witchcraft: If true magic were to hap-pen, both male and female deities had to be invoked, and according to some, both women and men had to be present, fulfilling their gender-prescribed tasks. A further conflict was that most neopagans valued secrecy, partly out of fear of persecution, but also out of a love of the concept of hidden lore, of mystical truths that could only be revealed to the initiated few. Feminist Witches, in contrast, tended to be more evangelical, wanting to get the good word out to their sisters. Far from insisting on long periods of training and gradual initiation into higher mysteries, feminist Witches hearkened back to a phrase from the WITCH manifesto: "You are a Witch by being female . . ." They encouraged one another to form covens of the utterly inexperienced, to make things up as they went along, and to publish accounts of what worked for them so that others could draw on their experience (Adler 1979:171–222).

The downside of the feminist/neopagan combination notwith-standing, overall the combination has proved to be a productive one. The success of the relationship owes much to Starhawk, a Witch, feminist, and widely read pagan author. Starhawk found Witchcraft and feminism around the same time, and though she saw them as having a real compatibility, she was not specifically drawn into one as the result of her interest in the other, as many women were. Having already been exposed to neopaganism, she was introduced to femi-nist Witchcraft in the early 1970s by Zsuzsanna Budapest (Budapest 1989:xiv). Starhawk's covens are not all separatist (men are allowed to participate and be initiated), but her writings are insistently femi-nist, and it is clear that she regards Witchcraft's attitude toward women and the female to be among its greatest strengths. In many ways, Starhawk has served as a translator and mediator between feminists and neopaganism: She has worked with gender polarity, but evolved away from it; she has developed convincing thealogical justifications for conceiving of Goddess as both monotheistic and polytheistic; she has carved out a central, indisputable place for women without excluding men; and she has praised flexibility and creativity while upholding the value of things taken to be tradition- ally pagan.

Today there is considerably less friction in the United States be- tween feminist Witchcraft and the broader neopagan movement than there was initially. There are several reasons for this, one of which is that over the past twenty years of cohabitation, feminist Witches have become acculturated to the neopagan world. Things that they initially found odd or off-putting—ceremonial tools and language, polytheism, male deities—have become familiar, even beloved to them, and in some cases have been incorporated into their practice. And for neopagans, feminists are no longer angry alien infiltrators in a settled world of happy, naked, dancing nature-worshipers; they have become a part of the scenery. Finally, controversy between the two parties has lessened in part because the feminists won their right to the Goddess. By sheer force of numbers and enthusiasm, their success drowned out all but the most hardened opposition. Neopaganism flourishes today, perhaps more feminist and less hi- erarchical in flavor than it was before, and feminist Witchcraft flour- ishes alongside and to some extent within it (Jade 1991:64).

In the feminist spirituality movement today, there is a subtle trend away from identifying oneself as a Witch. Partly this is a tran- sition into a more free-form type of spirituality precipitated by a growing conviction on the part of feminists that what they are doing counts as religion in its own right, without the added status con- ferred by an affiliation with neopaganism. As Anne Carson notes in the preface to her bibliography on feminist spirituality, "As the 1980s progress there seems to be less of an interest in Witchcraft per se among feminists, at least in terms of ritual practice, as we begin to leave behind one traditional structure in order to create our own visions and philosophies" (Carson 1986:9). Witchcraft has acted as a launching pad for a spiritual movement that is now far more di- verse, reaching far beyond neopaganism, into Native American religions, other world religions, New Age practices, and even— sporadically—Jewish and Christian feminism.

Notes

[1] This chapter appeared in an earlier form in *Living in the Lap of the Goddess: The Feminist Spirituality Movement in America*, by Cynthia Eller, published by Crossroads Press in 1993, and appears in this book with the permission of the publisher.

[2] Most neopagans believe that the witchcraft persecuted by the Christian church in sixteenth- and seventeenth-century Europe was in fact this underground pre-Christian religion. Far from having the malicious intent associated with medieval witches, modern Witches say that they—like their persecuted predecessors—are bending unseen forces for the good of all. Time and again they stress that they are not Satanists. At a workshop on "Feminist Wicca Philosophy" (Feminist Spiritual Community retreat, Maine, June 1990), Delores Cole gave a fairly typical disclaimer, saying that one cannot have Satanism without Christianity, that "Satanism is the death side of Christianity," and thus bears no relation to paganism.

[3] Some neopagans worship no deities or a Goddess alone, but I have never encountered any who worship only a male god.

Works Cited

Adler, Margot. 1979. *Drawing Down the Moon*. Boston: Beacon.

Budapest, Zsuzsanna. 1979. *The Holy Book of Women's Mysteries, vol. 1*. Oakland, CA: Susan B. Anthony Coven No. 1.

———. 1989. *The Holy Book of Women's Mysteries*. Berkeley: Wingbow.

Carson, Anne. 1986. *Feminist Spirituality and the Feminine Divine*. Trumansburg, NY: Crossing.

Christ, Carol P. 1980. *Diving Deep and Surfacing*. Boston: Beacon.

———. 1987. *Laughter of Aphrodite*. San Francisco: Harper and Row.

Daly, Mary. 1973. *Beyond God the Father*. Boston: Beacon.

———. 1979. After the Death of God the Father: Women's Liberation and the Transformation of Christian Consciousness. In *Womanspirit Rising: A Feminist Reader in Religion*. Ed. Carol P. Christ and Judith Plaskow. San Francisco: Harper and Row. Pages 53–62.

Denfeld, Rene. 1995. *The New Victorians*. New York: Warner.

Jade. 1991. *To Know*. Oak Park, IL: Delphi.

Kelly, Aidan. 1993. "An update on neopagan Witchcraft in America." In *Perspectives on the New Age*. Edited by James Lewis. Albany: State University of New York.

Kimball, Gayle, editor. 1980. *Women's Culture*. Metuchen, NJ: Scarecrow.

King, Ursula. 1989. *Women and Spirituality*. New York: New Amsterdam.

Lux, Anne Marie. 1988. "Witches nothing to be scared of." *Sunday Gazette* (Janesville, WI), October 30.

Morgan, Robin. 1970. *Sisterhood is Powerful*. New York: Random House.
———. 1977. *Going Too Far*. New York: Random House.
Purkiss, Diane. 1996. *The Witch in History*. New York: Routledge.
Rhiannon. 1983. Interview with author.
Shreve, Anita. 1989. *Women Together, Women Alone*. New York: Fawcett Columbine.
Starhawk. 1982. *Dreaming the Dark: Magic, Sex, and Politics*. Boston: Beacon.
Stone, Merlin. 1976. *When God Was a Woman*. New York: Harcourt, Brace, Jovanovich.

≈ **2** ≈

Woven Apart and Weaving Together

Conflict and Mutuality in Feminist and Pagan Communities in Britain

by Ann-Marie Gallagher

But if we reject materialism as a tool for feminist analysis, the effect is to suggest there are forces affecting our lives which we cannot understand or control. This denies us the power to pursue our political goals of understanding and changing the conditions of women's existence in the world.
  –Debbie Cameron (1995), on feminism and spirituality

. . . the goal of transcendence and the concept of sacredness being separate and external to the self are alien to feminist Witches. . . .
  –Wendy Griffin (1995) on feminist Witchcraft

INTRODUCTION
Setting the Frame

For pagan feminists, the assumption within paganism that feminism and paganism have enjoyed a common history and a common set of themes regarding the position of women in patriarchy has long been a puzzle. When we read about claims which emphasize informing influences of the movement which are held to be feminist (Hardman 1996:xii; Harvey 1997:70), we are reminded rather of the powerful messages regarding gender and sexuality within pagan praxis, issuing from the virtual orthodoxy of gender bipolarity in the British context, and our own painful experiences within the larger pagan community. But it is when we consider the manner in which paganism and issues around spirituality generally are regarded in the larger feminist community that we are presented with a wider picture of a relationship between paganism and feminism which is fraught with conflict. The strong signals of outright rejection of paganism and pagan women's interests coming from, predominantly, radical feminism are a source of pain to us, and no less so because they arise largely from a space in which one might expect to find more progressive and critical analysis. This chapter will address, briefly, the development of the historical and political roots of the discord between feminist and pagan communities in Britain. The main focus, however, will be upon the experience of pagan feminists, and in the interest of exploring the distinctive "deep" and radical feminism of pagan feminists, will give space to autobiographical evidence from interviews with pagan feminists.

The present framework

The differences between the way in which pagan groups in Britain and in the U.S. operate around feminist concerns is highly indicative of the historical specificity of the British situation. Whereas women from the States tell of feminist conferences which routinely incorporate women's ceremonies, in Britain, women's spirituality is viewed by some members of the feminist community in a somewhat derisory fashion. Mainstream paganism, on the other hand, is not automatically feminist-friendly and pagan feminists practicing a solely Goddess-centered spirituality often do not have an easy time of it. While there are Dianic or feminist separatist groups of Witches in Britain, it is fair to say that they have hardly impacted upon mainstream paganism. In order to discover why this situation exists in Britain, a brief consideration of the respective historical and ideological developments of paganism and feminism is required. It should be stated, however, that dividing paganism and feminism into wholly separated categories is highly problematic for pagan feminists. For pagan feminists the theories and practices offered by both paganism and feminism are not divided. The temporary division that occurs in this essay is offered merely as an artificial lens onto the causes of present conflicts.

HISTORIES OF FEMINISM, PAGANISM, AND THE GODDESS MOVEMENT

Woven Apart

It becomes clear, when one examines both the ways in which the Goddess spirituality movement in Britain locates itself as being outside mainstream paganism and the sense in which mainstream feminism marginalizes women's spirituality, that this relationship is not entirely as mutually funded as it might seem (Long 1994; Weaver 1989). Historically, there are at least three strands in motion in the formation of Goddess spirituality, paganism, and what claims to be "political" feminism. The main body of feminism in Britain in the 1970s and '80s, for example, came largely and broadly from within the movements of the '60s, including the New Left (Roseneil 1995). The long-established socialist tradition within the women's movement (Puttick 1997) and from which radical feminism in the British sense emerged, engendered a deeply ingrained legacy of a Marxist materialism whose project is often anti-spiritual and anti-religious. Talk of women's spirituality, in this climate, came to be seen as anti-materialist and part and parcel of a "false consciousness" which diverted women away from political activism. Elisabeth Brooke sees the division which she locates as happening in the 1970s between socialist feminism, of which radical feminism in Britain is now mainly constituted, and women's spirituality, as being conceptualized as a split between "soft" and "hard" action; "embracing Witchcraft was seen to be letting the side down" (in O'Brien 1994:13). Since the early 1980s, when the terms "spiritual" feminist and "political" feminist were launched into general usage within feminist discourse, the spiritual has been seen as the antithesis of the political. In this sense, the British development differs from feminist movements in the U.S., which in the '70s embraced Goddess and other woman-centered spiritualities more readily (Long 1994), and, ironically, looking towards Britain integrated paganism and Wicca early on into practices which were identified as specifically feminist. This difference in development meant that the American feminist appropriation and translations of paganism were bounced back in the early '80s to influence spiritual feminists, but not to any great degree the wider pagan community here in Britain.

Although the British scene produced Monica Sjöö and others writing about Goddess spirituality, it remains the case that there are no popular *specifically feminist* writers of the influence and magnitude of, for example, Starhawk, focusing on paganism and Witchcraft in Britain. Paganism in Britain, although developing rapidly at a time coincidal with the protest groups of the '50s, '60s, and '70s and with the women's movement, seemed only to be nominally influenced by them. Asphodel Long goes as far as claiming that the pagan movement "still does not in any way define itself as feminist" (Long 1994:23). That it is *ill*-defined is not in dispute; in the pagan community, it is still the case that pagan feminists challenging the orthodoxy of gender bipolarity are often openly derided and effectively marginalized. Both the timing of the pagan movement's emergence and its proudly vaunted inclusion of a goddess or goddesses made it a prime candidate to receive from and contribute to the growth of feminism in Britain. The evidence for this type of substantive cross-fertilization is sadly lacking, however. When one goes to pagan feminists' accounts of encounters with other pagans, with non-pagan Goddess-women, and with radical feminists, it becomes even clearer that the relationships among the feminist, Goddess, and pagan movements is not at all straightforward.

FEMINISM VERSUS PAGANISM
Sources of conflict

In terms of responses from some feminist communities to paganism, the most immediate example of tension is found where such communities take up causes which negate, disrespect, or seek to criminalize paganism in campaigns such as contemporary feminist allegations of "ritual abuse" of children by "Satanists." Given the marked tendency in such campaigns to conflate pagan practices and identities with that of the alleged Satanists, it is not difficult to see how, for pagans, alignment with ritual abuse campaigns are seen as incitement to religious hatred. My own attendance at a campaigning event offering a workshop on ritual abuse was enough to provoke one of the facilitators into attacking me for "openly" wearing a pentagram, stating that this was "like wearing a swastika at a holocaust survivors' meeting."[1] Confrontations of this type are encouraged by feminist campaigners' unwitting use of material

originating from fundamentalist Christian campaigns which are an-
tagonistic toward pagans. Whereas the instigation of a new witch-
hunt stands to affect all pagan women, we are told by radical
feminists that the interests of the pagan community cannot be put
above those of "survivors" of ritual abuse.

It is disappointing that a movement which takes great pride in
respecting women's *differences* should take this position in relation
to pagan women. Certainly there seems to be a general abandon-
ment of critical thinking in relation to religion and spirituality. Religion is not challenged in the case of minority ethnic women because
"for minority women particularly traditional religion may be an
important aspect of ethnic identity" (Cameron 1995:6). The possibility of minority ethnic women celebrating their *spirituality* and not
just their ethnicity within these religions, therefore, is discounted
and points to an effective "othering" of minority ethnic women and
a normalizing of white secularism. On the other hand, the tendency
within some strands of radical feminism to ridicule women's spirituality generally appears to arise from an assumed separation between the spiritual and the material. In differentiating between the
spiritual and material, Debbie Cameron (1995), an outspoken radical feminist opponent of what she terms "spiritual tendencies
amongst feminists," simply echoes the dichotomies found within
north/western patriarchal discourse.

This essay sets out to explore not only the ways in which paganism and feminism come into conflict; it also seeks ways in which
their mutual interests might be restored. In order to achieve this, it
is necessary to make more explicit the nature of the interface between feminism and paganism. It could not do so without reference
to the experiences of pagan feminists and their own many and varied
stories and accounts of living the reality of our spirituality and
politics.

METHODOLOGY
Setting the Warp at Seven Spokes

Feminist researchers Pam Cotterill and Gayle Letherby claim that
". . . research involves the weaving together of the researched and
the researcher" (Cotterill and Letherby 1995:6) and argue emphati-
cally for the interweaving of their auto/biographies in the interest

of what Cotterill calls "putting the subjective in the knowledge" (Cotterill 1992:605). I stand with this and take the position described by Liz Stanley and Sue Wise as the "morally responsible epistemology" constituted within and from the feminist research community, the precepts of which include ". . . recognition of the reflexivity of the feminist researcher in her research as an active and busily constructing agent . . ." (Stanley & Wise 1993:200). Weaving together the subjectivity and reflexivity of the researcher with the acknowledged subjectivity of the researched produces an approach which moves into alliance with what Kum-Kum Bhavnani identifies as a "feminist objectivity," an objectivity which retains and acknowledges the perspectival, the subjective (Bhavnani 1993:95). This is explicitly constitutive of the approach which I take in this chapter, an approach described as "intersubjective participatory methodology" (Stanley 1995:185). The term "participatory" has a particular resonance for me here; I am a pagan feminist interviewing other pagan feminists. In order to attain feminist objectivity, I am obliged to include myself in *reflexively* and, along with my six interviewees, provide a seventh spoke for the web on which they and I weave our accounts.

DEMOGRAPHICS
The Speaking Spokes

Over the course of three months in 1998, and as part of a much larger and ongoing project of interviewing pagan women in Britain and the British Isles, I interviewed six pagan women identifying as feminists. It is acknowledged that they are *only* six in-depth interview relationships, and in no sense representative of other pagan feminists, but ones which, of themselves, provide rich and active clues as to the particular relationship between feminism and paganism. The interviews were based on a number of questions around identity, experience, politics and practices, and in line with qualitative feminist interviewing techniques, interviews were often conducted following the flow of the women's own accounts, and sometimes questions arose spontaneously from them (Cotterill 1992:593).

The seven of us ranged widely in age, background, and experience. All of us are white and, at the time of the interviews, living in Britain. Agewise, there was a 22-year gap spanning 27 to 49. In spite of the occasional casting of paganism and Witchcraft as middle-class phenomena[2], five of us presented a working-class background and two pointed to middle-class upbringings. Of these, Linda pointed to an agrarian working class background in Ireland and Daniela a German middle-class upbringing. Daniela and Harper identified, like myself, as bisexual, Harper incorporating the term "queer." Shan, while married, eschewed the term "heterosexual" in favor of "connoisseur," explaining that twenty-five years of her life were spent "as a dyke" and some of this time as a separatist. Ann, Julie, and Linda identified as heterosexual. Although all the participants had experienced education at college level or above, the point at which we entered further and higher education differed considerably among us. In terms of pagan identities, Ann describes herself as pagan (non-aligned); Daniela as priestess and mystic; Harper as kitchenwitch; Julie as Witch; Linda as a spiritual and ethnic pagan; Shan as priestess, Celtic, Witch; me as "ditchwitch" (like Harper's description, a variation on "hedgewitch").[3] All but Shan and Julie worked solo, though most worked "occasionally" with other women.

All participants were happy to use the term "feminist" alongside their paganism, and as the interviews proceeded it became increasingly apparent that their own particular feminism was regarded as integral to their paganism. At first, this integration reflected my own experience and identity as a pagan feminist, and was a powerfully validating experience for me personally. However, in the course of all of the interviews the quite significant differences in the way that terminology around gender was being deployed, (a) alerted me to the dangers of assuming identical understandings of certain concepts, including, importantly, feminism; and (b) provided me with important clues about misunderstandings arising from women either not having access to linguistic refinements routinely employed within feminist discourse or choosing deliberately not to use them. These possibilities led me to interrogate my own understandings of what it meant to be a pagan feminist and, prompted by a couple of the women I interviewed, I co-opted a work colleague into putting me through the same process. Needless to say, my experience of being put on the spot (this time by a non-pagan feminist!) was somewhat different from that of my interviewees.[4] Nonetheless it was a valuable exercise in reflexivity in that it forced me to clarify my own position and, by extension, led me to take care around the terminology being deployed by other pagan feminists.

INTERVIEWS WITH PAGAN FEMINISTS
Weaving with Words

Issues of language
Speaking in another mother-tongue

The most immediate indication of the possibility of misinterpretation by me, by the women I was interviewing, and by non-pagan feminist commentaries arose in a question which focused upon a conflict commonly experienced within the pagan community, that relating to the problem of gendered "bipolarity." Shan offered, ". . . I don't ascribe to the idea that I have feminine and masculine within me. I have not one iota of masculinity in me. I am completely female. Every single one of my chromosomes is an X." She then totally threw me by stating, "To me, everything I do is feminine." Shan later revealed that she considered everything that women did as feminine because women did it, but did not ascribe to the patriarchal version which assigned some attributes as feminine and some as masculine in a more prescriptive manner. Here I found an important source of misunderstandings between what I had been used to term feminist references to "feminine" and "masculine" and what some pagan feminists understood by the terms. It also led me to review the response from another woman, Ann, when I asked whether she had any problems with gendered bipolarity. I had been rather surprised by her unproblematic "no," since it was something which had been an issue for the rest of us, until the more explicit explanation given by Shan raised the possibility that some of us were using the terms differently.

In retrospect, a problem around defining gender-related terms had already raised itself earlier in an interview with Linda, who struggled to explain what she meant by feminine. I was puzzled, since she had firmly stated that she had found problems relating to masculine-feminine bipolarity issues in the pagan community, to find her identifying a problem she perceived with "some pagan feminists" who she saw as tending "to deny a great deal of the feminine aspect of themselves," an aspect which she claimed she could see in me.

> AMG: I'm wondering what you're meaning by femininity here, because I wouldn't describe any one part of myself as feminine in the general kind of sense that's expected of that word.

> Linda: I don't mean that. . . . no, no, I don't. . . . no . . . but I don't know what other term to use and I don't mean femininity as in being a feminine person you know, kind of . . . wearing the clothes . . . what society dictates as feminine, oh god, you should know that I don't mean that (LAUGHS). You do know that, don't you?

Linda's struggle with the terminology continued a little further and ended in her suggesting she needed to go away and think about it after the interview. A personal discomfort around gender issues arose in the context of the interviews for me; although generally accepting of feminist aims to raise consciousness, I felt that there were serious ethical issues around challenging definitions I was eliciting from the women participating in the research. I became mindful of Daphne Patai's warning that, ". . . to turn interviews with other women into opportunities for imposing our own politically correct analyses requires an arrogance incompatible with genuine respect for others" (Patai 1991:148). I had to steer a careful course between attempting to bring clarity to definitions in the interests of avoiding misinterpretation and challenging them on what views they offered no matter how much I found myself in disagreement with them.

ISSUES OF POLITICS
Embodied spirituality and embodied politicality

That there was difficulty among pagan feminists in defining our terms and interpreting them between ourselves was a prime indicator that non-pagan feminists might misapprehend our different use of language elsewhere. A prime area of misconception presently is arraigned around politicality or our assumed lack of it. Both a difference between "acting politically" and "political activism" and a measure of modest or misunderstood labelling of what constituted politicality arose in the interviews. It was at the point of women defining their politics and then recounting personal autobiographical details that stories began to emerge of the distinctiveness of pagan feminist politicality. Linda, an Irish national living in England, described herself as an Irish Republican and a Marxist feminist, and revealed that she had been on remand in prison in Armagh women's jail in Northern Ireland for three months after being arrested during non-violent protests at the time of the prison hunger strikes in 1981.

> I think that there was a time when I was really heavily involved in politics, I mean with activism. I didn't really think a great deal about my spirituality, the feminism side, or the femininity. It was only actually when I was in Armagh [prison] that I soon began to feel more of a bond with women who were also in there. . . . And my spirituality was kind of really on the outskirts then. . . . I hadn't really studied anything academic until I went back to my MPhil[5] in '92 . . . when I began to really appreciate and identify more with my own spirituality and develop it further. . . . one was always on the outskirts of the other, so like now the spirituality has taken over so that my political links are now . . . on the outskirts. I'm not actively involved on a pretty much day to day thing like I used to be. So the active politics has really gone . . .

The intertwining of the political and the spiritual here is quite complex. At the beginning of her account, the coming into the spiritual via the political seems quite straightforward, but at the point at which Linda comes away from her birth-country where she has been immersed in day-to-day activism, her definition of her own politicality changes. Although she distinguishes between involvement and activism early on, she comes to describe her *political links* as being more in the background because of her partial withdrawal from activism, though she clearly is still an activist from her descriptions of continued involvement in campaigns around Irish Republican issues. Further into the interview, in her descriptions of her present life as a front-line animal rights advocate, it becomes apparent that Linda is a person who also *acts* politically. Her account of the present status of her politicality, however, appears rather self-effacing.

Similarly, Julie, when asked how she would described her politics, began by saying that she "wouldn't describe them in any way at all," but then went on to disclose a standpoint which saw "politics in everything." The view of politics as integrated and imminent matched both her description of her spirituality; "everything is connected to everything else," and her involvement in local campaigns against closures of libraries and homes for the elderly, though she wasn't sure whether this came under the descriptor of being active politically. Some reticence in assigning some actions as political was evident from Ann's interview; she described herself as "gearing towards left and socialism," but thought she was an "armchair anarchist," and felt that she should be doing more. Further on in the interview, however, she revealed active memberships in the Campaign for Nuclear Disarmament and the National Anti-Hunt Campaign against bloodsports and collecting signatures on petitions for these campaigns, adding that her present studies for a degree in Women's Studies prevented her doing more.

Where Shan had a very succinctly refined definition of her politics as "radical" and "subversive . . . not an activist," Harper expanded on a similar notion of subversiveness which she acknowledged as central to and profoundly embedded within her politicality and spirituality. She begins her self-analysis with a delineation of where she stands in relation to her socialism and her paganism:

> Something I could say on that is arguments I often have with socialists so I could include socialist feminists in that . . . well, coming from Marx's idea that religion is the opiate of the masses . . . my understanding is that Marx perceived of a time when, in this utopian state, religion as an organized infrastructure the way we know it now doesn't exist but spirituality as I understand it does, and that is the freedom of every individual to attain a sense of spirituality. In that sense I try and have my Witchcraft unstructured.

While Harper saw assumptions about her spirituality coming from encounters with other feminists, she described encounters with mainstream paganism with a similar sense of self-situatedness:

> There is a baseline from which I am suspicious of anyone who purports to tell me what I need to know. . . . So in that paganism does contain a body of knowledge that attempts

to educate me about what is and is not relevant in terms of spiritual progress, in terms of iconography, in terms of ritual, method, timing, setting, all of those things, I try and be very conscious when I use them that I'm not just blindly accepting of all of those. . . . I try to treat it as this really grand intellectual and spiritual smorgasbord from which I choose and select the things I like, the things that suit me, the things that enable me—in very much the way I try as a feminist to select from my social construction the things that I think empower me. So I try and approach my paganism with the same sense of agency that I approach my sexuality. . . . But I try consciously to select from that and synthesize on a personal level to produce a way of living on a spiritual and feminist plane that's more acceptable to me.

This sense of agency and subversiveness, of gleeful eclecticism found in Harper's and Shan's accounts, shone through all the stories of magic, spirituality, and politicality the women shared with me even if not always with the same degree of self-consciousness. Daniela for example, speaks of sifting through books on magic and feminism, ". . . when I read a book about magick [sic] or feminism, I discard the parts that have no value for me and integrate the parts that do. . . ."

PAGAN FEMINISTS AND EVERYDAY MAGIC
Weavers for Change

All of the women, in different ways, described approaches to and choices concerning political and spiritual practices matching Harper's "smorgasbord" approach. This wrapping-up of chosen forms of nourishment into one's spiritual and political web is suggestive of a high degree of accomplishment in the dismantling of hierarchical authorities and categories. There is a high level of conscious choice throughout their accounts, at points which are probably least expected by non-pagan feminist observers, at least those which characterize pagan feminists as gullible and credulous, and which probably do serve to alienate pagan feminists from sectors of the pagan community where hierarchy and strict lines of demarcation are elevated. As Linda recognizes: ". . . there are conflicts with other people's views of my feminism and my paganism and my paganism and other kinds of paganism, but no conflict within myself, no." At the same time, the interweaving of categories kept separate elsewhere under patriarchal conceptual frameworks speaks of a spirituality and politicality which is powerfully em-bodied, en-spir-ited, en-chanted and rooted in the everyday. Shan told me,

> . . . embodied is a word where I've encountered it recently, intellectually as I've returned as an old lady to this univer-sity stuff and I thought "you really had to say that?" (LAUGHS) I mean, it's so real to me, it's so natural to me that I just have great difficulty dealing with the other bit at all. I just about manage to realize that there is something called transcendence, though around the edges, very weakly.

And Julie,

> . . . it is all connected, that I am a whole person and just the same way that I would separate my different feelings, you know, angry, happy, sad and so on, I would say, my skin, my bones, my spirit, my emotions. That is all part of one thing.

It interested me to note that the Goddess most often mentioned in the interviews was Brighid, who is particularly beloved in Britain and Ireland as healer and as fierce protector of women. There is a third aspect she incorporates which may at first be considered oddly placed with these other two; she is patron of smiths and jewelry-makers. But a goddess who oversees the fashioning of hard metals into things both practical and beautiful seems a particularly apt choice for these women, who are constantly weaving transforma-tion within and about them, transforming understandings of the spiritual and of the political.

The processes of research, however, are never complete and per-haps particularly appropriately so in this case; as Diane Reay (1996:70) puts it, "interpretation remains an imperfect and incom-plete process. There are many possible readings of interview tran-scripts." The possibilities offered in the rich and varied tapestry of the web woven with these women's words are endless, and per-haps, rather than "cast off" the stitches of the web, I should leave some threads dangling from it, the better to pick them up and weave on later.

REFLECTIONS ON PAGAN FEMINISTS' WORDS
Patterns in the Web

Almost at the end of writing this piece, I light seven candles, one each for Ann, Daniela, Harper, Julie, Linda, Shan, and me. I then light two yellow candles, one for the many people upon whose work I have built, and one for Athena, whose owl feather I keep next to me and who has inspired my work from beginning to end. I think about the accomplishment with which the women I have interviewed break down the oppressive categories of patriarchy and my attention turns to Athena, upon whose energy I have drawn. She has been conceptualized within patriarchy as patron of intellect, wisdom, and battle, born out of the head of her father, thus avoiding the "messy" bodiliness of childbirth. She has been conceptualized, leaning on reconstructions of pre-Hellenic cultures by Goddess women, as patron of weaving, crafts, and childbirth (Spretnak 1979). In this circle of flames I understand that Athena represents a blend of these things to me; I am no happier eschewing her as intellect simply because it has erroneously occupied the prioritized domain of the masculine within an oppressive regime, than I am separating intuition, hand and body wisdom from intellect in the manner of the patriarch. And I realize that it is in this manner that pagan feminists are changing the world, shifting our praxis to a point where it undercuts even the false choices between constructionism and universalism offered by postmodern theories which currently bedevil feminism.

WEAVING ON
The Open Web

The materiality of our spirituality does not imply an essentialized, universalized premise for our affinities with the Goddess, with the earth, though proclaiming and sacralizing bodiliness in a culture which relegates women's bodies to disposable container status is, as Jane Caputi states, "a profoundly revolutionary act" (Caputi 1992:434). Growing our status as women through the empowerment of mythmaking, symbols, and thealogy does not imply that we are unable to politically situate ourselves; our grounded models of interconnectedness provide rich grounds in which to grow transformational politicalities.

Our thealogies, which are praxis- and experience-led, disclose a trust in human action to bring about change, and see the Goddess in the fire that drives us to work for equality and justice. The presentation of spirituality by radical feminists like Cameron as being solely dependent upon mysterious forces divorced from material realities proceeds from a patriarchal model of spirit/matter dichotomy which should, by rights, be given short shrift by any critically aware feminist analysis. Contrary to radical feminist claims that spirituality disempowers women and is inimical to feminist aims and objectives, pagan feminists demonstrate ongoing incorporation of a thealogy which, like feminism, is subversive and transformational. Leading from new understandings of the way in which patriarchy has constructed oppressive versions of reality at a deep, cosmological level, pagan feminists incorporate the politicality of feminist spirituality into our everyday lives.

Whereas some sections of the non-pagan feminist community do not perceive for themselves the need for a goddess or any other spirituality, it should be at least possible to accommodate a feminism which does, as a *different* feminist epistemology, secularist feminism being one such other. While we pagan feminists find ourselves speaking out in pagan communities for the recognition of women's issues and for the validity of feminist aims, we could use the solidarity of support from non-pagan feminists, both in engaging in the problematics of issues that are threatening to our communities, and respect toward our difference.

I promised to leave the web open, and not to neatly cast-off in the manner of closures approved of elsewhere, and in the manner of weavers, I offer up the motif of the web itself as a symbol and maker of connections:

Who is in my network,
what links us, to be exact?
Better ask to understand the force
that cuts through rock the water's course,
and binding like to like
makes also opposites attract (Susan Saxe 1983:65)

Notes

[1] February 28, 1998, a one-day conference titled "Women Fighting Back" in Manchester, Lancashire, England.

[2] For example, Tanya Luhrmann's (1989) influential work *Persuasion of the Witch's Craft: Ritual Magic in Contemporary England* (London: Picador), based on a study of groups in London in the 1980s, has sometimes been taken to indicate a middle-class hegemony among adherents of the Craft.

[3] The term "hedgewitch" usually denotes a Witch who is a solo-worker who interests herself in nature-magic. Harper explained her preferred identity of "kitchenwitch" as being patriarchy's worst nightmare (a Witch) inhabiting the space generally reserved for the domesticated woman. My choice of "ditchwitch" is equally idiosyncratic: I prefer the generally overlooked space between the kitchen and the hedgerow; the ditch. Ditches flow along paths and sometimes dip under them, and interesting things grow in them.

[4] Many thanks to Cathy Lubelska, Principal Lecturer in Social History at University of Central Lancashire.

[5] Masters Degree by research

Works Cited

Bhavnani, Kum-Kum. 1993. Tracing the contours: Feminist research and feminist objectivity. *Women's Studies International Forum*. Vol. 16:2. Pages 95–104.

Cameron, Deborah. 1995. Can you feel the force (and should you give in to it)? In *Trouble & Strife*, Vol. 31 (Summer). Pages 3–11.

Caputi, Jane. 1992. On psychic activism: feminist mythmaking. In *The Feminist Companion to Mythology*. Edited by Carolyne Larrington. London: Pandora Press. Pages 425–40.

Cotterill, Pam. 1992. Interviewing women: Issues of friendship, vulnerability, and power. *Women's Studies International Forum*. Vol.15:5/6. Pages 593–606.

Cotterill, Pam, and Gayle Letherby. 1995. Collaborative writing: the pleasure and perils of working together. An unpublished paper presented at the Women's Studies Network Conference, Stirling University, Scotland. July 4–8.

Griffin, Wendy. 1995. The embodied Goddess: feminist Witchcraft and female divinity. In *Sociology of Religion*. Vol. 56:1 (Spring). Pages 35–49.

Hardman, Charlotte. 1995. Introduction. In *Paganism Today*. Edited by Charlotte Hardman and Graham Harvey. London: Thorsons. Pages ix–xix.

Harvey, Graham. 1997. *Listening People Speaking Earth: Contemporary Paganism*. London: Hurst & Co.

Long, Asphodel. 1994. The Goddess movement in Britain today. *Feminist Theology* #5 (January). Pages 11–37.

O'Brien, Lucy. 1994. The wild woman within. In *Everywoman* (February). Pages 3–15.

Patai, Daphne. 1991. U.S. academics & third world women: is ethical research possible? In *Women's Words: The Feminist Practice of Oral History.* Edited by Sherna Berger Gluck and Daphne Patai. London: Routledge. Pages 137–53.

Puttick, Elisabeth. 1997. *Women in New Religions: In Search of Community, Sexuality and Spiritual Power.* London: MacMillan.

Reay, Diane. 1996. Insider perspectives of stealing the words out of women's mouths: interpretation in the research process. *Feminist Review* 53 (Summer). Pages 57–73.

Roseneil, Sasha. 1995. *Disarming Patriarchy: Feminism and Political Action at Greenham.* Buckingham: Open University Press.

Saxe, Susan. 1983. Ask a silly question. In *Reclaim the Earth.* Edited by Leonie Caldecott and Stephanie Leland. London: The Women's Press. Page 65.

Spretnak, Charlene. 1979 [1992]. *The Lost Goddesses of Early Greece: A Collection of Pre-Hellenic Myths.* Boston: Beacon Press.

Stanley, Liz, and Sue Wise. 1993. *Breaking Out Again: Feminist Ontology & Epistemology.* London: Routledge.

Weaver, Mary-Jo. 1989. Who is the Goddess and where does she get us? *Journal of Feminist Studies in Religion.* Vol. 5. Pages 49–64.

❦ 3 ❦

The Mutable Goddess

Particularity and Eclecticism within the Goddess Public

by Marilyn Gottschall

INTRODUCTION

Recently a friend of mine attended her first "pagan" ritual, complete with priestesses, circle casting, Goddess chants, and energy work. While this a-religious, lapsed Catholic approached the Goddess business with great trepidation, her reaction to the ritual was very positive. "I felt so comfortable; I didn't expect that. It all seemed so familiar."

I considered the possibility that my friend was really a Witch at heart, come home at last, but quickly rejected that notion because I had witnessed the same response from other friends on other occasions. Instead, her response confirmed my impression of Goddess worship as a highly idiosyncratic form of religious expression that appeals to a wide variety of people.

The American Goddess movement has evolved over the past twenty years in largely grassroots settings among women who have felt alienated from mainstream religious and political institutions. It has developed out of a complex web of interactions with vital, if marginalized, religious, social, and political groups. The Goddess movement drew breath and sustenance from New Age spiritualities, from the American neopagan movement, from feminist critics of mainstream patriarchal religious traditions, and from many thousands of individual women across the country who possessed a deep spiritual longing. It is in many ways the manifestation of that longing, the spiritual expression of numberless women who were determined to seek access to the sacred in ways that were meaningful to them.

The history of the Goddess movement and its relationship with those out of which it grew has been carefully documented by contemporary feminist scholars (Eller 1993; Neitz 1991), and by movement insiders (Adler 1986; Starhawk 1982). They provide us with much needed information about the burgeoning Goddess phenomenon, a form of religiosity which has heretofore been overlooked or inaccessible to scholars. One of the things that we are learning is that the Goddess movement is an exceedingly diverse body of practitioners which includes everything from strict Wiccan neopagans to loosely or non-affiliated women who have adopted some gynocentric beliefs and New Age practices. Some scholars even include post-Christian feminists into the mix, claiming that there is little difference between New Christian spiritualities and what is generally thought of as feminist spirituality (Woodhead 1993).

It is interesting that in the face of this diversity, the scholarly trend is to describe feminist spirituality and the Goddess movement as a new religion (see Eller 1993). While the categorization of Goddess worship as a religion brings needed attention to many of its practices, the generalities that are being constructed do not accurately reflect the diversity and fluidity that exists within Goddess worship. The impulse to categorize religious behaviors derives from what has been the dominant model in the sociology of religion, a "denominational model" (Roof 1998). This model assumes that formal religious traditions with their structured beliefs and practices are normative, and it seeks to categorize religious outcroppings in relation to mainstream religious norms. Thus scholars are put in the difficult position of constructing typologies amid religious phenomena that may be inherently ambiguous and contradictory. Scholarly discussions of new expressions of religiosity, including the Goddess phenomenon, are therefore often phrased in language that refers back, inevitably, to the "church" model. These phenomena are then interpreted as deviations from a norm that perhaps does not apply. Innovative practices and shifts in religious devotional patterns may thus be overlooked or misunderstood.

In 1986, however, Margot Adler had a different perspective of the Goddess movement, noting that the women's spirituality movement was already defying definition. It "is now so large and undefinable that it is like an ocean whose waves push against all shores" (p. 227). What Adler saw was the growing shapelessness of the Goddess movement, a form of cultural religiosity that was becoming increasingly diverse, more geographically widespread,[1] more eclectic in nature, and more dynamic in process.

This essay diverges from the trajectory of current scholarship on Goddess worship. It does not focus on the ways in which Goddess spirituality is distinct from mainstream religious denominations, i.e., nature-centered and gender-centered beliefs, magical practices, etc. My suspicion is that those who denominationalize Goddess worship make a case too strongly. While Goddess spirituality draws some measure of continuity from a core gynocentric symbol system and a canon of popular feminist spirituality writings, its inherent vitality and instability make it difficult to contain.

I would argue that Goddess worship is more reflective of the do-it-yourself, experienced-based ethos that typifies much of contemporary religious expression. As the Goddess movement expands, beliefs and practices are becoming increasingly idiosyncratic. Recombinations of symbol and culture appear to mirror the diversity of the individuals and communities who set about constructing their own meaning systems. I suggest, therefore, that we approach the Goddess movement as a highly syncretic, dynamic, and increasingly diverse form of popular religiosity that has emerged among women who occupy similar political, spiritual, and psychological neighborhoods. My understanding of Goddess spirituality has been shaped by my experience as a participant and observer in a Womenspirit community for over ten years and upon my research there.

THE WOMENSPIRIT COMMUNITY

Twice a year, round about the summer and winter solstice, Goddess worshippers gather for the day in Southern California to make-merry, visit, shop, and be entertained by belly dancers, drummers, poets, and vocalists. At other times in the year they gather to celebrate pagan holidays such as Hallomas and Lammas in large public rituals, or to study in small group workshops. Womenspirit events have become one important focal point among many in the geographically and spiritually diverse Goddess community of the Los Angeles metropolitan area.

At the core of Womenspirit (WS) is a collective of seven to twelve women that has been organizing public rituals, educational events, and solstice fairs since 1986. A loosely organized and eclectic group, the collective members bring a variety of spiritual interests, ritual practices and worship motifs to WS community events. Any given event might include a hybrid mix of Celtic traditions, ancient Near Eastern or contemporary Middle Eastern traditions, Latin American customs, African, Hindu or Chinese mythology, or a good dose of Wiccan practice. Their following consists of an equally diverse group of Witches, Goddess worshippers, neopagans, feminists, Unitarian Universalists, and assorted spiritual seekers.

WS states that its goal is to spark "the growth of Goddess Consciousness and Women's Spirituality," to provide opportunities for "personal growth, empowerment," and to "hope for planetary healing."[2] Towards this end it has created and hosted an impressive number of events. An average year sees two Solstice Fairs which draw upwards of a thousand people each; two to four public rituals[3] each of which is likely to attract 150 to 250 attendees; and anywhere from five to fifteen educational workshops,[4] generally with numbers appropriate to small group gatherings.

In an attempt to better understand the worship practices among WS followers, I distributed survey forms to attendees at the 1998 Womenspirit Summer Solstice Fair. I sorted the responses in search of a highly specific group of people, those who had attended WS events for more than one year, and those who had attended a range of events (at least fairs and rituals). My data are based on the surveys of 46 women and 4 men who met these criteria.[5] The participants responded to general demographic questions as well as more focused inquiries about their spiritual practice, their attendance history with and attitudes toward WS, and their understanding of religious community and its importance in their lives.

FINDINGS

My entire group of respondents could be described as long-time and committed participants in Goddess spirituality; seventy percent of the sample has participated in the movement for more than 5 years. The majority of respondents identified themselves as Witches and 88 percent employed multiple descriptive terms which included a combination of "Witch," "Goddess worshipper," and/or "neopagan." Only a handful noted their participation in other religious traditions[6]; however, 32 percent reported that they participate in New Age spiritualities.

Demographically this community resembles other Goddess communities. Seventy-eight percent of this group is over the age of 35, with the majority of respondents being between 35 and 55. They are for the most part white, female, and unmarried. Two-thirds of the WS sample described themselves as heterosexual.[7] Of those women, only 12 respondents, roughly 30 percent of the heterosexual women, reported being married.

Religious practice within this group is also consonant with accounts of the larger Goddess community. Ritual performance is integral to spiritual practice and it is conducted both individually in home-based practice and in collective ritual. The primary site of religious devotion for this sample is the home (96 percent); 86 percent reported that they have home altars, and a majority of those said that turning their homes into sacred space, using icons, altars, candles, incense, etc., was an important part of spiritual expression. Domestic devotional paths for almost all respondents include reading and studying, often on a weekly basis, prayer and meditation, spellcasting, candle magic, and divination.[8]

In general, Goddess spirituality is highly individualistic with personal belief and practice at its center. According to Eller (1993:8), feminist spirituality features a spirit of rugged individualism where "each woman is breaking her own spiritual path." When asked to select the most important components of their spiritual path, the WS sample overwhelmingly chose personal devotion (building altars, meditation, spellcasting, etc.) and personal belief over and above any other options including regular ritual gatherings, healing work, and magic. Notably, those characteristics that were most identifiably feminist—women-centered myths, feminist critique of traditional religious practice, and social action—did not rank high on this scale.

Eighty-two percent indicated that their personal spiritual path included a combination of beliefs and practices from other traditions, and they noted feeling no contradictions in doing so. The traditions most frequently cited were Buddhism (28 percent) and Native American (38 percent) but included an astounding array of practices.[9] As well, nearly 40 percent continue to celebrate Jewish and Christian holidays.

While their domestic worship involves performing ritual, ninety percent of respondents also cited ritual attendance outside the home as an important aspect of their devotional life. Slightly more than 80 percent ritually celebrate Wiccan sabbats (equinox and solstice), the moon cycles, and life events such as divorce, marriage, menopause, etc. While all but four of the respondents regularly participate in large WS rituals, the majority suggested that covens and pagan educational small-groups provide the primary means of ritual observance and their primary religious sustenance. In general the function of the coven is to meet regularly to do ritual, study, conduct healing work, give personal support, and celebrate. Significantly, 82 percent of coven members reported that they had a satisfactory spiritual community, whereas the reverse was true for those with only a loose affiliation to the Goddess community.

Although small groups form the basic social and devotional units within the movement, groups like WS which organize large gatherings also have an important place. Seventy-eight percent described WS as a religious/spiritual community, but none claimed it was central to their spiritual path. In spite of the lack of centrality of WS, almost all respondents attend *both* solstice fairs each year, and 70 percent attend one or two rituals. Many have been doing so for upwards of 5 years. They come because WS offers what they say they want in religious community: a central gathering place for fun and celebration (84 percent) and the opportunity to socialize with like-minded people (80 percent).

DISCUSSION

It is now a commonplace in contemporary sociological studies of religion that Americans are turning away from denominational affiliation. Spiritual seekers are turning more to experience-based, eclectic, do-it-yourself forms of religious expression. Mass media and the marketing of religious products and information have created a virtual shopping mall of beliefs and practices for the spiritually curious. This milieu enables and encourages seekers to create highly personal meaning systems by combining mainstream and alternative beliefs, values, and practices, and to fulfill their communal needs through loose affiliation with parachurch organizations (Wuthnow 1988; Roof 1993).

This turn away from denominationalism brings into light the propensity that everyday people have for the construction of their own private worlds of meaning. Charles Lippy (1994) asserts that people everywhere need to make sense out of their lives, and they do so by drawing on the symbols and processes available within their socio/religious context. Worlds of meaning are thus constructed and maintained in the personal practices and beliefs of everyday people—in the shrines that they visit, the rituals they conduct in their homes, the icons they revere, the healers they visit. Lippy calls this form of religious expression "popular religiosity." Popular religiosity

> ... appreciates individual blends of belief and practice without claiming that any one mix is normative. Religiosity accepts what people actually think and do without *a priori* judgments as to whether a specific belief or practice is really religious or not. (Lippy 1994:9)

Religiosity, as opposed to religion, is concerned with a spirituality that lies beyond the boundaries of institutional religions. Because the power of the sacred is often domesticated and constrained by the institutional and doctrinal structures of organized religion, Lippy sees popular religiosity as an attempt by ordinary people to reclaim access to the power of the sacred.

Popular religiosity is vital and interactive, particularly as it is expressed in the late twentieth century. Because it is not institutionalized, but local and inherently idiosyncratic, it results in a pastiche of custom and belief. It has no concern for conceptual consistency, doctrine, or structure. It is driven by the quest for access to sacred power and is characterized by adaptation, hybridity, and amalgamation.

Lippy's work is particularly helpful as we turn to examine Goddess worship practices. The devotional pattern that we find in the Goddess world—a committed domestic practice coupled with small group ritual and occasional attendance at public rituals and fairs—is not only similar to evolving patterns in the larger community, but it is conducive to the idiosyncratic practices that typify popular religiosity. While it is not my intention in this essay to make an extended argument for Goddess spirituality as popular religiosity, I hope to muddy the Goddess waters a bit by approaching some of the contradictions and particularities of the WS Goddess group with Lippy in mind. I will briefly look at (1) the ways in which individualized worship coupled with the small group practice fosters innovation and idiosyncracy, and (2) the ways in which the eclectic cluster of beliefs and practices is created, transmitted and diversified by its social institutions.

Personal Belief and Small Group Practice

Across the religious board, Americans are developing privatized and "personally tailored religious worldviews independent of religious institutions." People are searching for "simple, direct, and practical" experience of and access to the divine. They do so in order to gain some measure of control over their lives, and to establish some positive sense of social identity in a complex and alienating society (Lippy 1994:4).

Nowhere is this more the case than among the women and men who inhabit the Goddess movement. A turn to the Goddess provides a rich milieu of symbols, images, and beliefs from which to construct meaning and order in a life, and it places the individual at the center of devotional practice. We have already seen the high value placed on the personal belief system among the WS sample, even at the expense of doctrine, magic, and women-centered ideologies. This coupled with the value of the home as sacred space speaks to the idiosyncratic and highly individualized nature of this group. While drawing from a core of shared cultural symbols and mythology, WS followers prize, above all, their freedom to construct their own constellation of belief and practice.

One specific indication of the individualized and context-driven nature of Goddess spirituality appears in the relative disinterest in its overtly feminist aspects among a large portion of the WS group. Forty percent of the total ignored "feminist" and "feminist spirituality" as terms that described them. Similarly they declined to select feminist values like belief in the Goddess, woman-centered myths, social action, and feminist critiques of patriarchal religions when describing the important parts of their spiritual path. Their disinterest stands in marked contrast to Eller (1993), Adler (1986), and

Starhawk (1979, 1982, 1987), all of whom maintain that feminism is integral to the new religion of feminist Witchcraft/spirituality. There are a number of plausible explanations for this discrepancy including the possibility that as the movement expands and encompasses more people, earlier forms of "orthodoxy," either political (feminist) or religious (neopagan), become increasingly diffuse. Ultimately, ideological conformity which was once thought to characterize the movement loses ground to personal religious expression.

Religious identity and a sense of belonging to a community are also important pieces of Goddess worship, but the way in which that identity is articulated says a great deal about the cohesiveness, or lack thereof, among Goddess worshippers. Seventy-four percent of the WS sample referred to themselves as Witches. While some of the WS women are indeed initiated or certified Witches, many simply use the term as a form of self-definition to denote some kind of religious affiliation with the Goddess movement. This generic use of the term means that it no longer specifies particular religious practices, beliefs, or relationships. Generic and non-specific language allows adherents to "communicate to others that they are religious people," giving visibility and legitimacy to their beliefs without imposing doctrinal coherence or consistency (Lippy 1994:228).

As Americans drift away from denominationalism, small-group worship practice is proliferating across the religious spectrum. In order to replace the communal benefits of denominational practice, individuals find relief from the pressures of complex and alienating urban society by constructing and maintaining alternative religious communal affiliations. Worshippers are migrating to special interest groups, women's groups, and parachurch bodies which have no church affiliation but which provide support, intimacy, and the promise of access to the sacred (Wuthnow 1986).

In addition, there is a clear shift in American religious practice away from the centrality of doctrine and toward an experience-based form of devotion.[10] There is an increased openness across the board to mystical, magical, and/or alternative ways of experiencing the sacred (Roof 1993).

Small-group patterns in the Goddess movement are very much in keeping with the broader social phenomenon. The coven provides its members with the intimacy and support available in a close community; it opens a forum for teaching, learning, and sharing magical and psychological self-help techniques, thus providing a means to affect change in a life; and it assumes experience-based worship where participants pursue ecstasy and the means to channel its power. The coven is the cauldron, the primary institution within which spiritual needs and the will to power are articulated and mobilized.

The decentralized nature of the coven, however, serves as a vehicle for and virtually ensures the development of particularized beliefs and practices. While consistency of belief and practice is achieved in some measure through a canon of popular writings, each coven has its own individual constellation of methods, myths, and motives. While some are highly structured and attached to specific forms of ritual, many encourage innovation. In addition, many Goddess people participate in open circles or even in church groups (Unitarian Universalist) rather than in covens.

Because there are no central institutions in the Goddess world, groups like WS are valued not so much for spiritual or worship purposes, but rather for their ability to create public space where alternative communities can gather, socialize, shop, and/or play. WS performs a needed service by creating a fluid, temporary, and loosely affiliated social community without imposing doctrinal or membership commitments. People have the opportunity to come together with others like themselves whom they might never meet or see under any other circumstances. WS events counteract isolation and rejuvenate participants through their general atmosphere of merriment and celebration.

Eclecticism And Goddess Social Institutions

As noted, popular religiosity is characterized by its eclecticism, idiosyncrasy, and lack of conceptual coherence. Whereas theologians and religious organizations strive for logical and consistent systems of thought, ordinary people, including Goddess people, easily accommodate multiple and often contradictory beliefs and non-rational hopes. To the extent that people are exposed to a greater variety of religious symbol systems, their personalized beliefs reflect that variation. Due to increasing religious pluralism in the U.S. and the ubiquity of mass media, twentieth-century Americans have access to an unprecedented amount of religious information. Whether TV, bookstores, CDs, or the Hindu temple down the street, we are barraged with messages "about what is important in life and how to find happiness" (Lippy 1994:17).

We have already seen that the WS Goddess community constructs highly eclectic personal belief systems and that participants overwhelmingly approve of the eclecticism that they find at WS events. One might even make the argument that WS is successful because it is a conduit for new ideas, materials, and methods. Workshops import ideas and develop skills in the Goddess public, encouraging participants to integrate this information into their personal practice; the rituals not only mix traditions and practices, but they draw together men and women from diverse groups to worship in common. Each fair ushers in an array of new products, services, and entertainment. Goddess icons, CDs, magical paraphernalia, greeting cards and bumper stickers, books, jewelry, clothing, etc., all serve to market variations on the Goddess theme. The fairs feature performers who carry new trends and introduce diverse perspectives into the community. Entertainers include both local and nationally recognized vocalists, drummers, dancers, storytellers, and musicians.

Adler noted in 1986 that festivals and public rituals have "completely changed the face of the neopagan movement" by introducing thousands of participants across the nation to a repertoire of songs, dances, stories and myths, and ritual practices (Adler 1986:422). Applying her observations to the Goddess movement, we can assume that events like those that WS sponsors serve to expand the sites of religious innovation and democratize practice and belief. This inevitably results in an ever-widening community where innovation and change are normative. The increased openness and practical egalitarianism means that Goddess religiosity has evolved away from any means of control of the groups that contributed to its growth.[11]

The eclectic events that WS sponsors—which provide entertainment, education, and recreation—are a superb way with which to ensure the vitality and dynamic quality of Goddess spirituality. As fair-goers relax and enjoy themselves, and as ritual and workshop participants come together in mixed groups, they are absorbing a continually shifting mix of products and ideas, and they are participating in the rapid and inevitable process of change that accompanies any decentralized form of religiosity in a media- and product-saturated environment.

CONCLUSION

Overall I have tried to highlight several aspects of a Goddess community that are given to expansion, flux, and change in order to demonstrate that it is a highly dynamic and mutable form of religiosity. I have located its personalized devotional pattern within a religious community that values eclecticism, and that religious community within the forces of hypermodern society. My hope is that this shift in perspective enables us to search for the unending particularities with which Goddess worshippers approach the sacred.

Religion scholars once predicted that secular beliefs would prevail over religion, that the lure of science, technology, and the material abundance that they provide would fulfill the human need for meaning. They were wrong. The search for the sacred has rebounded, manifesting itself in novel and unanticipated ways. But contemporary religiosity doesn't look like the religion we are used to; it is the product of life in a fast-paced, highly diverse, and image-oriented society. Its forms are improvisational and particularistic, unexpectedly syncretic, and rapidly changing.

Roof suggests that contemporary religious expression is the "reflexive self-searching for something to hold onto in a fragmented, rootless world" (Roof 1998:9). If this is the case, it is unlikely that traditional forms of analysis possess the conceptual vocabulary to catch up to religiosity in the twenty-first century.

Notes

[1] While numbers of Goddess worshippers are commonly regarded as impossible to estimate with any accuracy, a *Time* magazine article in 1991 suggested that over 100,000 women in America were then participating in some form of Goddess worship. *Gnosis* (No. 48, Summer 1998) estimates that there are between 200,000 and 500,000 pagans in the U.S., but Neitz (1990) and Griffin (in personal communication) both claim that numbers typically do not include the women in the Goddess community.

[2] WS flyer.

[3] Rituals include an annual winter solstice celebration, and a variety of summer solstice, Hallomas (Halloween), spring, and harvest rituals.

[4] Workshops include: (1) educational events such as a regular Herstory series which features particular goddesses, Cakes for the Queen of Heaven study group, etc. (2) arts workshops such as mask making, rattle and drum making workshops, and (3) special purpose groups such as croning groups.

[5] The fact that WS events are open to men might raise the criticism that this group is atypical of the Goddess movement. While it is true that many covens in the larger community are "women only," and many practitioners are lesbian, significant numbers of heterosexual women and some men also participate in Goddess spirituality. Because the responses of the male participants in this study were not significantly different from the females', I included them in the sample, just as WS includes them in its events.

[6] Three reported affiliation with the Roman Catholic Church, one with a Protestant denomination, and two with Judaism.

[7] While sexual demographic information is impossible to obtain, scholars agree that the Goddess Movement has a higher proportion of lesbians than the general populace and that lesbianism tends to be normative (Adler 1986; Eller 1993).

[8] For an extended discussion of personal and group ritual, see Adler 1986; Budapest 1986; Eller 1993; Griffin 1995; Starhawk 1979, 1982, 1987.

[9] These included: Hinduism, tantra, yoga, Tibetan tara mantra, Eastern meditation techniques, acupressure, Chinese medicine, Catholicism and the Guadalupe myth, Judaism, Shinto, Gnosticism, Religious and Christian Science, ancient Egyptian, Mesopotamian, Canaanite, Phoenician, Babylonian, and African traditions, Wicca, and Celtic shamanism.

[10] See, for example, Donald E. Miller, *Reinventing American Protestantism: Christianity in the New Millennium* (Berkeley: University of California, 1997) for discussions of Pentecostal and charismatic Christians, and James R. Lewis and J. Gordon Melton, *Perspectives on the New Age* (Albany: SUNY, 1992) for discussions of New Age religions.

[11] Goddess eclecticism is perceived by some as a negative, and even threatening, feature to "orthodox" neopagans. One Los Angeles practitioner expressed sadness to me that the pagan religion was being "lumped in with New Age" and eclectic Goddess worship and that scholars were questioning the existence of those who were seriously involved with an older and "purer" form of nature religion.

Works Cited

Adler, Margot. 1986. *Drawing Down the Moon*. Boston: Beacon Press.

Budapest, Zsuzsanna. 1986. *The Holy Book of Women's Mysteries*. Volume I. Oakland: Susan B. Anthony Coven #1.

Eller, Cynthia. 1993. *Living in the Lap of the Goddess: The Feminist Spirituality Movement in America*. New York: Crossroad Publishing Co.

Griffin, Wendy. 1995. The embodied Goddess: Feminist Witchcraft and female divinity. *Sociology of Religion*. Vol. 56(1), Spring. Pages 35–49.

Lippy, Charles. 1994. *Being Religious, American Style: A History of Popular Religiosity in the United States*. Westport, Conn.: Greenwood Press.

Neitz, Mary Jo. 1991. In Goddess We Trust. In *In Gods We Trust*. Edited by Thomas Robbins and Dick Anthony. New Brunswick: Transaction Pub. Pages 363–72.

Roof, Wade Clark. 1993. *A Generation of Seekers: The Spiritual Journeys of the Baby Boom Generation*. San Francisco: HarperSanFrancisco.

———. 1998. Religious Borderlands: Challenges for future study. *The Journal for the Scientific Study of Religion*. 37 (14). Pages 1–14.

Roof, Wade Clark, and William McKinney. 1987. *American Mainline Religion*. New Brunswick: Rutgers.

Starhawk. 1979. *Spiral Dance: A Rebirth of the Ancient Religion of the Great Goddess*. New York: Harper and Row.

———. 1982. *Dreaming the Dark: Magic, Sex and Politics*. Boston: Beacon Press.

———. 1987. *Truth or Dare: Encounters with Power, Authority and Mystery*. San Francisco: Harper and Row.

Woodhead, Linda. 1993. Post-Christian Spiritualities. *Religion*. 23. Pages 167–81.

Wuthnow, Robert. 1986. Religious movements and counter-movements in North America. In *New Religious Movements and Rapid Social Change*. Edited by James A. Beckford. Beverly Hills: Sage. Pages 1–28.

———. 1988. *The Restructuring of American Religion: Society and Faith since World War II*. Princeton, N.J.: Princeton University Press.

༃ 4 ༃

Crafting The Boundaries

Goddess Narrative As Incantation[1]

by Wendy Griffin

Feminist theorist Helen Cixous has argued that:

> Women must write through their bodies, they must invent
> the impregnable language that will wreck partitions, classes,
> and rhetorics, regulations and codes, they must submerge,
> cut through, get beyond the ultimate reserve-discourse, in-
> cluding the one that laughs at the very idea of pronouncing
> the word *silence*. . . . (Cixous 1980:256)

Among the partitions that she would have women wreck are
those which delineate cultural understandings of gender. The social
institution that has historically had the most significant role in maintaining these understandings and in engendering us is religion
(Reineke 1995; King 1995). Religion structures reality and teaches us
what it means to be human (King 1995). It shapes social order providing a world-view through which we learn to accept certain social arrangements and reject others (Geertz 1973). It provides
sex-specific codes of conduct and expectations (see Gross 1996).
During the time of the Cult of Mary, for example, the Virgin mirrored the feminine ideal of the Catholic ethic. It functioned as a world-
view, a cultural narrative that linked both women and men to the
larger society and told them a story about how to act there.

BOUNDARIES

One of the most important ways that religion does this is through
the use of partitions, or boundaries. Mary Douglas (1966) argued

that the significance of boundaries lay in their power to define and separate things into opposites: order from disorder, cleanliness from dirt, the sacred from the secular or the profane. As boundaries are socially constructed, a form of cultural narrative, there is a precariousness about them. That which has the potential to destroy existing patterns by mixing with them, has the power to create a new pattern. The vulnerability of these boundaries results in rules being established to exaggerate and maintain the differences between what is within, and is acceptable, and what lies without and is unacceptable. Rules, formal and informal, keep the threat of pollution at bay. But Douglas (1970) reminds us that, as boundaries are mental constructs, potential danger always exists in the ambiguities and contradictions on their borders. Religion, more than any other social institution, patrols these boundaries. This vigilance is necessary because, if the borders change, so does that which was defined. Our cultural narrative would tell us a new story and alter the way we experience and understand the world (Douglas 1966).

The most frequent of all border images is the human body. Douglas argues that the social body teaches us how the physical body is to be perceived: ". . . there can be no natural way of considering the body that does not at the same time involve a social dimension" (1970:98). Feminist scholars add that it isn't just the *human* body that religion uses to demark difference. Because women carry the potential for order and meaning (life) and for disorder or chaos (death), it is the *female* body that is used (Reinke 1995).

When a society feels its boundaries are threatened, it attempts to restore social order by reinforcing or even redefining the boundaries more strictly. As the boundaries of the human body are violated during sexual intercourse, the defense of society's boundaries often involves restating or redefining appropriate sexual behavior, especially as it concerns the female body. Sometimes this is done in linguistic metaphor, such as Yahweh's accusation (Jeremiah 3:1,6) that Israel had "played the harlot." Sometimes the metaphor is physical, as in "maintaining purity" through genital mutilation. Women have been veiled, silenced, buried alive, stoned, and burned to death in an effort to maintain religious and cultural boundaries.[2]

DUALISM & THE FEMALE FORM

This kind of dualistic thinking where women are identified with the body, and men, consequentially, with the mind, was well defined by intellectuals from Aristotle to Descartes and has been thoroughly discussed by feminist scholars (for early examples, see Beauvoir 1961; Griffin 1978). In the past thirty years, feminist religious scholars have begun to argue that this concept is reflected in the cultural narratives of patriarchal religions that typically see transcendence and immortality as goals, define perfection as unchanging, and are anti-body and anti-nature (see Gross 1996). Christian feminist theologian Rosemary Radford Ruether points out that this otherworldly dualism results in women being

> ... identified with the despised body that constantly changes and finally gives evidence of its finitude by dying, and the entire natural world of change and decay is also rejected in favor of a spiritual, otherworldly ideal. Compounding the negative effects of women, the world of nature is symbolically and conceptually assimilated with the body and the female. (in Gross 1996:237)

As a result, the body must be disciplined, even mortified, and desire conquered (Griffin 1995), and that, of course, means that women must be controlled. According to theologian Melissa Raphael (1996:187) "women's bodies endanger men's spirits." They threaten men's souls.

Historically, women have been told this same cultural narrative, and the logical result is that we have become alienated from our own flesh. We have plucked, shaved, starved, veiled, corseted, sanded, lifted, and siliconed our bodies as we learn to objectify them and ourselves. Cixous reminds us of the results. "Censor the body and you censor breath and speech at the same time" (1980:250). Or, as Adrienne Rich put it so eloquently, "The woman's body is the terrain on which Patriarchy is erected" (1972:38).

Ruether also argued that

> Patriarchal religion is built upon many millennia of repressed fear of the power of female bodily processes. Any effort to admit the female in her explicit femaleness as one who menstruates, gestates and lactates, will create psychic time-bombs

that may explode with incalculable force. One can expect cries
of "witchcraft," "blasphemy," "sacrilege," and "idolatry" to
be directed at those who seek to resacralize the female body.
(in Raphael 1996:21)

That, of course, is exactly what is happening.

GENDERED SPIRITUALITY

Today, there are more flexible definitions of what it means to be
female or male. If being a man meant that one was the family pro-
vider, the current female labor force level in the U.S. of 46 percent
(Bureau of the Census 1995) challenges that image. If being a "good"
woman meant taking care of home and children, the fact that the
fastest growing family group in America today is headed by single
fathers forces us to rethink these definitions. Sociologist Meredith
McGuire (1994) posits that the core nature of gender identity has
become more open and fluid, giving us multiple options to explore.
She sees emerging gender issues as the epitome of contemporary
identity concerns. While religious rituals linking the gendered self
to the spiritual self are not uncommon, these typically reinforce
traditional narratives of gender identity. But the dramatic socioeco-
nomic changes which have reshaped the nature of family and work
coincide with the presence of spiritual rituals that *transform* gender
identity, and allow individuals to explore their potential more fully.

Drama theorist Elizabeth Bell tells us, ". . . metaphorical attempts
at 'writing the body' are cultural, historical, and linguistic textual
spaces of representation and identity" (1993:350). Writing the female
body is about presenting it in a way that teaches us something about
who and what women are supposed to be. If women "are" their
bodies, any attempt at transforming gender identity would require
rejecting the meaning behind traditional representations of the female body. In this act, women would purposefully redraw boundaries. And as the social institution most concerned with defending
meaningful boundaries, religion is facing considerable challenge.

GODDESS SPIRITUALITY

One of the most serious challenges comes from those spiritual groups
and networks of groups and individuals who are resacralizing the

female body through Goddess spirituality. This is an amorphous grouping of women and men (see Griffin 1995). Some of these people call themselves feminists, many do not, and many feminists disavow these groups. Some call themselves pagans, Wiccans, or Witches, others do not, and some Wiccans reify traditional gender roles rather than challenge them.[3] What members of this diverse group have in common is that they worship or, more commonly, *celebrate* a primary female divinity, some as an entity, others as an archetype. Some individuals and groups also revere a lesser male divinity. They typically participate in "Goddess rituals" and/or practice Witchcraft, meditation, and other energy techniques called *magic*. Although there is neither written dogma nor sacred book, this belief system functions as a religion (Lozano and Foltz 1990; Raphael 1996). The Goddess is also understood as immanent, the flow of energy linking all things and making the whole biosphere sacred. That, of course, automatically makes humans a part of, rather than apart from, Nature and sacralizes the female body. Because this theology (often referred to as *thealogy* because of the emphasis on female divinity) is so profoundly earth-based, and because of the need for linguistic convenience, I refer to these people as Gaians.[4]

METHODOLOGY

This chapter grew out of a larger project that began in 1988, when a student of mine invited me to attend a Wiccan ritual organized by her coven of Dianic (feminist separatist) Witches. After slightly over a year of doing participant observation with that group, I moved my focus to a larger, more loosely structured Goddess group (see Griffin 1995). Though my main interest is in women's groups, to date I have done participant observation with a wide variety of Gaian groups, in the U.S., Britain, and Mexico. My practice is to take extensive field notes as soon after an event as possible, tape-record indepth interviews, photograph and/or film when appropriate, and read the same materials that Gaians do. The data for this chapter were drawn from these triangulated sources.

WRITING THE BODY

In postmodern terms, Goddess spirituality functions as a new multidimensional, cultural narrative. It tells a new story, one that tells participants who they are and where they fit in. It teaches Gaians how to think and feel about things. It provides a new cultural vision of the world that shows them the way things could be and it shapes a new ethos that can guide what they do. Raphael points out that the words "magic," "image," and "imagination" all come from the Chaldean word *magdhjim*, meaning philosophy.

> Hence to visualize a different social patterning, whether past or future, but freed from patriarchal domination and re-aligned with the divine cosmic energies, is magically to conceive, gestate and give birth or consciousness to new conditions of possibility. This is the postmodern magic of (literally) making wishes come true. And it is a practice encouraged by the "reenchantment" of nature in postmodern science. . . . The world is (re)opened to magical suggestion. The energies of heavenly and human bodies, flesh and cosmos, are (re)made continuous with one another. Changes in the body affect changes in the world and vice versa. (Raphael 1996:27)

By combining the methods of sacred theater with power of religious ritual to deconstruct representations of the female, Gaians are redrawing the boundaries that distinguish order from chaos, the acceptable from the unacceptable. Their narrative results in an embodied thealogy that erases the boundary between mind and body and creates the possibility of an integrated self. In Douglas' terms, by altering the boundaries, they change the shape of the experienced world. It is no longer Descartes saying, "I think therefore I am." It is the Goddess saying, "As you think, so you become." It is narrative as incantation, and it all begins with the body.

In androcentric terms, the human body and the male body are collapsed and seen as identical, leaving the female body as a deviation from the standard. At birth and for the early years, it is typically considered in neutral terms. It may be seen as weak, but it rarely is seen as dangerous. That often changes with the physical developments associated with the arrival of a girl's first menstrual period. Historically, male-dominated cultures have created a *liturgy* for protection against the "bleeding woman," often backed up by strict enforcement of social and sometimes physical boundaries. As the girl's body becomes the woman's, it is defined by other conventions. Care is taken to make sure it is not seen as taller or stronger or more powerful than the adult male's body (Goffman 1979). This positioning of boundaries is part of the gender narrative of our culture. As the female body moves into full reproductive maturity, the meaning ascribed to its representation becomes the traditional "be fruitful and multiply"—under the appropriate circumstances, of course. A pregnant body is usually a message about fertility not sexuality, growing dependence not autonomy. When women cease to menstruate and are no longer physically fertile, the body is hidden. Sagging flesh and age-spotted skin are no longer dangerous, just distasteful. Beauty belongs to the young. These are some of the boundaries that Goddess spirituality makes a point of transgressing.

First Blood

Carol Christ is a widely read thealogian who was among the first to argue that women needed a female rather than a male divinity because of the effects of religious symbols on consciousness (Christ 1982). In her book *Laughter of Aphrodite*, she tells how she and a friend welcomed the friend's thirteen-year-old daughter, Claire, into the world of women. They were on the island of Lesbos and decided to go to Aphrodite's temple. On the way there, the women told Claire,

> Aphrodite is Goddess of transforming cosmic power, especially as it is known in sexuality, that she is by no means Goddess only of love and beauty. We tell Claire how lucky she is to be becoming a woman now when women are beginning to understand again that our bleeding is not a curse but mystery, sacred gift. We tell her our blood is not dirty, that in some cultures men even mimic women's bleeding in their rituals in order to participate in our power. (Christ 1987:192)

Once at the temple, they poured out a libation of wine at the threshold and then entered. Christ writes,

> Inside, I show Claire a beautiful carved image of a flower within a vaginalike oval shape. I tell her that she must understand that her vagina, her sexuality, is her own, that she may share it when she chooses, but she must never give her power to anyone. We pour honey for our sexual juices and red wine for our blood onto the flower. It glistens in the sun.

"Nothing about our sexuality is dirty," we say. "Remember this image. Hold it in your mind all your life." (193)

Few young girls get to go to Greece, but the concepts of celebrating a girl's "first blood" and welcoming her as she crosses the boundary into womanhood are important parts of resacralizing the female body. In 1990, three years after Christ's book was published, a ritual for girls who had recently begun to menstruate was held at the Michigan Women's Festival. This festival is an annual event attended by anywhere from six to ten thousand women. The first blood ritual was preceded by an all-day workshop where the girls talked about the biological facts of menstruation, what it was like to menstruate, their own attitudes toward their bodies and the stereotypes they had heard about women and menstruation. They made small pouches for themselves and filled them with different things that represented something to them about the change they had experienced in their bodies and lives. In the short ritual later that day, a younger girl who had "not yet begun to bleed" led the others on-stage, and then remained to one side as her companions stepped over "the threshold" and were welcomed and embraced by adult women. It was very simple, though it was in front of thousands of women who yelled, applauded, and helped them celebrate their young adult bodies. It wasn't Christ's book that inspired this, as the woman who organized the workshop and ritual hadn't read it. The book hadn't created the narrative, it simply presented an idea that was already there in the culture. In Goddess spirituality, women *experience* their bodies as sacred, and they want their daughters to as well.[5]

Growing from the Inside Out

For four cold days in May 1994, two hundred women gathered in the mountains outside Santa Cruz, California, for the first International Goddess Festival. Most of them were from the United States, but some came from elsewhere, five countries in all being represented. I had received a flyer announcing the event and decided to attend. One of the nights we sat huddled on the grass in front of a large stage while a series of musicians and dancers performed for us. Professional sound and lighting equipment had been rented for the event, and the moon that hung over the stage might have been part of a movie set, it was so full and low. The last act began with the eerie sound of *didgeridoo*, an instrument of the Australian Aborigine that is made of a narrow tree and traditionally only played by men. This night, a female musician crossed that gendered boundary and played the phallic tube. Onto the stage glided a tall woman whose long, red hair cascaded in waves down to the small of her back. Vivid pink chiffon hung in panels from her hips; otherwise, she was naked. She was also about eight-and-a-half months pregnant. As the didgeridoo sounded its breathy growl, she began to undulate in a slow, sensual bellydance. There was a moment of silence from the crowd, and then they screamed and whistled their approval. As the dance progressed, the woman reached into a large basket on the corner of the stage and pulled out a python that was almost twice her height. It twisted slowly around her, as though it were dancing, too, and the crowd went wild.

Later, an art student in her late twenties who had never been to a Goddess event but was familiar with some of the images gave me her impressions of that dance.

> Common culture takes the sex out of pregnancy. It covers it up. . . . I was surprised that here there was no contradiction between pregnancy and sexuality, and it made me think there is a different way to define sexuality . . . not based on other people. It seemed to be complete in and of itself. It was a type of strength without force, a very grounded beauty that was solid and self assured, rather than tentative and fleeting. . . . It was growing from the inside out, and had nothing to do with superficial attributes or unobtainable ideals against which women are traditionally judged.

Dancing with Giants

During these same four days, a large number of workshops were held, including one walking on stilts. This seemed rather superficial and frivolous to me, but I was informed that the teacher, a woman in her sixties who took up stilt-walking after having breast cancer, traveled the women's festival route giving these classes, called "Women Walking Tall." It seemed like great therapy and I thought nothing more about it.

Near midnight on the last night was a full moon ritual. We stood in a clearing deep in the heart of the redwoods, as heavy African drums began to play. Women swayed, some danced; no one seemed able to stand still against their rhythm. Suddenly, the circle opened and into our gathering strode giants. They were bare-breasted under the moon, wearing only extremely long pants made out of strips of cloth that fluttered like leaves as they moved. Intellectually, we knew these were women we had met, that they had stilts strapped to their legs inside their pants, leaving their hands free. But under the full moon in the middle of ritual, they were giants. And then they began to dance on the uneven forest floor. Faster and faster they danced around the circle, until we moved back to watch them in awe.

The same young artist wrote me later that

> Although the women were exposed and unsupported, they communicated an incredible strength . . . which I realized I was not used to seeing in . . . groups of women. . . . I felt incredible to be surrounded by women who were so big and imposing, but not threatening. I felt it was unique that these women had no one standing over them, nothing covering, above them, blocking them. They were it. There was no opportunity for comparison. It forced you to look up to women.

Bathing in the Cauldron

The last example took place in a small artists' community four hours north of Mexico City. Beginning in 1981, there has been a small but flourishing women's spirituality group there, which I located through the local English-speaking newspaper while on vacation in 1996. The unofficial coordinator of the group was Gerry, an American who had lived most of her life in Mexico, but who had studied in California with various Goddess groups. She allowed me to do an in-depth interview, invited me to a meeting of her group, and then told a small group of us to be at the hot springs outside town the next night.

Six Americans, five Canadians, and one Swiss woman met at the end of a dirt road and proceeded to walk in by foot, following a stone path that wove between thermal pools. It was another full moon, and in the distance I could see two men in sombreros tending a large fire. When we arrived at the fire, the men were gone. Four of us had never been to the place before and had no idea what to expect. Following instructions, all of us shed our clothing and entered a small building next to the fire. Water lapped at our ankles as we joined hands and proceeded in naked single file into the darkness. After a few moments, I realized the woman ahead of me was climbing steep steps. I could feel (but not see) a narrow arch on either side of me, no more than three feet across, and as I reached the top step, she began to descend. I followed and found myself in warm water up to my neck. It felt at first like I was in a cave, though I could feel the walls were made of brick and cement. In the faint light that came in, I could just make out that there was another narrow arch at the far end of the "cave" and women were again holding hands and passing through steps that were even steeper than before. The next chamber was very similar, though the water was hotter than the first. At the far end, I could see a faint glow illuminating another arch, just as narrow and perhaps fifteen feet high.

The final "cavern" was very different. The water here was very hot. Steam rose and disappeared out a round hole in the ceiling that was open to the night. The whole structure was round and there was a thin ledge just under the water, barely enough to sit on if one were careful. From somewhere outside, a light was turned on. It fell through the hole and against the wall and arch through which we had just entered, bathing everything in a soft, orange light. After allowing us to play a bit, Gerry announced we were going to do a "sound rainbow." Each woman took a turn floating or standing in the center of the "cave" as the rest of us circled her and sang out her name and two or three attributes or things she wanted for the coming year, such as: Sally, dance, laughter; Barbara, courage, strength.

The acoustics in that small space were amazing. Sometimes the sound was full and round, often it was unmelodic, and occasionally it was so beautiful it was almost painful. It bounced against the walls and echoed across the orange water. It filled the darkness of the second cavern, where women would go to cool down when the water in the last one got too hot. Sometimes, we could hear them as they chanted the names of goddesses, "Isis, Astarte, Diana, Hecate, Demeter, Kali, Inanna."[6] In the center of the circle, one by one, each woman received the "blessing" from the sound rainbow. Some women stayed until those of us circling had finished the song and even for several moments afterwards. Since there was no structure, the music ended when the energy was gone, the blessing/magic was done. Other women rushed the experience, as though it were too much for them to bear, too overwhelming. More than one woman looked close to tears after her turn. A woman in her late fifties told me later:

> The whole experience was beautiful, memorable. I loved it when the women sang to me. I felt supported by people that didn't even know me! It was like the sirens singing, only not the negative part; let's just "take care" of that old myth too! Everything was resonating and beautiful, and we were too.

After the "rainbow bridge," Gerry drew my attention to the arch. On either side of that narrow, slit opening sat a woman. One was the youngest among us: strikingly lovely, flat stomach and full breasts, the stereotypical blonde water nymph of a nineteenth-century painting. On the other side sat the oldest, a woman nearing seventy. She was La Calaca with a skull-like face, empty sagging breasts, and bald pubis. Gerry smiled and said, "They're beautiful. . . . I dream in female."

This theme of authentic beauty, as opposed to "man-made" beauty, ran through the talk of the woman who spoke of sirens in a follow-up interview.

> It was like we were all in a cauldron, only we weren't suffering. The steam was rising and the moon came in through the hole at the top. The sirens were very beautiful women, and so were we. Everyone looked beautiful, although we weren't. We were just ordinary people, fat and thin, old and young, but everyone looked beautiful. It felt secret, private, even though we were in a group. It just felt wonderful.

Her choice of the word "cauldron" is significant. Gaian mythos uses the cauldron to represent renewal, rebirth, and transformation.

CONCLUSION

In writing the body, whether this is done through verbal or nonverbal messages, women in Goddess spirituality are deconstructing the patriarchal religious metanarrative. They transform gender identity by subverting traditional meaning and representation of what it means to be female, simultaneously creating new definitions of appropriate gendered behavior for women. This process redefines the boundaries of what is acceptable. Girls learn their menstrual blood is sacred, their sexuality belongs only to them and there is nothing wrong or dirty about it. Women learn to think about pregnancy in a way that embraces strength and doesn't deny sexual desire. They "look up to women," admiring their strength and abilities, and their willingness to embrace new challenges. They learn that ordinary women can do extraordinary things. They see women as naturally beautiful, independent of artificial aids, age, or body type. They see a body of women supportive of other women.

Done in a spiritual context, this writing of the body provides "truth messages" (Ellwood 1993) that encode the world-view of Goddess spirituality. The body thus represented tells a new cultural narrative, one where Divinity is immanent, the female body is sacred, women are strong and authentically beautiful, mind and body are part of an integrated whole, sexuality is celebrated and not always linked to reproduction, and patriarchy is a temporary aberration rather than a natural condition. It is a narrative intended to heal us all, women and men, and reconnect us to a re-enchanted world.

It is still too soon to know what, if any, lasting effect this new narrative will have. Bloch (1997) has found the symbolic presence of the Goddess in the spiritual world-views of those in alternative spiritualities who *don't* identify as Goddess worshippers. And the growing numbers of practitioners in graduate schools in the United States, Canada, and Britain suggest that the influence of the Gaian narrative will increase. Its presence in mainstream culture may be far more significant. We can already see parts of the narrative seeping into our store of cultural images and transgressing traditional boundaries. For example, in the decade of the '90s, a popular daytime television soap opera had a significant Gaian character. Unfounded religious prejudice against Goddess spirituality was the basis for an evening prime-time episode of another, award-winning series. A major boundary was crossed when actress Cybil Shepard accepted her award at the nationally televised 1996 Golden Globe Ceremonies by thanking the "great Goddess in her many guises."

The mainstream press, both national and local, has covered the phenomenon, and Public Television shows a trilogy of Goddess films annually. *Star Trek* actor Leonard Nimoy introduced television viewers to a group of Gaians in a cable show he hosted on Witchcraft.

It isn't just the media. In 1992, several major Goddess groups were among the sponsors of and activists at the World Parliament of Religions. They coordinated a large public full moon ritual and blessing in Chicago's Grant Park. In 1993, many people were scandalized by a national conference that was attended by over 2,000 members of 32 Christian denominations coming from 49 states and 27 countries. Growing out of the World Council of Churches' Ecumenical Decade and put on by church women, the conference "reimaged" the divine as female. An unexpected backlash resulted in grants being cut from the funding organizations and the event being called the greatest heresy in the last fifteen centuries (in Matossian 1995:34). The boundaries had been violated and were quickly reinforced.

Nevertheless, in this time of the democratization and privatization of religion, it seems clear that the old metanarrative isn't working as well as it used to. Whether or not the women who are writing the body claim the label of feminist, transgressing the boundaries breaks up old cultural understandings and creates a new and a more feminist pattern. Whether or not Goddess spirituality continues to grow and become a major religion, it has already contributed to the new patterns that are developing. In Douglas' (1966) terms, the image of society is currently in flux and the shape of fundamental experience is being altered. Those who practice Goddess spirituality would probably call this "magic."

Notes

¹ I am indebted to Melissa Raphael (1996) for the phrase "narrative as incantation."

² And it continues today. In Afghanistan, the religious Taliban recently ordered all women out of the workplace and back to the home, forbade them an education, and even painted the windows of their houses black, in an effort to keep men from looking in at them and to maintain the women's

"purity." Of course, this not only makes women invisible, it effectively blinds them to the world outside as well.

3 There is an attempt to redefine masculinity as more nurturant and less dominant among many Wiccan groups. However, this challenge to patriarchy has not yet proven to be a serious one, as there have always been some men who are less dominant than other men without threatening male dominance as an institution.

4 All of those I have questioned on this topic are comfortable with the aggregate term "Gaian," though they prefer the name for their own individual path.

5 Just as many young girls won't make it to Greece, many won't make it to the Michigan Women's Festival. In some communities there are workshops and small rituals for them. Some girls have private family rites of passage.

6 A well-known Goddess chant by Deena Metzger and Caitlin Mullin.

Works Cited

Beauvoir, Simone de. 1961. *The Second Sex*. Translated and edited by H. M. Parshley. New York: Bantam Books.

Bell, Elizabeth. 1993. Performance studies as women's work: historical sights/sites/citations from the margin. *Text and Performance Quarterly*. Vol. 13, No. 4. Pages 350–74.

Bloch, Jon P. 1997. Countercultural spiritualists' perception of the Goddess, *Sociology of Religion*. Vol. 58, No. 2 (Summer). Pages 181–90.

Bureau of the Census. 1995. *Statistical Abstract(s)*. Washington, DC: U.S. Department of Commerce.

Christ, Carol. 1982. Why women need the Goddess: phenomenological, psychological, and political reflections. In *The Politics of Women's Spirituality*. Edited by Charlene Spretnak and Carol Christ. Garden City, NY: Anchor Books. Pages 71–86.

———. 1987. *Laughter of Aphrodite*. San Francisco: Harper & Row.

Cixous, Helene. 1980. The laugh of the Medusa. *New French Feminisms*. Edited by Elaine Marks and Isabelle de Courtivron. Translated by Keith Cohen and Paula Cohen. Amherst: University of Massachusetts Press. Pages 245–64.

Douglas, Mary. 1966. *Purity and Danger*. London: Routledge.

———. 1970. *Natural Symbols: Explorations in Cosmology*. London: Barrie and Rockliff.

Ellwood, Robert S. 1993. *Introducing Religion: From inside and out*. Englewood Cliffs, NJ: Prentice Hall.

Geertz, Clifford. 1973. *The Interpretation of Cultures*. New York: Basic Books.

Goffman, Erving. 1979. *Gender Advertisements*. New York: Harper & Row.

Griffin, Susan. 1978. *Woman and Nature: The Roaring inside Her.* New York: Harper & Row.

Griffin, Wendy. 1995. The embodied Goddess: feminist Witchcraft and female divinity. *Sociology of Religion.* Vol. 56, No. 1 (Spring). Pages 35–49.

Gross, Rita M. 1996. *Feminism and Religion.* Boston: Beacon Press.

King, Ursula. 1995. Gender and the Study of Religion. In *Religion and Gender.* Edited by Ursula King. Oxford: Blackwell Publishers. Pages 41–44.

Lozano, Wendy G., and Tanice Foltz. 1990. Into the darkness: an ethnographic study of Witchcraft and death, *Qualitative Sociology.* Vol. 13, No. 3 (Fall). Pages 211–34.

Matossian, Lou Ann. 1995. Re-imaging God. *On the Issues.* Spring. Pages 33–35.

McGuire. Meredith B. 1994. Gendered Spirituality and Quasi-Religious Ritual, *Religion and the Social Order.* Vol. 4. JAI Press. Pages 273–87.

Raphael, Melissa. 1996. *Thealogy and Embodiment.* Sheffield: Sheffield Academic Press.

Reineke, Martha J. 1995. Out of order: a critical perspective on women in religion. In *Women: A Feminist Perspective.* 5th edition. Edited by Jo Freeman. Mt. View, CA: Mayfield. Pages 430–47.

Rich, Adrienne. 1976. *Of Women Born: Motherhood as Experience and Institution.* New York: Norton.

୭୬ 5 ଚ୬

False Goddesses

Thealogical Reflections on the Patriarchal Cult of Diana, Princess of Wales

by Melissa Raphael

READING DIANA'S DEATH

When Diana, Princess of Wales, was killed in a car crash in Paris on August 31, 1997, many commentators were taken aback by the religiousness of the public response to her death. Flower-strewn shrines adorned with images of Diana appeared in the tunnel where she was fatally injured, outside her home in Kensington Palace, and in towns throughout Britain. In the week before her funeral there were all-night candlelit vigils, pilgrimages to her birthplace (that continue to this day) and visions of her presence. These phenomena made it possible for some Goddess women to claim that, in the late summer of 1997, we were witnessing the makings of a post-Christian goddess cult; that, in however unlikely a form, the Goddess was resurfacing in the global consciousness and that the West in particular was expressing its long-suppressed instinct to worship goddesses.

One grieving Goddess feminist noted that the flower-strewn route and the invoking of the Goddess of the hunt in her brother's oration lent Diana's funeral significant pagan undertones. Most significant to this Goddess feminist was the Avalonian symbolism of Diana's burial "on an island in a lake, facing the rising sun" (Henning 1997:1). Or again, while Asphodel Long (1997:2) denied that her own or the public's mourning for Diana constituted the birth of a goddess cult, this was for her "the stuff of myth." In the tragedy of Diana's ill-fated marriage and death, Diana took the part of

Goddess and the public, whoever they might be, took the part of the chorus. Long noted that Diana, named after the Goddess of the hunt, was herself hunted by a pack of patriarchal hunters and that her death recalled the mystery of Persephone. In a dark tunnel in Paris, Diana entered into the Underworld and, according to Long, would rise again in the uprising of all women against exploitation by husbands and in women's protest against the patriarchal alienation of feeling from public and private relationships.

And Long did not only trace the characteristics of classical Goddess mythology onto the events surrounding Diana's death, she also supported the oft-made claim by those who loved Diana that she was not merely on the side of the "down-trodden" but that she incorporated or represented their suffering in her own self: "she dealt with *my* grief, she understood *my* suffering." Or similarly, as some black women and men claimed, "she was Black at heart" (Long 1997:3).

Whether or not Diana *actually* achieved the status and qualities of a goddess in the week of mourning following her death is, to some extent, a technical question of definition and also of interpretation. In my own view, public reverence and devotion to Diana's corpse and to her photographic image went far beyond normal respect for the dead; indeed, the reverence reached such a pitch that it would not be inappropriate to say that she was rendered, if only temporarily, a goddess with a vast cultic following.

It seems clear that, however much orchestrated by the media, her death touched a collective mythological nerve. This was hardly surprising. As so many insisted at the time, Diana, if only by virtue of her times, was the most famous and the most photographed woman in the history of the world. As one television commentator claimed, the projection of Diana's image around the globe had taken her "beyond celebrity." Since the early 1980s Diana's image had been inscribed on the public consciousness so continuously that it had assumed some of the properties of an archetype of "perfect" womanhood—particularly that of the "fairy tale princess." And in the space of a few hours, Diana's sudden and violent death was to so fill the waking and often sleeping consciousness of vast numbers of people, that the archetype went from that of princess to Goddess. With the media constantly impressing on us that the entire world was in (something more than) mourning for Diana, it was hard to resist her becoming the all-absorbing reality—internal as well as external to the self—normally associated with the worship of divinity.

Diana's royal status uniquely contributed to her image's promotion into that of a patriarchal goddess. In Britain, popular absorption in the antics of the royal family amounts to a degraded form of paganism. Diana's non-ordinary status as by far the most luminous of a "pantheon" of royals would, of itself, almost inevitably have surrounded her death with the penumbra of the numinous. Diana glittered with precious stones and shone with fine rainment as sacred objects often do. She was compassionate and suffering and her death was tragic: fraught with mythological motifs of betrayal, hunting, blood sacrifice, the public lamentations of women. The mythography of Diana's death did not entirely lack a sense that her having been violently sacrificed to tabloid journalism had taught the public a moral and spiritual lesson. In the days following her death, the press mediated what they construed to be the public's repentance of their prurient, fatal interest in Diana's affairs and their vow to become better, more serious people in honor of her memory.

It hardly needs to be said that the death of *any* person of kind disposition, especially a parent of young children, occasions feelings of sadness and loss. That would be as true of Diana's death as anyone else's. However, over and above a legitimate sorrow at the death of a well-intentioned person and mother, it seems to me that the media and the public, in a kind of symbiotic loop, were sustaining a highly ritualized mourning for a false goddess—the very patriarchal mediation of the archetype telling us, I believe, something of what (*feminist*) thealogy means when it postulates *the* Goddess. Indeed, it may be that for many Goddess women, the contemporary cult of Diana was and remains an object lesson in what might be called negative thealogy, or what the Goddess is not. Although it may seem strange to talk of thealogy[1] and idolatry—the cult of false gods—in the same breath, a Goddess feminist could, I think, properly judge that devotion to one who, like Diana, succeeded so markedly in a patriarchal culture is an instance of patriarchal idolatry. It is of patriarchy worshipping its own image in the idols of its own creating.

If Diana has achieved something of the status of a goddess, she is a patriarchally constructed and mediated goddess whose appearance and moral qualities were wholly typical of those revered as marks of feminine sanctity in Western patriarchal, monarchical (mono)cultures: namely, whiteness, slenderness, pale skin, golden hair, material wealth and a high status in the social hierarchy, modesty (in which Diana, with her sweet smile and downcast gaze excelled), and the capacity to heal by bestowing comfort, not by magic nor any other learned technique. It is a property of patriarchal constructions of female sanctity that women of moral and religious virtue undertake the burdens of close physical contact with children, the sick, the old and the very poor, that is, those who are beneath masculine attention because they are without a useful function in an inherently exploitative patriarchal system. And it is no coincidence that it was for the giving of consolation and comfort, and despite (or in a post-Christian culture—*because of*) her excessive spending on her appearance and jet-set social life, that Diana became an icon.[2] One devotee, interviewed in a documentary film clearly intended to demonstrate Diana's status as a popular goddess, claimed that she had won his heart by being the only woman in public life who showed "womanly emotions" (Alwyn 1997). The contemporary popular cult of Diana epitomizes patriarchy's somewhat equivocal worship of femininity and reinforces an ideology of femininity as, like Nature, an object of mass consumption and as a public service.

For these reasons alone spiritual feminists should be suspicious of the cult of Diana since it exemplifies how (false and degraded) goddess cults can persist in patriarchal cultures. Such cults present a sharp contrast to Goddess feminism, which is non-cultic. During the week when central London became a shrine to a goddess, and most of my friends and acquaintances succumbed to what appeared even to them to be an unaccountable, wholly disproportionate and obsessive mourning, two things especially sharpened my focus on that contrast. First, that the love Diana had exhibited for the afflicted renewed a very old patriarchal discourse on the sanctity of feminine love, and second, that her death triggered in many a grief for *themselves* as much as for Diana, whom they did not know personally. That is, an ontological question arose concerning the relation of women to those whom they sacralize or regard as Goddess. It is to these two questions of how thealogy might authentically conceive of the Goddess's love and of her ontological relation to the women who celebrate her that this paper will now turn.

LOVE AND THE GODDESS

Countless contemporary women minister to the needs of children and the sick for free or for very low wages. Their doing so is normal and expected and reinforces the ordinary, basically profane, status of women within the patriarchal socio-religious order. Diana, however had the non-ordinary status of an aristocrat and a member of the royal family. In consequence, the many photographic images of her self-humbling in order to minister to the sick (and sometimes literally unclean) appeared to depict an almost miraculous act of grace that was usually received with quasi-religious gratitude. That she lovingly *touched* the afflicted was an act of gracious self-profanation; for it to be efficacious it had to assume her sacredness, or more particularly, the power of a kenosis or the self-emptying of sacredness. Of course the sacredness of any female thing under patriarchy is unstable and ambiguous. On the occasions when Diana *failed* to demonstrate these feminine virtues but showed herself to be an ordinary human being—quarrelsome, sexually and emotionally needy, narcissistic and manipulative—she was vilified by the media and by the public themselves. In short, she was desacralized: that is, made available to public exposure and derision—the very characteristic of any profane thing.

Without wishing to simply dismiss Diana's distinctively establishment philanthropy nor its maternal posture (it was surely preferable to callous disregard of those less fortunate than herself), thealogical conceptions of love and care have very different qualities to those sacralized by patriarchy. In thealogy, the sacrality of motherhood does not always consist of its being always caring and compassionate. In their Mother/Crone Goddess/self women are also sometimes angry, irritable and indifferent. Diana's self-professed ambition to be a "queen of hearts" entirely lacked this Crone aspect. Above all, thealogical love is not just about *feeling*; it is also about the demands of mutuality and political activism (Starhawk 1982:421).

Or again, when Carol Christ defines the Goddess as "the power of intelligent embodied love that is the ground of all being" (1997:v), she too gives a comprehensive account of moral/erotic love (the two are not distinguishable in thealogy) as a defining quality of women who realize their Goddess-self. Thealogical love is not a supernatural—nor even exceptional—choice. To love and be loved is not a mark of grace. Thealogy does not concentrate divine love in saints or moral heroes but diffuses it as a natural, though patriarchally diminished, property of the power generated in the connections of care and natural relationships of exchange between all embodied, natural beings. If one accepts Christ's contention that Nature is "intelligent and loving" (1997:156–57), Nature is not amoral and the moral/erotic manifestation of love rather than hatred or indifference is not non-natural.

Diana's love, by virtue of its patriarchal context and mediation, could only be arbitrarily directed toward whatever objects it happened to encounter in the course of a royal visit. But in a thealogy of connection, love is mutually empowering and mutually re-creative. It does not feed, as Diana's love did, on the traditional Christian assumption of brokenness: that humanity, by its nature, is subject to the chronic failure of relationships. For thealogian Christ,

> In Goddess religion, the source of morality is the deep feeling of connection to all people and to all beings in the web of life. We act morally when we live in conscious and responsible awareness of the intrinsic value of each being with whom we share life on earth. When we do so, we embody the love that is the ground of all being [namely, the Goddess]. (1997:156)

Empowerment born of thealogical love is systemic because Goddess women usually claim to experience life as an interconnected web where hierarchies of being do not exist and where the love directed to one is love directed to the whole and where the healing of a part is, at least a prolepsis of, the healing of the whole.

Whereas, in terms of actual political change, Diana's ministry of comfort left the world of those she touched largely untouched, the Goddess chant celebrates how the Goddess changes everything she touches (just as in P. L. Travers' surely proto-thealogical mythology, a great wind blew the fictional English nanny Mary Poppins' transformative magic into a patriarchal household!). And whereas even the most compassionate *patriarchal* touch assumes a hierarchy of touching subject and touched object, to say that the Goddess changes every (patriarchal) thing she touches is above all to rehearse a magico-political vision of a Goddess whose love is visible in all natural and political transformation. For in political thealogy, the self-realization and empowerment of women describe the loving will of the Goddess. Through a recognition that life consists in its connections, new social patternings emerge that will heal the ecological wounds upon the Goddess's own natural body, even as they heal all other natural bodies that exist within it. Political change is not, then, the historical product of single, powerful agents of consciousness, whether human or divine, but the continuous, regenerative, cyclic power of Nature characterized by its processes of sometimes cataclysmic, often imperceptible transformation.

Thealogy customarily personifies these dynamics of transformation as Goddess. As Mother-Goddess she gestates, births, nourishes and cares for all living things. And yet the Crone aspect warns us that Mother-Goddess' love is not, as Diana's was in her patriarchal context, a consolatory sop. Mother-Goddess love can be tender but it is also manifest in a furious will to justice for all her human and non-human children whose lives are used as fuel to power patriarchal economic, military, and political systems. Here, love is the motive force of justice and Goddess women urge love of the Goddess so that, in being loved and cherished by us, she, as weaver of the web of our natural and social ecology, can flourish in and for us.

Goddess-love is not, therefore, the one-way compassionate love of the privileged, the princess for the pauper, but a love born of mutuality. When women mother the Goddess with love, nourishment, and protection from harm, that is identical with the Goddess mothering them. The absolute immanence of the Goddess entails that the circle of love is unbroken. By its nature, Goddess-love cannot give any woman—or even the Goddess herself—hierarchical power over others. Thealogy's radically organicist world-view entails that the basis of patriarchal power, the subject/object relation, is weakened or disappears. Thealogical love empowers because it describes the egalitarian, organic connection or communion of subjects. In patriarchal religion, however, the condescension of "disinterested" philanthropic love usually disempowers, as Diana's did, by its reduction of persons to grateful objects. When the subject who loves has a non-ordinary status, the imbalance between subject and object assumes thealogically unacceptable proportions; the good impulse to love and be loved suffers gross political distortion.

BEING GODDESS

When unhappy, ill, and oppressed people claimed to have been one with Diana in her suffering, as she had with their suffering, theirs was, I think, an instance of false consciousness. Diana's royal/"divine" status accrued her the kind of hardly imaginable privileges that put an unbridgeable social and experiential gulf between her and nearly all other people on the planet. And this gap between her and "ordinary" women was not merely social, it was also ontological. For at the point of her death, when Diana's probable forthcoming could not betray her ordinariness and age could not carry her body beyond the parameters of a quasi-sacred youthful perfection,[3] Diana could uniquely represent the feminine, "acceptable" face of female divinity.

I say "uniquely" because patriarchal goddesses are, by virtue of being patriarchal, necessarily impossible aspirations. Patriarchy at once constructs an idea of female divinity and makes the realization of that idea by women dependent on criteria that are, in effect, beyond their reach. Diana's quasi-divine status was dependent, as I have outlined, on her enjoying an extremely exalted hierarchical status and on a particularly accurate performance of specific feminine virtues, neither of which are within most women's social capacity to enact. As is also evident in the Catholic cult of Mary, patriarchy, in Diana, at once offers an image of the female divine and takes away the conditions of its possibility. The net effect of doing so is to further reinforce women's sense of spiritual unworthiness, of being *less* than whatever female divinity might be.

In the week after Diana's death, pictures of her radiant crowned head appeared above office desks and shop counters, pinned there by the (usually low-paid) women who worked at them. To see these images gave me, at least, a sense of the profound alienation of women's sense of their own limited worth and that held up as of infinite worth by patriarchy. The contrast between Diana's radiance and their "ordinariness" was so absolute that the only way they could fully identify with the object of their veneration was negatively— through reflection on the times when Diana had suffered betrayal (usually at the hands of the men in her life). That is, their only means of identifying with her, or sharing in her sacredness, at the same time effectively sacralized the oppression of women.

Patriarchy is not monolithic and there is no doubt that some women (and men) have always negotiated with, reinterpreted, and subverted their own masculinist traditions.[4] Nonetheless, over the centuries patriarchal culture has largely succeeded in so purifying and moralizing female sanctity, setting it on so high a pedestal that it is out of sight and hearing. This kind of idealized, depoliticized concept of female sanctity cannot, then, interrupt the voluminous patriarchal discourse on the sacred and the exercise of its power. Masculine religio-political power has been preserved by the deceit that female sanctity is above and beyond women's customary, routine domestic commitments and biological processes. It is a deceit so successfully practiced that women under patriarchy tend to experience the sacred primarily as a lack.

But nor should the patriarchal feminine sacred be an aspiration for spiritual feminists. The latter would not, or should not, wish to identify with a "divinity" like Diana whose persona was constructed by patriarchal ideology and mediated under and through the patriarchal gaze. Spiritual feminism is rightly in search of usable models of female divinity. But spiritually and politically empowering images of divinity are not easily derived from mass culture. As a constructed object of devotion, Diana became merely a pastiche of female divinity, a collage of spurious mythological fragments quite unlike the Goddess as reconstructed into a political and psychic whole by contemporary spiritual feminism. Diana's glamour, for example, was achieved at considerable expense to her mental and physical health and had little or none of glamour's authentic and original magico-numinous resonance. Although most Goddess women themselves relish the creativity and expressiveness of self-adornment, the glamour that helped establish Diana's cult was merely that debased magic of cultivating a charming (emptily decorative) appearance that "sells" a woman at the highest possible price in the marketplace patriarchy establishes in *all* natural resources.

If patriarchal goddess cults alienate women from their own divinity, what, then, might a Goddess feminist properly mean when she says that she does not merely worship or celebrate the Goddess, but *is* Goddess? I use the word "properly" because there are surely

criteria by which one can judge whether a thealogical claim is feminist: that is, when it is liberative of women, and when it is not. When
thealogy describes women as Goddess this is, properly, both a spiritual and a political speech-act. Thealogy, which is an inherently
radical project, sees woman-power becoming Goddess-power in
systemic political criticism and in the envisioning and enacting of
a wholly Other political possibility.

Thealogy also describes an ecopolitical will to become Goddess
by a reintegration of the embodied self into the natural body of
Earth—the body of the Goddess. So that to know and celebrate the
Goddess/self is at once to know and celebrate female embodiment's
being precisely not perfect or static as in the patriarchal archetypes
of princesses and goddesses, but subject to the life-giving process of
continuous, seasonal, organic change. The power of the Goddess/
self is liberated in the liberation of the "wild woman" or "natural"
self from the alienations of masculinist, technocratic modernity (see
Raphael 1997). The motif of the wild woman which has been so
characteristic of thealogy in the 1990s is entirely Other to the im-
maculate self constructed and tamed by constant application of the
technologies of "beauty." The wild self is not merely unresistant to
the body's seasons, its natural passage of time. The Virgin-Mother-
Crone self *is* the Goddess, *is* Nature and therefore *is* that passage of
time.

Likewise, although the realization of the Goddess/self may require a long and strenuous process of casting off the alienating values
of the patriarchal mindset, the Goddess does not *come after* that
process. The Goddess is not a product but is indivisible from the
process of post-patriarchal female becoming. She is not, strictly, a
quest or an aspiration. She is not a divinity whose virtues we must
imitate, rather she is the defining property of what it means to be
in a politically and naturally transformative state in whatever social, historical, ethnic, or geographical context that might be. In this
sense the Goddess is not a *lack* but has an element of what is *not yet*
expressible or knowable. This is part of her mystery.

It must, of course, be emphasized that thealogy gives no single
account of (the) being (of the) Goddess. As a discourse, thealogy is
characterized by its refusal to pin down and dissect (and therefore
kill off) either its own discourse or the being of the Goddess. Where
some Goddess women will experience the Goddess as "real" in

having psychic, political, or metaphoric power,[5] others will tend to experience the Goddess as a divinity having a real existence separate from the women who embody her and to whom thealogical evocations of her might more literally apply. But thealogical realism and non-realism are usually continuous with one another. Starhawk's position is typical of most thealogians: "I have spoken of the Goddess as psychological symbol and also as manifest reality. She is both. She exists, *and* we create Her" (see Starhawk 1979:82; Alba 1993:19; Christ 1997:104).

Whether or not the Goddess is a real divine agent separate from the self, she is, arguably, more than the sum of the one or many women who invoke her. Her transcendence may be imaged (whether actually or metaphorically) as, most basically, the interactive energy or dynamic of the whole—the surge, pulse, or rhythm of the cosmos and of all social and natural relations. And even where many women find it helpful to personify Goddess-energy as a transcendent, emancipatory, guiding will, that will is not such as to require bowing or prostration before it. When Goddess feminists invoke the many ancient names of the Goddess, this is not so much an act of worship as an incantation that helps them name, own, and realize their Goddess-self in terms that are sufficiently archaic as to have lost much of their original contextual particularity and whose power is therefore sufficiently transcendentalized as to become available to any and every woman who chooses to translate or transpose them into the conditions of their individual personality and biography.

So the ways in which the Goddess may be said to be transcendent never arrogates the divinity/power of woman to herself as patriarchal goddess cults do. The Goddess is transcendent in summarizing all that is. But the Goddess is also wholly immanent in each element of all that is, so that women *are* Goddess in so far as they are alive and celebrate their aliveness by honoring and integrating life's ordinary, immanent relational, physical and intellectual demands and by treasuring its products (see Gottner-Abendroth 1991).

It has been my contention that the negative patriarchal cult of Princess Diana that flourished in the week following her death, and which persists in a self-replenishing flow of media images and words in her honor, can help Goddess feminism to outline a sharply contrasting positive thealogy. In this respect, Mary Daly's understanding of the Goddess as a "Verb" rather than a static noun that merely replaces the noun God is a particularly instructive one. For Daly, Goddess images name "active participation in Powers of Being." Like magic broomsticks, Goddess metaphors carry women into the Background: an Other time and space of postpatriarchal female existential self-realization (Daly 1985:xix). Like other celebrity-goddesses who have been adrift and often unhappy in the patriarchal cultures which produced them (one thinks of Marilyn Monroe), Diana is hardly a model for the Dalyan project. What Daly's thealogy suggests is that, for Goddess women, to be Goddess is not to be an object of reverence, but to be a subject whose life is characterized by its Goddessing.

CONCLUSION

When Diana died a spiritual response emerged and rapidly gained mass and momentum largely independently of the authoritative voice of the patriarchal religions. That interpretations of Diana's life and death were plural, highly individualistic, and made few explicit links between her life and death and traditional, mainstream Christianity is evidence of the increasingly post-institutional, post-traditional nature of contemporary Western spirituality. Post-Christian feminists might derive some encouragement from that. Nonetheless, a patriarchal religious ideology of femininity and of female divinity was mediated by a secular press and it seems as if the presence of a growing community of Goddess women and men in the West over the last twenty-five years or so has not yet made much perceptible impact on popular culture and popular religion.

This means that when women want to understand the divinity of their femaleness in the light of contemporary women's experience, there is a danger that they will be bought off by images of female sacredness which, like that of Diana, may be post-Christian but which remain politically and spiritually misbegotten. For a woman to be as much a victim of patriarchy as its product—as Diana was—is no guarantee of the helpfulness of her image or her experience within a feminist spirituality. Feminist conceptions of female spiritual/political empowerment may be derived, with some difficulty, from feminist readings of women in contemporary culture but should also, with Charlene Spretnak, affirm a postpatriarchal future for women: "We have barely tapped the power that is ours. We are more than we know" (Spretnak 1982:398).

Notes

[1] Thealogy may be defined as feminist reflection on the femaleness of the divine and the divinity of femaleness, and as ethical, spiritual, and political reflection on the interconnected meaning of all these. In Letty Russell and Elizabeth Clarkson (eds.), *Dictionary of Feminist Theologies* (London: Mowbray, 1996), p. 281, Charlotte Caron defines thealogy in a similar way as "reflection on the divine in feminine and feminist terms."

[2] Diana was not a practicing Christian (indeed, she had a somewhat post-Christian propensity for consulting psychics) and readings of her life fell largely outside a Christian interpretative frame. This relieved those who had an interest in establishing a goddess cult around the figure of Diana (especially the media) from the constraints of a prophetic discourse against wealth and privilege that would have put her expensive lifestyle into a spiritual and moral perspective and which constitutes Christianity at its liberative best.

[3] On the place of female physical perfection in patriarchal conceptions of the sacred, see Melissa Raphael, *Thealogy and Embodiment: The Post-Patriarchal Reconstruction of Female Sacrality* (Sheffield: Sheffield Academic Press, 1996), pages 75–123 *passim*.

[4] For me, a Jewish feminist who pursues an ideal of postpatriarchal Judaism, invocation of the goddesses of the Jewish tradition—particularly Lilith, Shekhinah, and Hochmah—is a way of naming a wide range of existential and political possibilities—namely prophetic rage, the will to contest and subvert, absence, carefree indifference, laughter, and sexual desire (Lilith), tenderness, repose, peacefulness and presence (Shekhinah), and the unity of all these in intellectual honesty and integrity (Hochmah/Wisdom). As for many postmodern Jewish feminists (if one must adopt a label) these ancient numina together offer the possibility of the *tikkun* (healing or mending) of not only the struggles and contradictions of the self under patriarchy, but also the *tikkun* of femaleness from patriarchy (at least as the latter is experienced by Jewish women). See further, M. Raphael, "Goddess Religion, Postmodern Jewish Feminism and the Complexity of Alternative Religious Identities," *Nova Religio* 2 (1998), pages 198–215. For analysis of the different types of Jewish feminism see Nurit Zaidman, "Variations of Jewish Feminism: The Traditional, Modern and Postmodern Approaches," *Modern Judaism* 16 (1996), 47–65.

[5] For Naomi Goldenberg (who is both an atheist and a thealogian), leaving Judaism and Christianity behind entails "growing out of" depen-

dence on external divinities, and accepting that gods and goddesses are psychological forces or archetypes, but which are no less real and powerful in their effects. (*The Changing of the Gods: Feminism and the End of Traditional Religions*. Boston: Beacon Press, 1979, pages 42–43.)

Works Cited

Alba, De-Anna. 1993. *The Cauldron of Change: Myths, Mysteries and Magick of the Goddess*. Oak Park, IL: Delphi Press.

Alwyn, Richard. 1997. *The Shrine*, dir., broadcast on BBC 2, December 30.

Christ, Carol. 1997. *Rebirth of the Goddess: Finding Meaning in Feminist Spirituality*. Reading, Massachusetts: Addison-Wesley.

Daly, Mary. 1985. Original Reintroduction, *Beyond God The Father: Towards A Philosophy Of Women's Liberation*. London: The Women's Press.

Göttner-Abendroth, Heide. 1991. *The Dancing Goddess: Principles of a Matriarchal Aesthetic*. Boston: Beacon Press.

Henning, Jan. 1997. Editorial, *Wood and Water* 60. Page 1.

Long, Asphodel. 1997. Diana in Paris—in memoriam, *Wood and Water* 60. Pages 2–3.

Raphael, Melissa. 1997. Thealogy, redemption and the call of the wild. *Feminist Theology* 15. Pages 55–65.

Spretnak, Charlene. 1982. The politics of women's spirituality. In *The Politics of Women's Spirituality: Essays on the Rise of Spiritual Power Within the Women's Movement*. Edited by Charlene Spretnak. New York: Anchor Books. Pages 394–403.

Starhawk. 1979. *The Spiral Dance: A Rebirth of the Religion of the Great Goddess*. New York: Harper & Row.

———. 1982. Ethics and justice in Goddess religion. In *The Politics of Women's Spirituality: Essays on the Rise of Spiritual Power Within the Women's Movement*. Edited by Charlene Spretnak. New York: Anchor Books. Pages 415–29.

೦೭ 6 ೦೪

High Priestess

Mother, Leader, Teacher¹

by Helen A. Berger

Women have a central leadership role within American Wiccan covens that are composed of both men and women. Wicca, or Witchcraft, as the religion is also called, defines itself as an earth-centered form of spirituality. Covens, small groups of typically five to thirteen people, are established by a high priestess (HPS) and high priest (HP).

Although Witches tend to be ambivalent about all forms of hierarchy, the HPS is normally acknowledged as the group leader. The HP is usually viewed as having the secondary role of advisor to the HPS. To help soften the notion of and help legitimize their leadership, women speaking about their role as HPSs use the metaphor of mother, often coupled with another metaphor such as teacher or analyst. Although the maternal metaphor might be viewed as relegating women to their traditional sphere, the image of motherhood is being reconstructed within Wiccan rituals and mythology to provide a socially acceptable but powerful image of women.

Bednarowski (1980), focusing on religions that have flourished within the Christian context, notes that the groups in which women are able to assert leadership share four characteristics: (1) the image of the divine has a feminine aspect; (2) the doctrine of the Fall is either denied or tempered; (3) traditionally ordained clergy are not required; and (4) marriage and motherhood are not stressed as the only or primary roles for women. Wessinger (1993) has suggested a fifth criterion—the expectation of equality for women. Wicca meets all five of these criteria.

WICCA

Although most participants acknowledge that Wicca was created in the 1940s in the United Kingdom, they view their religious practice as a return to or a re-creation of a pre-Christian, pan-European form of paganism in which the Goddess(es) of fertility and the God(s) of the hunt are venerated (Adler 1978, 1986). Wicca was transported to the U.S. from the United Kingdom in the 1960s. Most of the early U.S. adherents were white, middle-class women and men who had been influenced by or were participants in the counter-culture. Since the 1970s, women in the second wave of feminism have been drawn to the religion's worship of goddesses as well as gods. Some of these women have joined women-only groups, which venerate the Goddess to the exclusion of the gods. Most of these women, as well as the men who continue to join the religion, like those who joined before them, are white and middle class.

In inclusive groups—that is, groups that have both men and women as members—both male and female deities or forces are worshipped.[2] However, in these groups the Goddess is a more central figure than the God force. Although in ritual both are acknowledged and welcomed into the circle, the image of the Goddess is more often invoked. Images of the Goddess or Goddesses are more numerous on altars and in the homes of Witches. Wicca, therefore, exceeds Bednarowski's first criteria for a religion in which women are leaders. Beyond having a feminine aspect, the divine is *primarily* female.

Similarly, Witches go even further than is suggested by Bednarowski's second criteria—rejecting not only the doctrine of the fall, but what they view as Christian anti-sexual and anti-sensual attitudes that have developed from the concept of Eve—the first woman—as temptress and, therefore, responsible for the fall. Laura, a woman in her twenties, who at the time of our interview in 1987 had been a solo practitioner for four years, stated, "I like it in Witchcraft where it says you are divine as you are right now. That all you have to do is recognize that divinity within yourself. . . . You should love and respect other people and the world you're in, you should enjoy life, enjoy sexuality."

People who become HPSs and HPs are usually trained in covens. This training varies from group to group, but most often involves the HPS, HP, and sometimes other coven members who are knowledgeable about a particular technique or area of magic or ritual teaching about magic, the creation of rituals, and the mythology that surrounds the rituals. As initiates progress through their training, they are typically encouraged to take a more active role in the creation and running of rituals. Participants are also expected to read key books and to create their own "Book of Shadows," that is, a handwritten book of rituals and magical practices. As people gain in knowledge about Wicca, they progress through three degrees—first, second, and third. The attainment of each degree is acknowledged by a ritual. After completing their training, some individuals hive off—that is, they form their own covens, in which they become the HPS or HP. However, some individuals are self-initiated and learn ritual and magical practices from books, journals, and/or courses at occult bookstores. As no formal training or credentials are required to become leaders of a coven, some self-taught individuals subsequently form groups and teach others what they have taught themselves. In 1987, Laura noted,

> When you say whether or not you're a Witch, it is a very gray area because some Witches would say only if you have been initiated into a coven. Some would say if you had been initiated into the Craft in general, regardless of whether or not you belong [to a coven]. And there are people who just say I'm a Witch, and who's to dispute them?

There is a growing debate within Wicca about the need for more formal training of HPSs and HPs, and some groups are working toward this end (Berger 1995). Nonetheless, training still remains primarily in the hands of the HPSs and HPs of covens. Once initiated, all Witches are viewed as clergy—that is, capable of leading a ritual. Only those who head a coven take the title of HPS or HP.

Witchcraft is an amorphous religion, with no central bureaucracy to determine orthodoxy. Although there can be as many forms of Witchcraft as there are participants, in actuality there is a good deal of consistency across groups and participants. The major division is between all-women's groups and inclusive groups; yet there is a growing similarity in these groups as Witches interact on the Internet, through newsletters made possible by desktop publishing, and at large festivals where several hundred people come together for a week or a weekend. This consistency has meant that feminist issues and concerns have become more clearly integrated into American Wicca, because all-women's groups, as well as feminists who joined inclusive groups, have a national forum in which to raise issues of sexism in personal and ritual practices.

Almost all of the women and most of the men I have interviewed have stated that they consider themselves feminists. Many of these individuals view their participation in Wicca and the veneration of the Goddess(es) as one aspect of their feminism. Those individuals who have not taken the label "feminist" maintained that they are sympathetic to issues of women's equity. As there are many different forms of feminism, not all those who claim to be feminists or sympathetic to the movement would agree about what constitutes feminism.[3] Nonetheless, what I see as a common thread among the groups and individuals that I have studied is that women's empowerment is stressed in covens and in rituals, as is their exploration of nontraditional jobs and gender roles. For example, members of covens I have studied have encouraged women in their group to question the division of household labor in their heterosexual relationships, as well as to reassess their career goals and to apply to medical schools or graduate programs. American Wicca, therefore, can be seen to meet or exceed both Bednarowski's and Wessinger's criteria for a religion in which women's leadership flourishes.

METHODS

The research for this paper is based on an eleven-year participant observation study of Witches on the northeastern coast of the United States, which began in October 1986. During this period I formally and informally interviewed over a hundred members of this new religion. For the first two years of my study, I joined the Circle of Light coven as a researcher.[4] I continued to participate in some of the Circle of Light coven's rituals and gatherings until it disbanded in the fall of 1996. I have also been involved to varying degrees with eight other inclusive covens.

In addition, I interviewed seven HPSs specifically about their leadership roles: Laura, one of the original members of the Circle of Light coven, who at the time of the interview was the HPS of her own group; Maeve Rhea, the HPS of MoonTide coven; Trish, who was trained by Maeve Rhea but subsequently became the HPS of her own coven; Judy Harrow, the HPS of a New York-based coven;[5] and Mevlannen and Iontas, two HPSs trained by Judy Harrow. Mevlannen, who is ritually married to Judy, continues to head her own coven in Canada while working with Judy's coven part-time. At the time of the interview, Iontas was HPS of a coven in upstate New York. More than a decade ago I interviewed Judy Harrow and Laura about their participation in Wicca. Both the earlier interviews and the more recent ones I conducted with these women are referred to in this chapter. I also informally interviewed Arachne, the HPS of the Circle of Light coven, about her experiences as head of that coven.

All seven of these HPSs are white, middle-class women who have been Witches for more than ten years. At the time of the interviews two of the women were working part-time at home while caring for their young children, one women was between jobs and the other four had white-collar jobs, such as administrative assistant, engineer, or manager. The women range in age from their early thirties to their late fifties.

LEADERSHIP

In inclusive groups the coven is usually formed by the HPS and HP, who then solicit participants from the larger Wiccan community. Although members of these groups are suspicious of hierarchy, the HPS is customarily acknowledged as the center of the coven. Iontas' HP, Hawk, in a 1997 interview relates:

> In our coven the HPS holds the authority and she sets the agenda—if she says to go east we go east and if anyone else in the coven disagrees we are free to leave her, but at that point that is it. Those leaving her cannot reconstitute the coven. If on the other hand we choose to stay in the coven, we go east—we can complain loudly if we wish but we best be complaining while we are walking.

Hawk spoke of this in a lighthearted fashion, noting that in practice his HPS, who is also his romantic partner, does ask for his input. He feels that part of his job as HP is to offer her his views on how the coven should be run and suggest positive and negative points of any decisions that she is considering. Iontas, his HPS, asserts that it is "much like an accommodation in any intimate relationship—any long-term relationship." She notes that while the decisions are ultimately made by her, she consults all members of the group and considers their ideas, needs, and desires.

Similarly, Laura, whose HP is also her husband, reports in a 1997 interview:

> His attitude is everything boils down to the HPS, and his role is the consort—to help and guide and advise. He may give me his opinion on something and if I really disagree with it and say we really have to do X and he thinks Y is a better idea—we end up doing X. Because even if he doesn't like it he will shut up and go along with it. His attitude is you're the HPS. If you screw it up, you can come crying to me and I'll tell you I told you so but that is the way we will do it. On the other hand, that doesn't happen very often.

Judy Harrow, an HPS for seventeen years, said in a 1997 interview that decision-making in a coven

> looks very much like a consensus decision-making procedure. Whenever it stops looking like one, in a sense, it means something went wrong—because everyone should feel they matter. . . . However, ultimately someone has to take responsibility for the decision. . . . It is hard for my democratic side to come to that conclusion, because it says hierarchy is a bad thing, but unfortunately that is the way it is.

Eller (1993a, 1993b) and Bednarowski (1986) have similarly noted that in all-women's groups, which at times deny the existence of any hierarchy, one woman who is more interested and capable of leading a ritual, organizing a gathering, or holding a coven together frequently becomes the de facto leader.

As participants in what they define as a feminist form of spirituality, Witches are opposed to patriarchal power—that is, "power over." Instead, they speak of individuals having "power to"—that is, the power to gain control of their own lives without the oppression of others. Starhawk, the most widely read of Witches writing in the English language, suggests adding a third category of power: "power with" or influence.

> The power of a strong individual in a group of equals, the power not to command, but to suggest and be listened to, to begin something and see it happen. The source of this power-

with is the willingness of others to listen to our ideas. We
could call that willingness respect, not for a role, but for each
unique person. (Starhawk 1987:10)

The distinction between power over and power to is a common
one within feminist literature. However, when individuals take
charge of a group, the distinction may become blurred. Starhawk's
discussion of power-with is an attempt to distinguish leadership
within covens from domination. The typical justification for some
individuals' being HPSs and HPs in inclusive groups is that these
individuals have power *to* help others develop spiritually, psychologically, and magically. The HPS and HP are viewed as guides for
the people they are training. Judy Harrow in a 1997 interview contends that:

> . . . the HPS is a leader to a small group of people that we
> work with on their spiritual growth. We do teaching, we need
> to keep aware of the group dynamics stuff, try to keep aware
> of each individual's development, acknowledging skills and
> also their weak spots. We do all the things that involve being
> the main or bottom line for a small and very intense spiri-
> tual group.

Part of acknowledging an individual's development and skills
is determining whether an initiate will be invited to continue with
the coven and whether she or he will be permitted to progress
through the first, second, and third degrees. Throughout their life
course, Witches are expected to work on their self-development, as
personality quirks may be a hindrance to full spiritual and magical
development. The HPS is expected to help people become aware of
their problems and provide social, psychological, or magical exercises to help them grow. An individual always has the right to leave
the coven, form her or his own, join another, or work as a solitary.
As covens have a high turnover rate—most covens survive for only
a few years—many people do choose to leave.[6] However, as long as
the individual remains in a coven, the HPS has a good deal of power
or influence in the person's life.

Issues of power, domination, and self-empowerment are central
to Wicca. Many of the rituals and magical exercises are aimed at
empowering and strengthening individuals. For example, in the
Circle of Light coven, everyone was asked to do affirmations by

writing a brief positive statement about her- or himself, which were then to be repeated in front of a mirror twice a day. Every six weeks they wrote a new affirmation. At a number of Samhain (Halloween) rituals I attended, individuals were asked to think about the things in their lives that they wanted to eliminate at this time of the year when the earth's greenery is dying and the days are becoming shorter. Participants wrote a list of changes they wanted to see evoked in the coming year, meditated on them, and then cast them into a ritual fire. In both these instances, the magical or ritual act was aimed at empowerment of individuals to change their self-perceptions and their lives.

All the HPSs I have spoken to view their role as empowering their coven members through their own leadership. Some scholars have noted that women's leadership style, in both mainstream religions and secular organizations, differs from men's in that it is more nurturing of subordinates and more cooperative (Wallace 1992; Nason-Clark 1987; Ice 1987; Gilson and Kane 1987; Naisbitt and Aburdene 1990). Other scholars argue that neither the leadership styles of women ministers nor those of successful women in corporations differ significantly from those of men (Robb 1985, Kanter and Fassel 1977). However, Kanter and Fassel contend that organizations that are feminist, such as *Ms* magazine, actively work toward a management style that is inclusive and anti-hierarchical and that attempts to help each person develop her or his abilities (Kanter and Fassel 1977). Similarly Lehman's (1993) research suggests that women ministers who were trained after 1970 when feminist concerns were incorporated into some seminary courses are more likely to adopt a ministerial style that is empowering of their congregation than either men in general or women who were trained prior to 1970. The different ministerial style of women trained after 1970, according to Lehman, serves both as a response to the gender discrimination that they have experienced in their churches and as a "legitimation for change" (Lehman 1993:7).

Robbins and Bromley (1992) have argued that new religions are social laboratories for the development of alternative cultural responses to social issues. The growth of feminist concerns within seminary training for mainstream religions has, at least in part, been influenced by the women's spirituality movement, particularly through the work of scholars such as Carol Christ and Naomi

Goldenberg (Lehman 1993; Neitz 1991). It is, therefore, not surprising that there are similarities between the ministerial styles of mainstream women ministers and Wiccans. Nonetheless, there are differences institutionally, as Wiccan covens meet in small groups in people's homes instead of in churches, and structurally, as American Wicca does not have the entrenched patriarchal system of mainstream religions. These differences are important, as covens can be viewed as places where women as HPSs, within a religion that recognizes women's authority, are experimenting with leadership styles that implicitly question hierarchy and power relationships.

JUST LIKE A MOTHER

Trish, an initiated Witch for eight years when I interviewed her in January 1997, was about to start her own coven. She told me,

> The HPS is the main leader—she basically organizes everything to do with the coven. She sets the goals for people most of the time. . . . Sometimes it is hard: you have to be the bad guy, you have to get people to see things they don't want to see and that is tough. I've seen Maeve [her HPS] have to do that a lot, with good results in the end but the toughness is real hard—and that is the same as being a mother.

Initially in the Circle of Light coven, Arachne and three other people—another woman and two men—acted as the "elders," or leaders, of the groups. Within the first year, however, the other female "elder" left the group and a more traditional structure of an HPS and HP developed. Even during the first year, however, it was clear that Arachne was acting as the HPS and increasingly taking the central role in the coven. During that year Arachne, in consultation with the other elders, asked Laura, an urbanite, to get more closely in touch with nature by tending a garden. Laura's husband was asked to do volunteer work in a hospital to develop his compassion. He subsequently reflected in a joking manner on the experience:

> I said, "you've got to be kidding. I'm compassionate. I don't kick old ladies. I feed scraps to stray dogs—whatever." . . . I grumbled the whole time. I don't believe I'm doing this . . . . I did it for about six months, and it did what it was

supposed to do. It got the point across to me, and I was rather
glad that I did it. (Darcie 1993:116–17)

Many Witches I have spoken to similarly feel that they have
benefited from the input of their HPS. Maeve Rhea, speaking of the
HPS who trained her, stated "that woman really was there for us,
she really gave her all."

The image of mother is being reconstructed by American Witches
to include the activity of confronting people's weaknesses to help
them change. The image, however, also involves more traditional
notions of motherhood, such as being available to coven mates emotionally and spiritually. Laura commented on what it is like to be an
HPS:

> I always thought that being HPS of the coven is you are the
> mother of the coven. . . . Sometimes that could be you're
> sitting down to dinner and you get a call from a covener
> who is weepy and upset about something, and it means
> dinner goes cold while you sit and listen to them. It is not
> something to resent—it's just part of the package.

The maternal image reappeared in each of my interviews with
women who were HPSs. When three of Maeve Rhea's coven members recently hived off she said that she felt like a grandmother,
watching the women she had helped train take charge of their own
groups. Some of the women I interviewed are mothers—others are
not. Nonetheless, the image of their activity as similar to mothering
appears in their accounts of being HPSs.

The use of the maternal metaphor within Wicca is consistent with
Sered's (1994) cross-cultural study of religions dominated by women,
in which she found that these religions tend to emphasize interper-
sonal relationships, particularly those of motherhood. She insists this
tendency is the result of neither genetics nor hormones but is consistent with women's lived experience. Cross-culturally most women
must be concerned with issues of motherhood—either as an activity
to carry out or something to avoid, to limit, or to seek. According to
Sered, mothering therefore becomes a central image in women's
religious experiences.

Sered contends that religions dominated by women share two
characteristics. The first is that the image of motherhood is seen
from the adult women's perspective, not from children's view of

mothering. Mothers, therefore, are viewed as sexual and with needs and desires of their own. The second characteristic is that as mothering is an adult role for women, it is usually conceptualized as one of power. In most societies, including American society, mothers are thought to have more power than daughters or sisters. However, as Sered notes, although there are some similarities, there is also enormous variety in cross-cultural conceptualizations of motherhood.

Proctor-Smith (1993) suggests that Ann Lee, the founder of the Shakers, provided a liberating role for women within her religious sect by reformulating the concept of mother "in a radically new way, distanced as much as possible from the institution of the patriarchal family" (1993:29–30). Wiccans provide a more open and direct challenge to traditional conceptions of motherhood and of womanhood than was witnessed among the Shakers. However, like Ann Lee they use the image of mother as a starting point for their critique.

Within Wicca the Goddess is viewed in her three aspects as the maid, the mother, and the crone. She has been described in this way:

> THE PRIMAL AND SUPREME DEITY of the ancient world, the oldest and most universally worshiped was the Great Mother, Mother Earth. . . . The Goddess is diversity. She represents both darkness and light and her worship is the reconciliation of opposites. We recognize no such thing as a "Good Goddess" or an "Evil Goddess." (G'Zell and G'Zell 1996: 25–26)

The Goddess who is spoken of as the mother is at once strong, sexual, independent, loving, the bearer of life and joy, as well as the bringer of change through the destruction of the old.

When the HPSs I interviewed spoke of their role as in some ways like mothers, they describe the role as one of power—not of docility. Trish speaks of the mother as the one who needed to be "the Baddy." Judy Harrow views the mother as the person who ultimately takes responsibility. Laura sees the mother as the person who is central. The mother is described in traditional terms as nurturing of their coven mates' abilities, but also as one who teaches and encourages people to confront their entrenched habits and change them. The notion of the mother as the agent of change is consistent for Witches with the crone aspect of the Goddess. This is the aspect of wisdom, but also of destruction and death. The destruction is viewed, by

Wiccans, as necessary for renewal, for growth, and as part of the natural cycle of life. Although it is traditional for mothers to be viewed as guiding their "young" as they grow, the notion of confrontation evokes a stronger image—one of an analyst, who forces his or her clients to examine their behavior so that they may gain control over it. Furthermore, the HPS goes beyond traditional images of motherhood in two other ways. First, she takes the role of organizational leader of the group. Second, the image of motherhood within Wicca, as is consistent with Sered's findings cross-culturally, includes sexuality. Sexuality is celebrated at Wiccan festivals and rituals and is viewed as part of all three aspects of the Goddess—the maid, the mother, and the crone.

While accepting the image of motherhood as a central one for women, Witches are transforming it, broadening it beyond the notions of nurturing and loving. This image of the mother is consistent in some respects with the role of mothering at the end of the twentieth century—one in which mothers are advised to be involved in their children's education and be aware of their children's psychological state. But while the women who are taking on the role of HPS in some ways see it as like mothering, they also note that it is a self-empowering role of leadership. Maeve Rhea asserted, "it's always good to be the alpha female." Mevlannen contends that what she gains is "a sense of connection, and a better sense of myself. This is what I do [even] during a period when my professional work is at a standstill." Judy Harrow in my 1986 interview with her notes:

> I have a need to feel that I am making a real contribution in this world. . . . I think that is probably a real need for everybody. You know, Freud said that the two greatest issues of life are love and work—making the difference, expressing yourself, having an outlet for creativity. I also have the same need as everyone else—to make money and pay the rent. But what I do to make money and pay the rent does not satisfy that other need in any kind of fullness. So I have to do something else beside my day job.

The role of HPS is an avenue for these women to express themselves and to take a leadership role, a role that may be denied them in their mundane lives. Even for those who are successful in their careers, the role of HPS provides an outlet to experiment with leading a group in which female authority is acknowledged.

Coven members vary in their appraisal of the success of their HPS's leadership style. For instance, Iontas felt her first HPS was not able to help her develop her abilities fully and therefore she sought out instruction from Judy Harrow. Laura, who during her training was asked to till a garden, did not think the gardening had been beneficial. She never grew to enjoy the activity and felt that the request negated an understanding of her true connection to nature. Although Laura completed her training in the Circle of Light coven, and therefore technically hived off, a rift has developed between her and her former HPS and HP. A similar rift divides Trish from her former HPS from whose coven she hived off. The intimacy of the coven makes it ripe for disagreements and hurt feelings. Furthermore, the use of the metaphor of the mother in the late twentieth century carries with it the notion of bad mothering or inadequate mothering.

The term *mother* has a double edge in another way as well. It brings with it traditional images of kin relationships and responsibilities—as Laura said, being there for others even if your food is getting cold. Yet, the image of mother is being refashioned within Wicca to provide an alternative view of womanhood—one that is empowering. The Goddess is the mother, the bearer of life and of death.

CONCLUSION

A coven is, among other things, a place in which a woman can explore her leadership skills as an HPS. Within this context women are attempting to create a form of leadership consistent with their feminist ideals, which focus on anti-hierarchical and consensus-based social relationships. There is a parallel between the leadership styles within Wicca and women ministers in mainstream churches who have been trained since the introduction of feminist concern into seminary training. However, within Wicca, women's leadership role is developing within a religion that recognizes female leadership as legitimate.

In developing their leadership style, Witches turn to an old image, that of mother. The mother is viewed in traditional terms as loving, giving, and helping others in their development. But the concept of mother within this new religion is also being refashioned to include a more empowering image for women. This reconstructed image of motherhood is one in which women are viewed as sexual adults, whose role involves the confrontation of others' weaknesses and in which their own leadership is legitimated. This image of motherhood is consistent with the Wiccan image of the Goddess in her triple aspect—powerful, sexual, demanding of change, and loving.

Most HPSs do not view their role solely in terms of mothering. They regularly note that their work as coven leaders is also like being a teacher or an analyst. The metaphor of mother provides one way in which these women can start to think about creating a new form of leadership that builds on what have been considered women's traditional strengths.

Notes

[1] An earlier version of this paper was presented at the 1998 meetings of the American Sociological Association in San Francisco.

[2] Neitz (1991) makes a distinction between Feminist Witches and neopagan Witches. I prefer to use the terms *women-only* or *all-women's* groups and *inclusive* groups, as among the groups I studied both types claim to be feminist.

[3] For a discussion of schools of feminist thought, see Rosemarie Tong (1998, *Feminist Thought: A More Comprehensive Introduction*, second edition, Boulder: Westview Press) and Alison Jaggar and Paula Rothenberg, editors (1984, *Feminist Frameworks: Alternative Theoretical Accounts of the Relations between Women and Men*, second edition, New York: McGraw-Hill).

[4] Fictitious names have been used for groups and for individuals throughout this paper, unless otherwise noted.

[5] Judy Harrow gave permission and requested that I use her full name in my work.

[6] Some breaks within the coven are a natural evolution of individuals completing their training and hiving off. Other ruptures can be acrimonious or the result of work, family, or educational opportunities requiring people to move to another part of the country.

Works Cited

Adler, Margot. 1978. *Drawing Down the Moon*. Boston: Beacon Press.
———. 1986. *Drawing Down the Moon: Revised and updated*. Boston: Beacon Press.

Bednarowski, Mary Farrell. 1980. Outside the mainstream: women's religion and women's religious leaders in nineteenth century America. *Journal of the American Academy of Religion* 48 (June). Pages 207–31.
———. 1986. Women in occult America. In *The Occult in America: New Historical Perspectives*. Edited by Howard Kerr and Charles L. Crow. Urbana and Chicago: University of Illinois Press. Pages 177–95.
Berger, Helen A. 1995. Routinization of spontaneity. *Sociology of Religion*. 56(1). Pages 49–62.
Darcie. 1993. 'Coming home': reflections on conversion to Wicca. In *Modern Rites of Passage: Witchcraft Today*, Book Two. Edited by Chas S. Clifton. St. Paul: Llewellyn Press. Pages 105–28.
Eller, Cynthia. 1993a. *Living in the Lap of the Goddess: The Feminist Spirituality Movement in America*. New York: Crossroads.
———. 1993b. Twentieth-Century women's religion as seen in the Feminist Spirituality Movement. In *Women's Leadership in Marginal Religions*. Edited by Catherine Wessinger. Urbana and Chicago: University of Illinois Press. Pages 172–95.
Gilson, Edith, and Susan Kane. 1987. *Unnecessary Choices: The Hidden Life of the Executive Woman*. New York: William Morrow.
G'Zell, Morning Glory, and Otter G'Zell. 1996. Who on Earth is the Goddess? In *Magical Religion Modern Witchcraft*. Edited by James R. Lewis. Albany: State University of New York Press. Pages 25–34.
Ice, Martha Long. 1987. *Clergywomen and Their World Views: Calling for a New Age*. New York: Praeger.
Kanter, Rosabeth Moss, with Diane Fassel. 1977. Some observations of women's leadership in organizations. In *Men and Women of the Corporation*, by Rosabeth Kanter. New York: Basic Books. Pages 299–303.
Lehman, Edward C. 1993. Gender and ministry style: things not what they seem. *Sociology of Religion* 54(1). Pages 1–11.
Naisbitt, John, and Patricia Aburdene, editors. 1990. *Megatrends 2000*. New York: William Morrow.
Nason-Clark, Nancy. 1987. Are women changing the image of ministry? a comparison of British and American societies. *Review of Religious Research* 28. Pages 331–40.
Neitz, Mary-Jo. 1991. In Goddess we trust. In *In Gods We Trust*. Edited by Thomas Robbins and Dick Anthony. New Brunswick: Transaction Publishers. Pages 353–72.
Proctor-Smith, Marjorie. 1993. In the line of the female: Shakerism and feminism. In *Women's Leadership in Marginal Religions*. Edited by Catherine Wessinger. Urbana and Chicago: University of Illinois Press. Pages 23–40.
Robb, Carol S., editor. 1985. *Making the Connections: Essays in Feminist Social Ethics*. Boston: Beacon Press.

Robbins, Thomas, and David Bromley. 1992. Social experimentation and the significance of American new religions: a focused review essay. *Research in the Social Scientific Study of Religion* 4. Pages 1–28.

Sered, Susan Starr. 1994. *Priestess, Mother, Sacred Sister: Religions Dominated by Women*. New York and Oxford: Oxford University Press.

Starhawk. 1987. *Truth or Dare: Encounters with Power, Authority, and Mystery*. San Francisco: Harper and Row.

Wallace, Ruth. 1992. *They Call Her Pastor: A New Role for Catholic Women*. New York: State University of New York Press.

Wessinger, Catherine. 1993. Introduction. In *Women's Leadership in Marginal Religions*. Edited by Catherine Wessinger. Urbana and Chicago: University of Illinois Press. Pages 1–22.

೭೫ 7 ೧೯

Thriving, Not Simply Surviving

Goddess Spirituality and Women's Recovery from Alcoholism

by Tanice G. Foltz

INTRODUCTION

The Goddess spirituality movement, which can be traced back to the early 1970s in the U.S., is currently enjoying tremendous visibility through weekend retreats, women's spirituality conferences, and music festivals, and it is gaining exposure in university academic programs. A point of discussion among feminist theologians, Goddess spirituality embraces such groups as Wiccans, pagans, and Gaians, all of whom celebrate the Goddess and practice an earth-based spirituality.

This paper explores the relationship between Alcoholics Anonymous (AA), Goddess spirituality, and women's recovery from alcoholism. In earlier research I discovered that Goddess spirituality practitioners were using their spirituality circles to supplement their AA meetings or as a substitute for AA (see Foltz, 1994). The women indicated that their participation in Goddess spirituality and Wiccan circles had helped them with their sobriety and had deeply affected them. This unexpected finding invited further inquiry.

METHODS

This chapter is based upon research conducted at a pagan festival and a womyn's music festival, both taking place in the Midwest and attended by people from around the country.[1] In 1995 I conducted in-depth interviews with ten women, eight of whom attended one of the two events, and two who responded to an ad I placed in a pagan newspaper. A year later I distributed a survey questionnaire from a Twelve Step tent at the women's festival and, out of 100 responses, collected 52 that were pertinent to this research.

The interviewed women ranged in age from 26 to 51, with 60 percent between 36 and 44. Three were married, two divorced, and five single. Six identified themselves as heterosexual, three as lesbian, and one as bisexual. All had attended college, half had Bachelor's degrees or more, and over half earned less than $20,000 annually. The women surveyed ranged in age from 16 to 55, with 56 percent between the ages of 40 and 50. In contrast to the interviewees, 72 percent identified themselves as lesbian, 20 percent bisexual, and 8 percent as heterosexual.[2] Only 10 percent were married, 50 percent were single, 19 percent woman-partnered, and 21 percent divorced. Over 87 percent had attended college, with 45 percent earning a Bachelor's degree or more, 19 percent had graduate degrees, and 56 percent earned less than $20,000 a year.

GODDESS SPIRITUALITY AS HEALING

Goddess spirituality considers the Divine Feminine to be immanent in all forms of life, and thus it acknowledges a deep spiritual connection between humans and the natural world. It honors the seasons of nature and women's cycles, both associated with phases of the moon. Women's bodies are revered as life-giving and their biological changes are celebrated in rites of passage. Goddess spirituality honors women's wisdom, and its rituals facilitate profound self-communication, trust, and women's bonding (see Foltz and Griffin 1996).

Meredith McGuire (1994:275) refers to Goddess (or women's) spirituality as "gendered spirituality" because it "serves to express, produce, or transform the individual's gender identity itself . . . toward some alternative ideal." Griffin (1995) has observed that Goddess spirituality provides sacred imagery which can transform one's way of looking at and being in the world (see also Lozano and Foltz 1990). Since a primary focus of Goddess spirituality is establishing spiritual connection with one's self, as well as with all beings, it has at its very core an intention of healing. Eller (1993:10) offers a fitting definition: "Healing is a metaphor for any form of self-transformation, whether emotional, physical or mental. It is the name given to the overall effort to gain self knowledge and marshal personal power."

Janet Jacobs claims that women's alienation is at the heart of the Goddess spirituality movement. She views the movement as having arisen from women's dual alienation from the devalued "female self" and from "the dominant patriarchal culture" (Jacobs 1990:377). Her work on sexually-abused women provides evidence that women feel transformed and empowered by their experiences with Goddess symbolism and ritual (see Jacobs 1989).

According to feminist thealogian[3] Christ (1982), "Women need the Goddess" to gain respect and reverence for their own bodies, to know and act on their own will, to understand their history, and to create bonds with women. Starhawk, prominent Witch, psychologist, and leader in the feminist spirituality movement, clarifies the centrality of a female Divinity in women's self-acceptance and empowerment:

> The importance of the Goddess symbol for women cannot be overstressed. The image of the Goddess inspires women to see ourselves as divine, our bodies as sacred, the changing phases of our lives as holy, our aggression as healthy, our anger as purifying, and our power to nurture and create, but also to limit and destroy when necessary, as the very force that sustains all life. Through the Goddess, we can discover our strength, enlighten our minds, own our bodies, and celebrate our emotions. We can move beyond narrow constricting roles and become whole. (Starhawk, 1979:9)

Goddess spirituality provides women with a compellingly strong role model as well as a female image women can draw upon to become reintegrated, whole, and re-sacralized—in short, empowered. This gendered spirituality that is feminist stands in contrast to the male-oriented gendered spirituality of the Twelve Steps of Alcoholics Anonymous (AA).

122/ TANICE G. FOLTZ

ALCOHOLICS ANONYMOUS
An Overview

Alcoholics Anonymous is a self-help treatment program for recovering alcoholics, cofounded by Bill Wilson who wrote the Twelve Steps (AA, 1976). A member of the evangelical Oxford Group, his religious beliefs are evident in AA's philosophy. Although AA claims to be secular, it has been compared to a cult (Bufe 1991), a sect (Fox 1995; Jones 1970), and an "identity transforming organization" (Greil and Rudy 1984), complete with conversion and testifying processes.

Quaker psychologist Kasl (1992:5), contends that AA's Twelve Steps and *Big Book* do not adequately serve women's needs, since they were based on the experiences of 100 white men and one woman. Rather, they refer to shortcomings and reinforce weaknesses in a setting where traditional gender norms put women at a disadvantage.[4]

Nevertheless, the majority of women in this study still participate in AA meetings while practicing Goddess spirituality. Because women do attend AA as a treatment option, it is important to understand what elements they consider to be obstacles to their recovery.

MAJOR PROBLEMS ENCOUNTERED

As newcomers to AA, the women felt scared, lonely, and isolated, but they soon discovered that AA meetings provided structure, fellowship, and social support. Like the women surveyed, interviewees initially experienced a "spiritual awakening" and an increase in their self-confidence. But eventually they began questioning the patriarchal language and hierarchical relations of AA's Judeo-Christian orientation.

Language, Hierarchy and Judeo-Christian Orientation

The first of the Twelve Steps, "admitted we were powerless over alcohol, that our lives had become unmanageable," prompted the response, "I am not powerless!" as it contradicts the ideal of self-empowerment. Kasl (1992) understands the Twelve Steps as aimed at humbling alcoholics, a good approach for men with stronger egos, but potentially oppressive for women.

Kate, a 42-year-old mother, wife, Witch, and recovering alcoholic/cocaine addict, discusses her concerns:

> I had problems with the Lord's Prayer and the "God give us serenity" and the empowerment thing—the fact that you had to give up your power. And that you had to admit that you were defenseless and you were powerless. And I kept saying to myself, "How can I start out right by saying, 'I am powerless,' and then expect to have the power to do this?" I mean I couldn't reconcile those two things.

Courage, a 42-year-old pagan and divorced mother, also found it difficult to accept AA's concept of "a Power greater than ourselves."

> For me the concept of higher power, it ties into morality and authority outside of one's self. And I think that authority outside of one's self doesn't work for me. For me, I work with inner power. And that inner contact for me helps for connection and community, and that's where I get my direction—not from outside people telling me what to do or saying the way things should be.

Although AA claims to be spiritual and not religious, its God-language belies this claim in several steps. The language of the third step, "Made a decision to turn our will and our lives over to the care of *God as we understood Him,*" requires the acknowledgment of inadequacy as well as dependency on a male Divinity. This stands in opposition to Goddess spirituality's emphasis on taking responsibility, and its belief that immanent in every being is an aspect of Divinity that is female. Because the God-language is highly charged, many women devise strategies to neutralize it.

Brigit, aged 51, wife and mother, has been sober 15 years and still attends AA meetings. When she reacted to the God concept her friend suggested that she "think of it like 'the Force' in Star Wars." She did that for a while and then later changed it to electricity, translating the God concept to something neutral. Even though Brigit now considers herself a Dianic Wiccan,[5] she will not use the term "Goddess" at AA meetings because she fears "it might be inflammatory in a mixed meeting." By keeping her true beliefs veiled, she continues to work the steps without bringing attention to herself.

Daphne, who draws on Dianic Wicca, Native American spirituality, and Eastern religions, provides another example. Single, aged 36, and just coming out as a lesbian when she was getting sober, it took her about six months in AA to begin to question the references to the Judeo-Christian God, as well as the heterosexual orientation of the meetings. In response to her concern, a friend asked her, "Which do you want more, your recovery or your politics?" After thinking about the implications and desiring to get sober first, she said: "So I went through my *Big Book* and changed every *He* to *She.*" By using these slightly subversive, non-confrontational strategies, the majority of women found they could successfully "get along" during AA meetings, and avoid rocking the boat while remaining true to their own beliefs.

A major source of concern for interviewees was closing AA meetings with the Lord's Prayer. Here Brigit relates her feelings as well as the strategy she and her women friends developed:

> I don't like saying the Lord's Prayer at the end . . . that's real patriarchal to me. . . . And so there's three people I know that go to my WomanSpirit and are very into women's spirituality and Wicca, and we, to ourselves, sing "We are a Circle" and we stand up and hold hands while everybody else is saying the Lord's Prayer.[6]

Clearly these women are attempting to modify AA's concepts to fit their own beliefs without creating any tension within the meetings. Others, however, would like to see some changes made in AA.

Nenoc, aged 27, a recovering drug addict and pagan, tried to affect change. Having attended a large young people's AA meeting for about five years, Nenoc was "really turned off by the Lord's Prayer." When she requested a more neutral closing, the group split: one adamantly defending AA's tradition, and the other considering change. In the end, Nenoc's suggestion ignited such a controversy that the meetings collapsed. This abrupt ending over the Lord's Prayer highlights AA's rigidity and its limited spiritual tolerance.

Intolerance to Wicca, Paganism, and Feminist Spirituality

In her study of Pagans in AA, Fox (1995) found that participants often encountered religiously based prejudice at AA meetings. To deal with this, they either switched meetings, stayed silent about their religious identities, or challenged AA's religious sectarianism. In my survey, 87.5 percent of the women felt they could not express their own religious or spiritual beliefs at AA meetings: In fact, one woman wrote she was told "not to explore Goddess images, but to stick to standard churches to get my spirituality in place." Several women who questioned AA's concepts or who shared their identities as Witches or lesbians were shunned or rejected outright at AA meetings.

Georgia, 36, Witch, mother, and recovering drug addict and alcoholic, provides a disturbing example. Georgia had been attending AA meetings for over a year when her picture appeared in *Time Magazine* with a pagan group for "Earth Day." At her next AA meeting, she was told to leave and not come back until she "quit that crazy religion." Although she complained to the main AA office, she felt so humiliated she did not return. Publicly ostracized and expelled by AA members, Georgia was left to rely on her Wiccan spirituality and her friends to keep herself sober. This is a potentially frightening prospect for recovering alcoholics who believe they must attend AA meetings to maintain their sobriety.

Dependency and Dogma: Another Addiction?

Because the success of AA depends on people coming to meetings, it emphasizes the importance of playing an active role (working the steps) toward recovery. One mechanism of establishing and maintaining commitment is the threat that the alcoholic will "never make it" without AA meetings. A regular part of talk at AA meetings includes a multitude of dogmatic slogans that defy challenge.

Suzanne, a 30-year-old lesbian college student, now a Dianic Witch, says even though she felt good about "the sense of commonality and community" she found in AA, she had problems with the dogma. She explains: "I mean that there were several old white men sitting around the table preaching kind of a hard line towards AA about 'take the cotton out of your ears and stuff it in your mouth' and 'put the plug in the jug.' And just meetings, meetings, meetings."

Other slogans include "utilize, don't analyze," and "your best thinking got you here," both implying that participants shouldn't think too much. Courage addresses this aspect: "And if I said anything at all that questioned the steps, I got, 'It's not broken, don't fix it,' 'it saved my life' in a very doctrinal way." She was concerned that AA was so dogmatic it was not able to "address new issues as new things came up."

Daphne talks about her belief in AA's dogma. "Years later, I had to do a cleansing of what I internalized there . . . and that was the message that 'You'll never make it outside of here sober' you know, 'You'll never make it if you don't go to meetings, and if you don't do this, then you'll get drunk.'" In fact, these messages created a "big fear about not being there." This carefully instilled fear may lead some to question if AA is yet another addiction.

Laughing Womyn, 36, a Dianic Wiccan Priestess and women's spirituality leader in her local community, eventually came to see AA meetings as another dependency to replace alcohol. She explains: "And that's one of the things that really took me away from AA too, is that I saw a lot of old timers being addicted to the meetings. And I didn't want to trade one addiction for another." She continues, "Once I got my feet under myself emotionally . . . then AA became kind of a weight around my neck; it ceased to be a supportive growthful [sic] place for me at that point, and I had to go find some other options." An option she chose was creating a women's full moon circle that became so popular it attracted between 30 and 50 women for over six years.

Mixed Meetings, Male Dominance

Many of the women interviewed observed that men tend to dominate in mixed-gender AA meetings, and the women surveyed agreed. A majority (87.5 percent) revealed a concern that "men ran the show" and 88 percent felt "uncomfortable speaking in a group of men." In fact, one woman wrote: "I was able to speak, but often had to force myself to do so. . . . (there was) no deep understanding." Further, 86 percent of the women felt that an AA meeting was "no place to discuss the source of alcoholism or addictions," and 80 percent felt their lesbian or bisexual orientation would not be tolerated in regular AA meetings.[7] What the women perceived as their primary recovery needs were often left unmet by AA meetings, and thus Goddess spirituality was welcomed as a spiritual supplement, and in some cases a substitute for AA.

GODDESS SPIRITUALITY
A Feminist Recovery Alternative

The combined results of the interview and survey data show that between 40 and 45 percent of the women in this study supplemented their AA meetings with Goddess spirituality. Of the women surveyed, 29 percent stopped attending AA altogether, though continuing with their Goddess practices. Among the interviewees, 60 percent fell into this category. These findings compelled me to ask, "What does Goddess spirituality provide for recovering alcoholic women that is missing from AA?" Three overlapping themes emerged from the data: a holistic approach, a healing spiritual community, and women's celebration.

Holistic Approach: Addressing the Whole Self vs. the Alcoholic Self

A primary theme is that Goddess spirituality is concerned with the "whole self"—the psychological, spiritual, emotional, and the social. This means it goes beyond AA's focus on the alcoholic self, reaffirmed with each greeting, "My name is Sue and I am an alcoholic." A criticism of AA is its disease focus, accompanied by a lack of sensitivity to the whole person. AA's party line is that a person's body chemistry makes her "allergic" to alcohol. This explanation completely excludes the discussion of any social factors that might contribute to alcoholism.

Of the women surveyed, 96 percent felt their alcoholism or addiction was related to abuse they experienced while they were growing up. Sixty-three percent reported having experienced childhood sexual abuse, 63 percent physical abuse, and 98 percent experienced emotional abuse. Although I did not ask questions about sexual abuse during the interviews, 40 percent of the women volunteered they had experienced this childhood trauma. They also related that these kinds of events were considered "irrelevant" or inappropriate for discussion at AA meetings.

Daphne articulates that she often resisted going to AA meetings because she couldn't talk about how her experiences with incest, homophobia, rape, and molestation continue to affect her sobriety. She explains, "Well no, you come in and talk about your sobriety, you talk about alcohol . . . and you didn't talk about this other stuff. 'No this isn't therapy. . . . you come here to stay sober. Get sober and stay sober.' And we were saying 'Hey look, we can't stay sober unless we talk about this stuff!'"

Kate has her own views about AA as a treatment program. She felt that abuse issues had most definitely influenced her addictive behavior. As a child she had been physically and emotionally abused by her father, and sexually abused by her brother from age twelve until she left home to get married. When her own children reached puberty, she began drinking heavily and shooting cocaine. Kate discusses her understanding of this behavior:

> What I believe is that I had a self destructive problem going on here as a result of not being able to process the pain I had as a child, and that I used alcohol to numb and deaden my feelings, and that progressed to a point where I was actively trying to kill myself. . . . Once I understood the underlying cause of my pain . . . I wanted to find out how to function healthy [sic]. So from there on out my premise with all of these people was that "You're treating the symptom, you're not treating the disease, the problem."

Spiritual Community and Safe Healing Environment

Daphne offers her experience of AA meetings: "There were people I cared about, but it really wasn't enough to feed me. . . . I didn't get to go deep enough and I didn't feel enough community . . . in terms of shared reverence." Like Daphne, many of the women interviewed were not spiritually satisfied with AA, and they either joined or started a Goddess spirituality group to be part of a woman's spiritual community.

What they found is that Goddess spirituality affirms women's reality, and it also creates an environment conducive to the development of trust among women. As one of the survey respondents wrote, "A woman-centered spirituality helps women celebrate themselves without having to filter through all the male and patriarchal language and attitudes of AA," and another, "I felt much freer to talk about issues related to recovery than in AA."

Courage's group provides an illustration of women's spiritual community. Courage had attended AA for nearly fifteen years and always disliked its dogma, especially what she calls the "power over" concepts. Unlike those who were content to quietly modify AA's God concepts, Courage experienced so much dissonance that she started an alternative Goddess-oriented recovery group to address women's issues. She created what she calls a "working circle . . . to get more a sense of community, and it's not just community around substance abuse, but it's community around the really whole life." The group is not just for recovering alcoholics but for "every sort of trauma, self-inflicted or outer inflicted" and "there's no issue about whose addiction is worse or anything like that." She related that many types of recovery issues are represented, but the women don't identify themselves "by choice of substance or coping behavior. We tend to identify by our woman-ness and by our personhood. . . . So we support each other in our full expression of who we are." She continues:

> It's much more about just affirming who each of us is. . . . It's the wholeness of our experience. We know that we are altered in some really intense way because of some things that we've experienced, and we honor the negative things that have happened. And we know that some of them are really horrible . . . but we do know we've grown from them, and we often do ritual around it.

Courage conveyed that the women acknowledge the situations in which they have given up their power and through Goddess ritual and affirmation they reclaim their strength. She observes:

> I found a healing that's happening. . . . it's a very profound healing, the trust is very very strong, and women say that they can say anything and not feel constrained. . . . And they've often commented that they've spent years at AA groups and other recovery groups, and they've never felt the kind of safety or comfort that they feel in this space. . . . I think I see a healing in the trust . . . and then I think I see healing of self-judgment, negative self-judgment.

For these women, trust issues are of paramount importance in the healing process. Goddess spirituality circles can provide "a safe place" where women can address "core issues" not discussed in AA.

Suzanne's experience exemplifies the physical and emotional healing that can happen in women's separate spiritual space. As a child, Suzanne was her "father's concubine," a role that left her locked in silence for the better part of her life. She claims to have literally found her voice within her women's spirituality circle, which offered a safe place to learn to trust and to begin to speak.

Suzanne was brought up Catholic and says she "felt disempowered because women had no place in the church," except for becoming a nun, and "nothing in the way of positive role models for women to take on." But once she began attending her women's spirituality circle she found "it fills my creativity, my longings, my needs, my ideas—going into a group of women, being honored, being appreciated, and really feeling empowered." Although for a long time she didn't say a word, she gradually became more vocal, and now she has gained so much confidence that she is often called on to lead the circle. Here she reflects on her circle as having played a decisive role in her healing, especially with respect to her childhood abuse:

> It has a self-healing aspect to it, because I found my voice, like I said before, I feel a lot more empowered, I feel a lot more calmer in my body, relaxed. I grew up in a severely abusive home, and so fled many many times—tried not to come back to my body. So grounding has been very important for me to learn. . . . I mean being able to stay in a calm centered place, be in touch with my surroundings, being in touch with people—not dissociate—just staying in the here and now and being comfortable in my body.

Like Suzanne, others have acknowledged that women's spirituality groups allowed them to break though the silence they had held about sexual abuse, incest, or rape. They discovered that Goddess spirituality awakened in them a self-respect which allowed them to enjoy their bodies, possibly for the first time in decades, without feeling overwhelmed by guilt and shame. Not only did they gain a sense of trust, but they were able to rebuild a sense of self-esteem, confidence, and inner strength that AA could not foster. Overall, the women in this study found the safety and nonjudgmental support provided by Goddess spirituality groups to be invaluable in their progress with issues of abuse.

Celebration of Women

Goddess spirituality exhibits a third quality that AA does not: It truly honors, affirms, and celebrates womanhood. This combination provides an empowering focus for keeping sober. Suzanne describes how the circle was important to her recovery:

> I was able to tune into the spiritual side of myself. . . . So I'd say especially Dianic Wicca has been a really transformative power in my life . . . in the women's spirituality circle, whatever I had to say was not only welcomed, but sometimes celebrated, and I was honored just specifically because I was a woman.

Brigit talks about the importance of being a co-creator of ritual in her WomanSpirit group. She says "I can be a part of planning it and that helps, whereas in a church you're sitting on the outside and you're kind of looking into the celebration . . . and with WomanSpirit if I care to I can be the celebrant, the person who's doing the celebrating, the High Priestess. . . ." And since she's always wanted to be a "real part of her religion" this is a new and exciting role. She continues:

> My life wasn't worth living and then this wonderful stuff comes into my life, and now I'm happy, and I'm sober. . . . We (she and her husband) are having a ball and I really attribute it to my women's spirituality and to my sobriety because I've gotten past the dogma of what my sobriety used to mean and now it's just this beautiful way of life, absolutely beautiful. . . . Like with the full moon I can renew my gratitude in a ritualistic way: I can remind myself on a monthly basis about how happy I am that I'm a recovering woman. . . . there's so much to feed my spirit and to feed my emotions and to help heal me.

Brigit emphasizes it's not the dogma that's keeping her sober but rather a feminine-based spirituality which helps her to celebrate her sobriety as well as her womanhood.

This theme of celebration is emphasized in a follow-up letter sent by Laughing Womyn, who writes:

> I've gone to Pagan AA meetings at the Womyn's Festival and didn't find them to be satisfying. I think some of what I need

that AA doesn't provide is to regularly be in an environment
where life is ecstatically celebrated. That's another big piece
of what group rituals give me. It does more than any other
thing in my life to help me believe life can be joyful and I can
thrive rather than simply survive. For me to stay sober and not
suicidal I need to be happy and very engaged in life. Some
people seem to do okay with a quiet contentment or simply
a lack of chaos, that's not enough for me!

DISCUSSION

This chapter has shown AA to be inadequate for many women
because of its narrow focus, its intolerance to alternative spiritualities, and its unwillingness to deal with women's issues. For example,
Miller, Downs, and Testa (1993) found that nearly 90 percent of
alcoholic women had been physically or sexually abused as children, and Russell (1984:183), in examining the prevalence of child
sexual abuse, found that 28 percent of females under the age of 14
had been subjected to "incestuous and/or extrafamilial sexual
abuse."[8] Given this factor and its strong correlation with women's
alcoholism, it is possible that survivors of such trauma may find
their way into the Goddess movement, as witnessed in this study.
AA's patriarchal tendencies and inflexibility stand in contrast to
Goddess spirituality which attracts women with its holistic approach
and its attention to women's special needs.

The women in this study are in the process of breaking new
ground by creating their own women's spirituality-based health care
alternatives. Through their actions the women are saying they want
a feminist spiritual community, they want a safe environment where
they can explore their deepest core issues, they want connection with
a female Divinity, and ultimately, they want self-empowerment.
Rather than identifying as helpless alcoholics, these women are
reclaiming their power, redirecting their lives, "accomplishing" stronger gender identities, and celebrating their womanhood.[9]

Goddess spirituality is steadily proliferating throughout American culture, and as social scientists it is our responsibility to study
its potential—especially for women. Because AA is missing a key
spiritual component for many women, we need to take a closer look
at Goddess-oriented recovery groups as therapeutic alternatives to

AA. Clearly, in the absence of suitable treatment programs, women are creating solutions to get what they need. Through Goddess spirituality, women are actively participating in their own healing and recovery in a meaningful and joyful way, and they are thriving, not simply surviving.

Notes

[1] This spelling of women with a "y" indicates feminist and separatist leanings.

[2] This difference in sexual orientation may be due to the different natures of the two festivals; whereas the pagan festival attracts men and women, a mostly heterosexual crowd, the womyn's music festival is exclusively women and about 80 to 85 percent lesbian.

[3] Thealogy means "the feminist knowing of the sacred" (Starhawk 1979:18). Thealogians are those religious philosophers who study Goddess spirituality.

[4] Kruzicki (1987) notes that women alcoholics are more socially stigmatized than men and they are often intimidated from speaking in mixed-gender treatment groups. When they do, their issues are often ignored (see also Jarvis 1992). To deal with these problems, Kasl (1992) developed the "Sixteen Steps to Discovery and Empowerment."

[5] Feminist and separatist, Dianic Wiccans worship the Goddess and exclude male gods.

[6] The chant "We are a Circle" was created by Starhawk. The lyrics are "We are a circle within a circle with no beginning and never ending."

[7] Although some women attended gay-lesbian, all women, and backroom meetings, they were unable to meet the needs met by Goddess spirituality.

[8] Thirty-eight percent reported at least one such experience before age 18.

[9] McGuire (1993) discusses the notion of people "accomplishing" an idealized gender identity through their participation in religious movements; she sees the "identity work" involved as an important part of the process of achieving health.

Works Cited

Alcoholics Anonymous 1976. *Alcoholics Anonymous*, 3rd edition. NY: Alcoholics Anonymous World Services. (Original, 1939.)

Bufe, Charles 1991. *Alcoholics Anonymous: Cult or cure?* San Francisco: See Sharp Press.

Christ, Carol 1982. Why women need the Goddess. In *The Politics of Women's Spirituality*, edited by C. Spretnak. Garden City: Doubleday. Pages 71–85.

Eller, Cynthia 1993. *Living in the Lap of the Goddess*. New York: Crossroad Publishing Co.

Foltz, Tanice G. 1994. Give me that old time religion: Women, Witchcraft, and healing. Presented at the Association for the Sociology of Religion annual meetings, Los Angeles.

Foltz, Tanice G., and Wendy Griffin. 1996. She changes everything she touches: Ethnographic journeys of self discovery. In *Composing Ethnography*, edited by C. Ellis and A. Bochner. Thousand Oaks, CA: AltaMira Press. Pages 301–29.

Fox, Selena. 1995. When Goddess is God: Pagans, recovery, and Alcoholics Anonymous. M.S. Thesis, Psychology, University of Wisconsin, Madison.

Greil, Arthur, and David R. Rudy. 1984. Social cocoons: Encapsulation and identity transforming organizations. *Sociological Inquiry* 54: 260–278.

Griffin, Wendy. 1995. The embodied Goddess: Feminist Witchcraft and female divinity. *Sociology of Religion*, 56:1. Pages 35–48.

Jacobs, Janet. 1989. Effects of ritual healing on female victims of abuse: A study of empowerment and transformation. *Sociological Analysis*, 50:3. Pages 265–79.

———. 1990. Women-centered healing rites: A study of alienation and reintegration. In *In Gods We Trust*, 2nd ed., edited by T. Robbins and D. Anthony. New Brunswick, NJ: Transaction Publishers.Pages 373–83.

Jarvis, T. J. 1992. Implications of gender for alcohol treatment research: A quantitative and qualitative review. *British Journal of Addiction* 87:9. Pages 1249–61.

Jones, R. Kenneth. 1970. Sectarian characteristics of Alcoholics Anonymous. *Sociology*, 4. Pages 181–95.

Kasl, Charlotte Davis. 1992. *Many Roads, One Journey: Moving beyond the Twelve Steps*. NY: Harper Perennial.

Kruzicki, Joan. 1987. Dispelling a myth: The facts about female alcoholics. *Corrections Today*, Vol. 49. Pages 110–14.

Lozano, Wendy G., and Tanice G. Foltz. 1990. Into the darkness: An ethnographic study of feminist Witchcraft and death. *Qualitative Sociology*, 13:3. Pages 221–35.

McGuire, Meredith. 1993. Health and spirituality as contemporary concerns. *The Annals of the American Academy of Political and Social Sciences*. 527 (May). Pages 14–154.

———. 1994. Gendered spirituality and quasi-religious ritual. In *Religion and the Social Order*, Volume 4, edited by D.G. Bromley. JAI Press, Inc. Pages 273–87.

Miller, Brenda A., W. R. Downs, and M. Testa. 1993. Interrelationships between victimization experiences and women's alcohol use. *Journal of Studies on Alcohol* Supplement 11. Pages 109–17.

Russell, Diana E. H. 1984. *Sexual Exploitation*. Newbury Park, CA: Sage Publications, Inc.

Starhawk (Simos, Miriam). 1979. *The Spiral Dance: A Rebirth of the Ancient Religion of the Great Goddess*. San Francisco: Harper and Row.

ꙮ 8 ꙮ

Feminist Witchcraft

A Transformatory Politics

by Susan Greenwood[1]

INTRODUCTION

Feminist Witchcraft has developed out of the 1960s feminist critique of existing patriarchal world religions, which are seen to have suppressed, de-valued and denied women's religious experience. Feminist Witchcraft, in common with all magical cosmologies, has a holistic philosophy; the symbol of the Goddess unites the individual with the universe, being both microcosm and macrocosm. Its origins are located by practitioners within a golden, matrifocal age, whose mythology reveres women and Nature, before urban cultures of conquest with their patriarchal religions divided spirit from matter, shattering the former symbiotic wholeness with their emphasis on a divine force outside the world. Judeo-Christian traditions were seen to have deepened the split finally establishing the duality between spirit and matter. Women became identified with nature, sexuality, evil, and the Devil and had to be controlled, while the male God was uncontaminated by birth, menstruation, and decay and was removed to the transcendent realm of spirit. The basis of much feminist Witchcraft ritual practice is therefore about re-connecting with this previous state of existence, of healing the wounds of patriarchy. The practice cannot be separated from politics—a politics of re-clamation and re-invention of lost tradition. Much feminist Witchcraft practice concerns healing, both the individual and the planet. In this chapter, I examine feminist Witchcraft practice, the search for wholeness and identity, which is in stark contrast with the postmodern fragmentation of the self, where the subject is heterogeneous, decentered and never a whole.

My interest in feminist Witchcraft stemmed from my involvement with feminism in the late 1970s. This was the time in Britain when vague ideas about "the Goddess," ideas which later became known as feminist Witchcraft, were being articulated. Feminist Witchcraft was created in the U.S. in 1971 by a group of women who called themselves the Susan B. Anthony Coven No. 1. This group produced a pamphlet called *The Feminist Book of Light and Shadows* which later became Zsuzsanna Budapest's *The Holy Book of Women's Mysteries*, published in 1980. In addition, in 1979, feminist Witch Starhawk published a self-help manual for celebrating the seasonal rituals of the Goddess entitled *The Spiral Dance: A Rebirth of the Ancient Religion of the Great Goddess*. This book was instrumental in many small groups of women getting together to explore an experiential spirituality which was relevant to their own lives and one which was "uncontaminated" by patriarchy.

I joined one such group in the early 1980s, but after a few months a friend and I decided to form our own group, using Starhawk's *The Spiral Dance*. It was after a couple of years of feminist Witchcraft practice and some time later after I had stopped practicing that I registered for postgraduate study. I wanted to research what I felt were important and interesting issues that were raised by feminist politics in the area of "magical spirituality." I started anthropological fieldwork among magical groups in London part-time in 1990, moving into a year of full-time involvement in 1992–93. During this time I became a member of two Wiccan Witchcraft covens and one feminist Witchcraft coven as part of the research.

Much contemporary writing on postmodernism postulates an anxiety concerning notions of identity and the self. This contrasts with feminist Witchcraft's claim to offer a sacred space within which a harmonious "whole self" may be found. Postmodernity is said to be characterized by the loss of the Enlightenment belief in a true self—the emancipation of the rational ego through knowledge, scientific research, and progress. Postmodernism is skeptical of "grand narratives" of "truth" and what are seen as their accompanying essentialist concepts, such as gender identity and universal oppression. In addition, it has been suggested that a postmodern feminism would replace unitary notions of woman and feminine identity with "more complex and pluralistic constructions of social identity" (McNay 1992:121).

The issue of identity in relation to postmodernism is therefore problematic in a study of feminist Witchcraft because feminist Witchcraft draws extensively on notions of an essential "true self." This is often conceptualized as a project of self-discovery within a politics of shared oppression. Feminist Witchcraft's ideal of an essential true self is firmly located within a *primordial* holistic world-view of the Goddess embodied in Nature. The issue of finding the true self (through the feminist Witchcraft ritual process) is central to the practice and is, I suggest, a response to what is generally termed "the postmodern condition"—which may be experienced as fragmentation and discontinuity. A search for a coherent and stable self in the midst of such apparent chaos may be an incentive for some individuals to become engaged in magical practices.

RE-INVENTED HISTORY

The history of re-invented[2] feminist Witchcraft started in the 1970s. In 1973 Mary Daly wrote in *Beyond God the Father* that:

> The unfolding of God, [then], is an event in which women participate as we participate in our own revolution. The process involves the creation of new space, in which women are free to become who we are, in which there are real and significant alternatives to the prefabricated identities provided within the enclosed spaces of patriarchal institutions. ([1973] 1986:40)

Two differing branches of feminist spirituality emerged: those keen on reforming orthodox religions, and those who looked to pre-Christian primordial goddesses that inspired a perception of the universe as organic, alive, and sacred (for examples, see Ruether 1983; Plaskow 1989). It is the latter, in the form of feminist Witchcraft, on which I shall focus.

For feminist Witches, seeing deity as female is a political statement as well as a spiritual reality. Ursula King writes that, "The worship of the Goddess is a self affirmation of the strength and wholeness of women; it suggests immanence and encompasses a holistic understanding of nature as the earth is seen as body of the Goddess" (1989:140–41).

The awareness that the Goddess is All and that all forms of being are One is central. Starhawk writes, "when the earth lives in us, as we in her, our sense of Self expands until we can no longer believe in our isolation" (1990:136). By analogy, feminist Witchcraft uses myth and folklore to suggest a common human history by suggesting that matrifocal societies were stable and unified; individual identity was unproblematic, being defined by total symbiosis with Nature. This is a re-discovered "hidden history." Eleanor Gadon (1990:xii–xiii) charts the history of Goddess cultures as, "Before the onslaught of patriarchy and the suppression of the Goddess, all that lived was bound into a sacred fabric, 'the larger web of the life force,' part of a whole."

But for feminist Witches there is a way out of the discontinuity of the present alienating culture. The profound discontinuity of the present is expressed as a distancing from patriarchy which is seen to be responsible for social alienation and fragmentation of the self. According to Starhawk, "the pain within us is a mirror of the power structures outside us" and we "must create situations in which we can be healed" (1990:97). The "situations" for healing are the Witchcraft ritual and involve *experiencing* the body.

Bodily experience is the very essence of feminist spirituality and is seen as the locus of women's power. The body is thus the source of self-affirmation and identity. Female bodies are seen to be the repository of special magical powers associated with the menstrual cycle. The womb is a mystical holy grail and cauldron of rebirth. These elements within the practice create distance from some feminist political ideals as women's spirituality sometimes slides into an escapism of the oppressed.[3] Patriarchal culture identifies femininity with communal, affective relationships, with care and mutual relatedness, and has, since Plato, associated femininity with the body and matter, while masculinity is associated with culture and spirituality. An emphasis on an essentialized femininity can re-enforce cultural stereotypes and help create a new mythology of women by their identification with nature (for example, see Haraway 1990). Nature and the Goddess become symbolic of an essential femininity, the antithesis of patriarchal society.

THE OCCULT SUBCULTURE

The British occult subculture is composed of many practices, ranging from a general study of "earth mysteries" to Druidism, Witchcraft, high magic, and chaos magick, all of which can be very broadly defined as paganism. Due to constraints of space, the focus of this chapter is on Witchcraft. Witchcraft is a nature-based practice, which commonly draws on shamanistic techniques of chanting, dancing, and drumming to induce altered states of awareness. It divides into Gardnerian Witchcraft and Alexandrian Witchcraft (which ideally work with equal numbers of men and women) and feminist Witchcraft, which is either Dianic (in Britain these groups are usually women-only and often lesbian) or liberal (those which include men).

The introduction of feminism into the occult subculture, via feminist Witchcraft, has brought dissension by its inclusion of politics. Feminist Witchcraft has drawn on many elements of Wicca, but ultimately its aims are very different. In 1954, Gerald Gardner wrote *Witchcraft Today*, in which he claimed that Witchcraft was a paleolithic fertility religion, magical practices developing later in Egypt. A traditional coven is made up of "six perfect couples, who are preferably husband and wife, and a leader" (Gardner 1988:114–15). In actual fact Gardner, a retired customs official, had invented his own version of Witchcraft using a mixture of folklore gained from overseas travel and a knowledge of Masonic and high magic ritual (see Kelly 1991; Hutton 1991). The Goddess, in this view, is a symbol of the feminine force of life who, in *partnership* with the God, creates polaric balance and harmony in the world so that life may continue.

To illustrate this point, I offer a Spring Equinox Gardnerian ritual that I participated in that was held in a very well-appointed basement flat in southwest London. The large studio lounge had an ochre circle of thirteen moons painted permanently on the floor. To the north was a rough-hewn altar laden with bowls for salt and water, flowers, a bell, a feather, Goddess and God figurines. Candles marked the other directions. The ritual[4] was a celebration of the equal powers of light and darkness. It began with the priest.

Priest: Today, we stand poised between the powers of Light and the powers of Darkness. From today the powers of Light will wax and the powers of Darkness will wane. . . .
Priestess: Behold the Cauldron of Cerridwen,[5] womb of the Gods and of men, awaits now the seed of the Sun.
(The Priestess and Priest place their hands round the top of the stang [forked stick] and plunge it upright into the cauldron.)
Priest: The Spear to the Cauldron
Priestess: The Lance to the Grail
Priest: Spirit to Flesh
Priestess: Man to Woman

Gardnerian and Alexandrian Witchcraft represent a dynamic balance of masculinity and femininity based on the notion of fecundity; polarization of the sexes is central, not a politics concerned with stripping away patriarchal domination.

All practices of Witchcraft raise power within a ritual circle but, in addition, feminist Witches share the feminist ethic of connectedness through shared oppression and the myth of a communal golden age. Urban city life produces fragmentation, loneliness, and distance from kinship networks; Witchcraft groups can replace these relationships. The appeal of the feminist version of Witchcraft lies in this ability to offer connectedness through the Goddess as a *political symbol,* and this forms a crucial difference in comparison to Wicca. But feminist connectedness may deny difference. The ideal of community, which many feminist Witches see as incorporating mutual identification and close relationships, privileges unity over differences and other points of view. This privileging may be problematic. Iris Young (1990) argues that community is an unrealistic vision for transformative politics in mass urban society. She states that an analysis of the concept of community reveals that desire for unity or wholeness in discourse generates borders, dichotomies, and exclusions and in particular denies differences; she believes that another political vision is necessary which does not suppress or subsume differences.

THE INTRODUCTION OF POLITICS
INTO THE SUBCULTURE

Having a history in the women's liberation movement, feminist Witchcraft ideology, in theory, cannot drop the connection between politics and spirituality; the politics of re-claiming the self are central to its practice. In the early 1970s, ideas of the Witch as a patriarchal freedom fighter were used by American radical feminists. According to Rachel Hasted writing in the magazine *Trouble and Strife* (1985), the original WITCH (Women Inspired to Commit Herstory) group accepted ready-made "facts" about the witchcraze in Europe and claimed that nine million Witches were burned as revolutionary fighters against patriarchy and class oppression.[6] They drew on the work of Jules Michelet, Matilda Joslyn Gage, and Margaret Murray. Each of these writers contributed to the idea that there was an underground women's spirituality movement, originating from matriarchal times which had been suppressed by patriarchy. The French historian Jules Michelet wrote *La Sorciere* in which he interpreted Witch hunters' records as a massive peasant rejection of Christianity, which took the form of a rebellion: Pagan priestesses led a doomed peasants' revolt against the oppression of a Christian ruling class (1862). Matilda Joslyn Gage, a radical leader in the U.S. Suffrage Movement, wrote in *Woman, Church and State* that Witchcraft and the occult were a form of knowledge based on the worship of a female deity which was outlawed by a jealous patriarchy (1893). Margaret Murray's *The Witch-Cult in Western Europe* claimed that European Witchcraft was an ancient pre-Christian fertility religion, which had survived among the peasantry (1921).

Feminist magic, drawing on these images of rebellion, has come to be seen essentially as a way of changing patriarchal thought forms of "power over" and domination. During the early 1980s, Greenham Common air base was the center of a new feminist awareness which combined feminist political insights with a reworking of magical techniques. Women protested against the nuclear missiles located within the base by covering the surrounding wire fence with string and wool webs, in which they entwined memorabilia and photographs of children and loved ones. Hundreds of women practiced, most perhaps unknowingly then, a powerful magical ritual by linking hands around the whole perimeter of the air force base and chanting songs for peace. It was felt that planetary crisis was nigh, due to the patriarchal forces of war and destruction. This was a time of growing awareness of the connection between feminist politics and spiritual values. Starhawk (1979, 1982) voiced new ideas about spirituality which were politically relevant and accessible to women.

For feminist Witches, spirituality lies in healing the wounds of patriarchy and finding a new sense of self that is identified with the Goddess therein. The Goddess is the symbol of a holistic interconnectedness of all of creation. I will share a feminist Witch's experience from my fieldnotes to show how she sees the holism of the Goddess. Leah was a teacher in her late thirties and explained her introduction into the "Craft" to me. She was around in the 1970s at the beginning of the first stirrings of feminist Witchcraft in San Francisco. She had a Jewish upbringing but could not relate to the maleness of God and so she became an atheist. In the early 1970s, she had a spiritual awakening from the effects of a hallucinogen. She saw the face of God, "except it was a woman's face." She felt an explosion of female energy that permeated her and she realized that she was the same as everything else. "I felt myself dissolve into molecules. I was the steps and the trees and the stars." It was this experience that meant that she did not have to go on "living a miserable life as an atheist," and it was from there that she got involved with the Craft. She explained her views of Witchcraft to me:

> . . . the fact that Witchcraft is a religion based on nature worship and deity as manifested primarily, though not exclusively, as female is a political fact. The fact that our God is a Goddess, that manifestation we choose to have in front of us is various shapes of female as well as male, and that the earth is female, is political. . . . The fact that we take and look at deity as a female and we take this into ourselves is a very political act, where spirituality as a whole is still owned and defined by men. . . . Women should be able to be prime movers . . . although we don't have recognition in the outside world, except as Satanists, which is not what we are, that's what people equate Witchcraft with. The fact that we do it all is a political act, an act of personal transformation when a woman or a man are no longer able to think of God in exclusively male terms. It changes the relation to everything, other people, the planet, everything. That small difference of saying "she" instead of "he" is enormous.

But some Wiccans do not like the mention of politics in any shape or form.[7] Another informant believes that all politics are a taboo area:

> You can't bring politics into the Craft—this is what's destroy-
> ing the Craft. It is non-political. Craft is a family—everything
> has its place. Religion and politics destroy and bring chaos.
> . . . You can't have all-female [groups] because you need
> balance, you need yin and yang. Dianic Witches are playact-
> ing, there is no ultimate balance, so you get "bitchcraft." Ev-
> erything has to balance and produce, this is what it's all
> about—reproduction.

By contrast, feminist Witchcraft by its very nature is a challenge to the political social system of patriarchy. Engaging in feminist ritual therefore becomes a political act. This is based on the central tenet of magical practice—that the microcosm (the individual) is a part of the macrocosm, and that work on the microcosm will have an effect on the macrocosm. Feminist Witchcraft is a practical politics; it is about making changes *from the inside*. In Britain, many come to practice feminist Witchcraft from radical feminist politics. During periods of complete exhaustion or "burn out" they come to view the "soft option" of feminist spirituality in different terms.[8]

SEXUAL POLITICS

The issue of politics, especially sexual politics, has divided groups because the central tenet of Wicca is sexual polarity, which is based upon the ideology of fertility and fecundity. The most important Wiccan ritual of polarity is called The Great Rite, in which the Goddess and God meet in sexual union (this may be actual or sym-bolic). The Great Rite forms the basis of the highest initiation ritual, the Third Degree, in Wicca. The High Priest draws down the energy of the Goddess into the High Priestess, who then becomes her per-sonification. In contrast, the feminist Goddess is a holistic unity of interchangeability and flow and there is no hard dividing line be-tween femininity and masculinity. Her essence is connectedness, to the extent where some would claim that all duality, including mas-culinity and femininity, is the product of patriarchal social construc-tion, and therefore inseparable from power relationships. Starhawk does not describe the essential quality of energy flow that sustains the universe as a male/female polarity. To do so would, "enshrine heterosexual human relationships as the basic pattern of all being, relegating other sorts of attraction and desire to the position of deviant. . . . Goddess religion is about the erotic dance of life playing through all of nature and culture" (1989:9).

WITCHCRAFT AS HEALING

The feminist Witchcraft ritual utilizes shamanistic techniques such as dancing and drumming to obtain trance states. Shamanistic techniques are particularly appropriate because they are seen to be primordial, allowing feminist Witches to locate their spirituality at humanity's beginnings. The historian of religion Mircea Eliade writes that ecstatic experience is a "primary phenomenon" fundamental to the human condition that has been changed and modified with different forms of culture and religion (1974:504). This primacy and the fact that shamanism is a process which has been observed in "classless" societies is particularly relevant to feminist groups which claim to be egalitarian in their practices. Ritual is a way of becoming "unpossessed" from patriarchy. By connecting to the Goddess through ritual, the Witch becomes empowered—she finds her own power within.

But most importantly, she can become unpossessed by the alienations of patriarchal culture. Healing involves coming to understand the way that domination has been internalized. Shamanic healing typically involves the destruction of the old identity or ego; this is often experienced as a crisis when the old patriarchal patterning is unable to explain the new experiences gained through Witchcraft ritual. This destruction of the old and the initiation into Witchcraft is often related to, and experienced as, the Sumerian myth of the Goddess Inanna, who journeyed into the Underworld to find Ereshkigal, her dark sister, who is really the repressed part of herself. Inanna is what Perera (1981) calls a many-faceted symbolic image representing wholeness. She combines earth and sky, matter and spirit. This myth introduces important magical ideas. It encourages an exploration of the self; it introduces the notion of a dialectics of change—nothing is static in the movement from ordinary world to Underworld and its connection with the changing seasons of the year; and it encompasses the notion of the unconscious as a realm, a universe to be explored, charted, and finally understood.

This last aspect concerns the process of initiation into the mysteries, which essentially means discovering the unity with nature and the cosmos and the rhythm of life, death, and rebirth. The descent to the Underworld is when the Witch has to face who she really is, beneath the patriarchal facade. A Witch also has to face her own anger, fear, destruction, and death.

PURIFICATION FROM PATRIARCHY

A typical feminist Witchcraft ritual involves cleansing and purification. This normally involves passing around the circle a goblet of salted water in which participants can leave any thought, feeling, or emotion they wish to be rid of. I attended one really spectacular purification. It was Samhain (Halloween), which is the Witches' New Year. The feminist coven in which I was a participant observer had created a magical circle in the overgrown garden of a south London Victorian mansion earmarked for demolition. The entrance to the circle was guarded by two life-size paper skeletons dangling from the branches of overhanging trees. To the north of the circle was the altar, a large table crammed with apples, pomegranates, candles, and a sheep's skull. In the east, the symbolic place of rebirth, was an elaborate, round sweatlodge, while to the south was an enormous pumpkin lantern. The west was dominated by a large mirror, beneath which was a water bucket full of apples (these were for apple bobbing when the ritual circle had been closed). In the center a large bonfire blazed.

The ritual centered on the purification in the sweatlodge. We were going to sweat out all our fears and bad feelings and would thus face the new year feeling refreshed and positive. The entrance to the sweatlodge was a tunnel and we each crawled into the darkness within, one by one. Those who were claustrophobic went last so that they could get out quickly if necessary. We sat in the near-total darkness; the shadows from the fire outside made patterns on the domed roof as we huddled together "like piglets in the womb of the Mother." We sweated out our anger and negativity, we howled and screamed out our feelings. It was a very elemental sensation of direct contact with the dark and the earth; we had re-established our connection with her. After about an hour we crawled out, one by one, making babyish noises to symbolize our re-birth, to be hosed down by icy water before being dried by the heat of the bonfire. Then the circle was opened by lighting the candles in the four quarters, invoking their spirits: of air in the east, fire in the south, water in the west, and earth in the north. The Goddess and God were invoked and the ritual proceeded with singing, drumming, and dancing. At one point we each left the circle in turn via a special gateway made of looped and tied twigs to gaze into the scrying mirror in the west. We asked ourselves questions like, Who am I? What do I want in the future? What do I want to leave in the past? After a few minutes I faced the circle and shouted a name I chose to call myself. Then I shouted everything that I was leaving in the old year. The coven shouted my name as I re-entered the circle and I jumped over the fire, to symbolize the new start to my life. I was greeted with hugs from the coven members.

Purification is the first stage on the path of the dissolution of patriarchal oppression and rebirth of the true self. For feminist Witches the idea of an authentic self is a powerful one, encompassing a notion of freedom from restraining social authority, gender roles, and oppression. It implies a fluid categorization, a flexible technique to discover who you really want to be rather than what you should be. Through the use of magic, nature spirits and animal powers aid an inner development. The ultimate aim of feminist Witchcraft spirituality is the connection with the true self; this is seen to liberate the individual's latent power and potential.

CONCLUSION

In this chapter I have argued that feminist Witchcraft rituals claim to offer a space to find a true self, a new stable identity located within the body, in a changing postmodern world. The body has become the main site of a postmodern attack on classical Enlightenment thought. Michel Foucault writes that there is no natural or pre-social body and that it is impossible to know the body outside of cultural meaning. By the "practices of the self" the subject "constitutes" her- or himself. These practices are not invented by the individual but are "patterns" in culture (1988:11). In Foucault's later work he answered criticism that the deconstruction of a constitutive and rational subject led to conceptions about a docile body empatterned by culture, and he shifted his theoretical focus from the body to the

self and political resistance (McNay 1992). Foucault's political resistance involved an "ascetic invention of the self" by exploring the
limits of subjectivity and an "interrogation of the boundaries of
identity." By using the ancient Greek notion of *epimeleia heautou*,
which means "taking care of one's self," as a knowledge and technique of working on the self, mastery of the self was possible (1988).

For feminist Witches, the quest for the true self starts from a
psychoanalytic search of the individual self, to find the personal "self-
hater" of the power structures of domination.[9] This is said to lead
to an understanding which enables the Witch to find her/his own
"power within." The ideology of the possibility of finding the true
self within is often compelling for those searching for identity, but
the practice does not always live up to these ideals. "True" self-
identity, or the quest for it, may be subsumed by the power of others
within the magical group (see Greenwood 1996a, 1996b, 1998a,
1998b). The issue of relations of domination *within* feminist Witchcraft groups, counter to the ideology of egality, is an important one.
These issues concerning the use of implicit power raise further
questions about the nature of such a politics of rebellion.

Notes

[1] I would like to thank Olivia Harris, Pat Caplan, Stephen Nugent,
Nickie Charles, and Felicia Hughes-Freeland for helpful comments. Thanks
are also due to the magical practitioners I interviewed, and those who al-
lowed me to share their rituals. A version of this chapter originally ap-
peared in *Practising Feminism: Identity, Difference and Power*, edited by Nickie
Charles and Felicia Hughes-Freeland and published by Routledge in 1996.
The research was funded by the University of London Central Research
Fund and the Economic and Social Research Council U.K.

[2] I use the term "re-invented" here to account for the feminist adaptation of traditional Witchcraft that is itself an invention.

[3] Ioan M. Lewis (*Ecstatic Religion*, London: Routledge, 1989 [1971]) and
Pamela Constantinides (Women heal women: spirit possession and sexual
segregation in a Muslim Society, in *Social Science Medicine*,1985, 21:6 [685–
92]) have associated women's ecstatic experiences with political impotency
and discrimination. For radical criticisms of Lewis' thesis, see Bruce
Kapferer (*A Celebration of Demons*, Oxford: Berg, 1991) and Janice Boddy
(Managing tradition: "superstition" and the making of national identity
among Sudanese women refugees, presented at the ASA Decennial Conference, Oxford, 1993).

⁴ This ritual was compiled by Ken Rees, who kindly allowed part of it to be reproduced here.

⁵ According to Doreen Valiente, Gerald Gardner's High Priestess, the cauldron is a symbol of transformation, and the British goddess Cerridwen brewed a Cauldron of Inspiration for a year and a day (D. Valiente. 1986. *An ABC of Witchcraft*. London: Robert Hale. Page 58).

⁶ W.I.T.C.H. stood for different things in different groups around the country. In one group, for example, W.I.T.C.H. meant Women's International Terrorist Conspiracy from Hell.

⁷ Following a more general awareness of ecological destruction, mainly from high-profile media coverage, many Wiccans are becoming more involved with environmental issues, e.g., local campaigns to collect litter from sacred spaces/woods, specific environmental groups, but politics remain relatively more peripheral to their practice.

⁸ This information was suggested by research conducted on radical and revolutionary feminist groups in London by anthropologist Sarah Green (now at Manchester University). Green notes that there is a split between the "spiritual" types and the hard-line political types within the feminist community, although she says that there is some overlap (personal communication).

⁹ Foucault is critical of psychoanalysis, arguing that the disclosure of the inner self and the unconscious desires leads to a more efficient regulation and normalization of sexuality through the production of self-policing subjects (M. Foucault. 1978. *The History of Sexuality*. Harmondsworth, England: Penguin).

Works Cited

Budapest, Zsuzsanna. 1990 [1980]. *The Holy Book of Women's Mysteries*. London: Robert Hale.

Daly, Mary. 1986 [1973]. *Beyond God the Father*. London: The Women's Press.

Eliade, Mircea. 1974 [1964]. *Shamanism*. Princeton: Princeton University Press.

Foucault, Michael. 1988. *The Care of the Self: The History of Sexuality*, Vol. 3. London: Penguin.

Gadon, Elinor. 1990. *The Once and Future Goddess*. Northampton: Aquarian.

Gage, Matida Joselyn. 1982 [1893]. *Women, Church and State: A Historical Account of the Status of Woman through the Christian Ages*. New York: Arno Press.

Gardner, Gerald. 1988 [1954]. *Witchcraft Today*. New York: Magickal Childe [*sic*].

Greenwood, Susan. 1996a. The magical will, gender and power in magical practices. In *Paganism Today*. Edited by G. Harvey and C. Hardman. London: Routledge. Pages 277–96.

————. 1996b. The British occult subculture: beyond good and evil? In *Magical Religion and Modern Witchcraft*. Edited by J. Lewis. Albany: SUNY. Pages 191–203.

————. 1998a. The nature of the Goddess: sexual identities and power in contemporary Witchcraft. In *Nature Religion Today*. Edited by J. Pearson, R. Roberts, and G. Samuel. Edinburgh: Edinburgh University Press. Pages 101–10.

————. 1998b. Gender and power in magical practices. In *Beyond the New Age*. Edited by S. Sutcliffe and M. Bowman. Edinburgh: Edinburgh University Press. In press.

Haraway, Donna. 1990. A manifesto for cyborgs: science, technology, and socialist feminism in the 1980s. In *Feminism/Postmodernism*. Edited by Linda J. Nicholson. London: Routledge. Pages 190–233.

Hastead, Rachel. 1985. Mothers of invention. *Trouble and Strife* Magazine.

Hutton, Ronald. 1991. *The Pagan Religions of the Ancient British Isles*, Oxford: Basil Blackwell.

Kelly, Aidan. 1991. *Crafting the Art of Magic*. Vol. 1: *A History of Modern Witchcraft 1939–1964*. London: Llwellyn.

King, Ursela. 1989. *Women and Spirituality*. Hampshire: Macmillan.

McNay, Lois. 1992. *Foucault and Feminism*. Cambridge: Polity.

Michelet, Jules. 1862. *La Sorcére*. Paris.

Murray, Margaret. 1921. *The Witch Cult in Western Europe*. Oxford: Oxford University Press.

Perera, Sylvia. 1981. *Descent to the Goddess*. Toronto: Inner City Books.

Plaskow, Judith. 1989. Jewish memory from a feminist perspective. In *Weaving the Visions*. Edited by Judith Plaskow and Carol Christ. New York: Harper and Row. Pages 39–49.

Reuther, Rosemary Radforth. 1983. *Sexism and God Talk: Toward a Feminist Theology*, Boston: Beacon.

Starhawk. 1982. *Dreaming the Dark: Magic, Sex and Politics*. Boston: Beacon.

————. 1989. [1979] *The Spiral Dance: A Rebirth of the Ancient Religion of the Great Goddess*. San Francisco: Harper and Row.

————. 1990. *Truth or Dare*. New York: Harper and Row.

Young, Iris. 1990. The ideal of community and the politics of difference. In *Feminism/Postmodernism*. Edited by L. Nicholson. London: Routledge. Pages 300–23.

ᘒᘒ 9 ᘒᘒ

Healing in Wicca

by Vivianne Crowley

An important characteristic of Western religions of the postmodernist era is healing (Ellwood and Partin 1988). This is true both for religious revivals such as Christian fundamentalism and for what are termed "New Age" spiritualities. Indeed, Orion's (1995) interesting North American study claims that the healing motif predominates in Wicca. The preoccupation with healing is found within Wicca, but Wiccans are not seeking solely to be healed. The Wiccan Witch is a healer.

Anthropologists distinguish between ritual and operative Witchcraft—Witchcraft as a religious practice and Witchcraft as a means of performing magic. Healing others is a traditional part of operative Witchcraft and a major focus of modern Wiccan activity. Wiccans may carry out healing magic alone, but it frequently takes place in the context of group or coven rituals; particularly at the thirteen Full Moons each year when groups often meet primarily for "magical work" or the practice of spellcraft.

Leading British Wiccan authors Janet and Stewart Farrar (1984) describe four types of healing carried out by Witches. Two—herbalism and psychology—involve no "magical powers." Herbal medicine is a recognized form of complementary treatment and psychological approaches to healing are common to both conventional and complementary medicine. Farrar and Farrar give practical advice about herbal cures and where to find out more about them. They say less about psychological healing than does the store of knowledge that they draw much of their practice from—the Gardnerian *Book of Shadows*, a collection of spells and rites hand copied by Witches from their initiators and left purposely unpublished.

The *Book of Shadows* recognizes that emotional well-being influences physical health in a mind-body continuum. It advocates a number of healing practices that can be termed "psychological" and involve belief by the patient in the practitioner. These include:

- allowing a sick person to believe a Witch has the power to cure him or her, i.e. faith healing;
- placebo potions;
- hypnotism;
- amulets—these are seen as working through the sick person's belief in them;
- prayer (this may be to the Christian God or to a saint if the patient believes in them);
- assisting the sick to help themselves by encouraging them to dwell on "happy thoughts."

Practitioners are also encouraged to dwell on "inner joy" so their own health will improve. In short, as well as the use of magical power and herbal remedies, the *Book of Shadows* encourages the use of the psychological tools of the traditional village healer, some of which are still used in conventional medicine.

Farrar and Farrar describe two other less-recognized forms of healing—auric healing, a form of spiritual healing or laying on of hands, and spells. What is the rationale for these types of healing? Wiccans believe in and practice magic: the science and art of causing change by non-physical means not as yet accepted by science (Crowley 1997). The Wiccan world-view is that the material world is comprised of energy and that energy can be manipulated by mind and by the Witch's own *etheric energy*. Etheric energy exists on the border between matter and mind. Wicca accepts the idea, common to the Western magical tradition and similar to Hinduism, that there is an energy field around the human body. Physical and emotional illness will manifest as damage to the etheric energy field or aura. A skilled magical practitioner believes she or he can detect this damage, use it to diagnose underlying illness, and repair the damage by transmitting energy to the aura of the person being healed. Healing the aura will in turn heal the physical or emotional illness which has caused the auric damage.

Auric healing requires the presence of the person being healed. Healing spells involve transmitting energy over a distance and do not require the physical presence of the patient. The concept is of creating a temporary circuit which allows the transmission of energy from the Witch or Witches to the recipient. To assist in this process, attempts may be made through sympathetic magic to create a "link" with the person being healed. If the individual is aware of the healing activity, she or he may be asked to provide a photograph or an object which has been in contact with her or him, such as an item of clothing or jewelry. Witches may also make a wax doll to represent the recipient and create the link, possibly incorporating his or her hair or nail clippings; although this is less common in modern covens. Objects that have been in physical contact with someone are considered to be impregnated with his or her etheric energy which in turn retains links to his or her aura. They act as channels for energy transmission to the person being healed. In the absence of these etheric links, Witches visualize the individual requiring healing. The visual image acts as a "homing device" to direct healing energy to the right recipient. Alternatively, in a group situation, healing energy may be directed toward one coven member who has an emotional link with the recipient. That coven member will visualize the recipient and project the group's healing energy toward him or her.

Wiccans frequently discuss the ethics of spellcraft. Most subscribe to the *Wiccan Rede*: "An it harm none do what you will." In other words, if it does not harm anyone or anything, then magic is permissible.[1] This may seem to leave considerable room for maneuver, but in reality the situations in which magic can be practiced legitimately are limited. Most covens consider it acceptable to use magic to help themselves and others with the problems of everyday life— providing magic is backed up by appropriate action on the material plane. Examples might be finding a job, gaining a college place or acceptance, and finding a new home.

When it comes to other magical activity, healing features highly in Wiccan magic-making, though here, too, it is recognized that healing is not straightforward. An illness may be a presenting symptom of underlying problems of a psychological nature.

> Magic is a simple force but applying it skillfully is difficult. In seemingly simple situations, there can be many complex factors. Even if someone has asked for healing, there can be many barriers within the person that can prevent it. On one

level, he or she may want to be well. On another level, the illness may be serving the individual in some way. It may bring attention to the neglected. It may be a way of hiding from a relationship, job or another aspect of life that someone finds untenable. (Crowley 1997:67)

Within Wicca, healing, "making whole," can be seen as having three major dimensions—healing others, healing self and healing the environment—all of which are inter-related. First, let us consider the healing of others.

HEALING OTHERS

The link between Witchcraft and healing is an age-old one; although traditional village Witches in Europe, like their counterparts elsewhere, were amoral in their practice. They were as ready to cause disease, if paid the right fee, as to affect cures. In modern Wicca, ethical constraints mean that the focus must be on healing rather than the reverse.

Wiccan interest in healing is bolstered by the many Wiccans who work in the healing professions. Margot Adler in her 1985 U.S. survey found that the biggest occupational grouping within Paganism (11 percent) was computer professionals.[2] This is not true within Wicca in Britain, nor I suspect in other European countries. In Britain, it is the caring professions that feature most highly amongst entrants to Wicca in the '90s. In a survey of 111 entrants to a Wiccan training group in 1993–95, 22 percent worked in medicine, complementary medicine, social work or care. Only 5 percent worked in computing.[3] A recent U.S. study (Orion 1995) shows similar figures for the healing and helping professions. In her sample of 153 attendees at Wiccan gatherings, 22 percent were involved in healing and helping professions, compared with 13 percent of the U.S. population overall. Computer professionals were significantly over-represented, comprising 10 percent of Orion's group compared with 4 percent of the U.S. population overall; but they represent a smaller group than the "helpers and healers." Wiccans in the healing and helping professions are likely to meet those needing physical or emotional healing. The impetus to use magical powers as a means of helping people is therefore strong; especially if, as Orion (1995) suggests, the majority of Wiccans are dissatisfied with conventional medicine.

In studying Wicca, most academics assume that magic does not work. A Witch's belief in her or his powers must therefore be mistaken, an example of cognitive drift (Luhrmann 1989), regression to childish wish fulfillment (Faber 1993), or other self-deception.

> I would suggest that the cult of Witchcraft has been designed at the deep unconscious level to undo the realities that attend the passing of the symbiotic stage and the dawning of separation and smallness. . . . the cult of Witchcraft has been designed to restore the past in a fantastic, wish-fulfilling, idealized form that reunites the practitioner with the symbiotic object and with the omnipotence and narcissism which accompany the before-separation interplay. (Faber 1993:67)

To translate the "psychoanaleze" of Faber's Freudian critique, Witches are deluded, infantile fantasists with an "obsessive, ongoing need to deny their separateness and smallness" (Faber 1993:68).

An alternative explanation to Witchcraft as delusion would be to call upon non-Newtonian explanations of cause and effect and conclude, as Witches do, that magic may and can work. Our understanding of mind-body interaction is still limited, but there is ample evidence that belief in the effectiveness of a cure is a significant spur to recovery. There is also some evidence (see Benor 1990) that spiritual healing, such as that practiced by Witches and Wiccan covens, is effective. Many medical practitioners and nurses have received training in recent years in the form of auric healing known as "therapeutic touch." Wiccan practitioners may be reinforced in their healing activities by positive feedback from those they have helped. Even where healing magic is unsuccessful, the practitioner will be rewarded by a sense of personal virtue for having tried, the more so because magic requires effort.

A non-believer could argue that cognitive dissonance is relevant here. Concentration, visualization, and entering an altered state of consciousness are all parts of the essentially shamanic practice which healing spells involve. These states of consciousness are pleasurable in themselves and entering them, regardless of purpose, provides positive feedback. To enter these states with the aim of helping others provides a justification for the practice. These altruistic aims will enhance the practitioner's sense of worth and belief in the practice. Another rewarding feature of the healing experience for the practitioner is the sense of social cohesion derived by ritual activity with a group of like-minded people. Regardless of the efficacy of the treatment, the incentive to practice healing is strong.

Those familiar with Wicca will know that healing others is engaged in particularly enthusiastically by new Witches and Wiccan groups. To understand why, we must put ourselves in the position of new Wiccan coven members. They are likely to believe that they have or might have magical powers: They are unlikely to have become involved otherwise. They want to try out their powers using the magical techniques they are gradually acquiring from their coven practice. There are ethical and group norm constraints as to how these powers can be used. Healing is therefore a highly acceptable purpose. It is altruistic and it benefits others. It is a legitimate outlet for Wiccan magical activity.

Healing has other appeal. By demonstrating their intentions of helping others, Witches are claiming for themselves the "moral high ground." Witchcraft is treated by outsiders with suspicion. It is stigmatized and associated with malice. There are considerable incentives for Witches to demonstrate to themselves, and to outsiders who know about their activities, the purity of their intentions and that they are ethical people, with a positive morality who are socially concerned.

In carrying out healing, practitioners are affecting, or believe they are affecting, change. Healing activities are thus a source of empowerment for Wiccans. This may be particularly appealing to women who are struggling with patriarchy. The image of the traditional Witch as "martyred healer" is a powerful one in contemporary Witchcraft, particularly in the United States where the percentage of women in the movement is much higher than in Europe. American Witch Starhawk in *Dreaming the Dark: Magic, Sex and Politics* (1982) gives a highly romanticized image of the traditional Witch. She is portrayed as an old woman, herbalist, and midwife whose healing hands and soothing voice charm away suffering. She is struggling through the forest to help a young woman in childbirth. Her neighbors have turned against her, accusing her of Satanism, but despite her fears for her own safety, she nobly risks all to help the young woman who needs her. Here is someone with whom women can identify—a lone woman struggling against the male medical and spiritual establishment. The healer is a heroine. This theme is found in many songs sung at Wiccan gatherings.

> I am a strong woman,
> I am a story woman,
> I am a healer,
> My soul will never die.[4]

This song was created at the anti-nuclear demonstrations outside the U.S. air base on Greenham Common in Berkshire, England, in the 1980s. Strength, creativity, and healing ability are seen for women as being linked. One leads to the other.

SELF HEALING

Wicca enables people to heal and empowers the healer. Wiccan practice may therefore foster healing within the practitioner. Here I am focusing primarily on healing in the sense of emotional healing. Wiccans, of course, need healing from physical ailments, too. However, setting aside for the present any paranormal claims, it is in healing of emotional damage that the processes involved in Wiccan participation may be most helpful.

For those low in self-esteem, and this is often the case for women, Wicca is a means to empowerment. In the Wiccan context, damaged egos learn a sense of power and control in an environment where a high value is placed on the feminine and where the Divine is made in woman's image. Janet and Stewart Farrar, two of Wicca's best-known practitioners, claim, "Now the purpose of Wicca, as a religion, is to integrate conflicting aspects of the human psyche with each other . . ." (Farrar and Farrar 1984:146). In other words, the aim of Wicca is to make whole. Here the Farrars place Wicca very firmly in the category of postmodernist religion. This is a long way from the original concept of Wicca promulgated by one of its "founding fathers" Gerald Gardner—of Wicca as ancient fertility cult in the Margaret Murray mold (Gardner 1954).

Often Wiccan covens are entered through rituals of initiation. These contain elements common to the rites of passage of all cultures—liminalism, a frightening ordeal, disorientation, and then "rebirth" into a peer community of adults; although in Wicca the frightening and painful aspects of the process are toned down for

158 / Vivianne Crowley

modern Western consumption. Aspects of the initiation process may be healing in the sense of enhancing self-esteem. The initiate enters what may be seen by her or him as an elite group—a semi-secret sorority/fraternity of skilled practitioners of the magical arts. Acceptance by such a group is a boost to the ego. In the standard initiation rite[5], acceptance involves a senior member of the group kissing the newcomer's feet in welcome—an unusual experience in Western society. The initiate is welcomed into a circle of the "chosen and preferred" by apparently high-status people with magical knowledge. The message is that she or he will become one of them.

Other aspects of the symbol structure of Wicca are likely to precipitate healing processes. Symbols are of circles, cycles, balance and wholeness. The Wiccan circle contains symbolism similar to that of a Native American healer's sand painting. Wicca's seasonal festivals mirror the cycles of Nature[6] and of human life. The messages in the sabbat liturgies are that the life is cyclical bringing pain, darkness, illness, and then relief, recovery, strengthening. After death is rebirth; after suffering, renewal; after despair, hope; after sickness, health.

Like other spiritual paths, Wicca facilitates religious and mystical experience; experiences which are associated with self-actualization and increased well-being. Self-actualization refers to experiences of transcendence, divine unity and mystical "highs." Elizabeth Puttick (1997a) points out in her study of *Women in New Religions* that many people are drawn to alternative spirituality specifically because they are seeking such experiences.

Carpenter's (1994) study of 52 participants at the 1993 Pagan Spirit Gathering using Hood's (1975) Mysticism scale showed a relatively high level of mystical experience compared with the samples reported by Hood.[7] This is perhaps unsurprising given that Hood's Mysticism scale includes many items directly related to the type of experiences fostered by Wiccan ritual.[8] These ritual practices are designed to induce altered states of consciousness and experiences such as timelessness and spacelessness, being absorbed by something greater than oneself, joyfulness, peace, sanctity, oneness, a new view of reality, unity with the Divine, interconnectedness, communication through symbols rather than language and a sense of all things being alive.

Research[9] shows that the intrinsically religious experience higher levels of mental health and well-being, responsible social behavior, purpose, personal competence and control, and lower levels of depression, guilt, worry and dogmatism. Similar positive findings have been shown for those who have religious and mystical experiences. In a U.S. survey (Greeley 1975), participants completed a Norman Bradburn Positive Affect Scale[10] designed to measure psychological well-being. Reports of mystical experience correlated .34 with "positive affect" (perceived psychological well-being) and -.34 with negative affect—distressing thoughts, emotions, symptoms, etc., which are consistently related to traditional indicators of poor mental health. Hood (1977) found that mystical experiences were correlated with high scores on an Abraham Maslow-based measure of self-actualization. In Wiccan activity, the individual is exposed to situations likely to foster mystical experiences that are highly correlated with self-actualization as defined by Maslow (1943, 1970) and form the pinnacle of his human Hierarchy of Needs. Therefore it would follow that these experiences are therapeutic and likely to be healing in themselves.

Self-healing may also take place more directly. A coven is a group of intimates. It is a quasi-family grouping and has the advantage of being a chosen rather than an imposed family. There are likely to be similarities between members in personality, tastes, and values. Indeed, compatibility with the group will be high on the list of prerequisites for the would-be newcomer. Rituals happen in conditions designed to foster intimacy. The usual rules of clothing are broken. Participants may be *skyclad* (naked) or dressed in special robes. The setting is darkness lit by candles; the imagery of the circle in which rituals take place is womb-like.

The circle heals the original mother-child separation, a precursor to the adult sense of alienation and anomie that many experience in industrialized Western society. Faber, from his psychoanalytic perspective of Wicca, views this as infantile regression. Others more sympathetic to Goddess-based religion might view it as a move forward.

In a Wiccan circle, which may be construed as a circle of friends or a family grouping, it is legitimate to ask for help from others. Indeed, this may be actively encouraged. Typically, in a Wiccan circle people ask for healing after a broken relationship, a bereavement, when stressed, and to assist in recovery from illness. The one asking for help is not perceived as burdening others. She or he is providing an opportunity for others to demonstrate their loving kindness and to use their magical talents. Healing activity benefits both giver and receiver. It creates connectedness.

HEALING THE ENVIRONMENT

Interconnectedness is important in Wicca, not only with other humans, but also as a psychological linking with Nature, a "belongingness" with all creation. Healing may be important here in the sense of healing the "split" between Self and other, human and other. Well-known British Witch Doreen Valiente described her rationale for the practice of Witchcraft in her after-dinner speech at the 1964 annual dinner of *Pentagram*, a Witchcraft magazine.

> What witches seek for in celebrating these seasonal festivals is a sense of oneness with Nature, and the exhilaration which comes from contact with the One Universal Life. People today need this because they are aware of the tendency of modern life to cut them off from their kinship with the world of living nature; until their own individuality is processed away, and they begin to feel as if they are just another cog in a huge, senseless machine.
> It is the reaction against this feeling which is attracting people's interest in Witchcraft today. They want to get back to Nature, and be human beings again, as She intended them to be. (Valiente 1964)

A sense of being "made whole" by connecting with Nature is seen as offering "peace of mind, as well as physical satisfaction" (Valiente 1973:135). Moreover, "peace of mind" and "contact" with Nature is not construed within Wicca as a one-way process. Nature reaches out to and is concerned about humankind. In a ritual text,[11] the Wiccan Goddess invites connection.

> I, who am the beauty of the green Earth
> and the white Moon amongst the stars,
> and the mystery of the waters,
> and the desire of the heart of woman and of man,
> call unto thy soul: arise and come unto me . . .

In Wicca, humankind and Nature are viewed as one. To heal Nature is to heal humankind and vice versa. As well as healing self and others, another frequent outlet for Wiccan magical energies is "healing the Earth."

From the 1980s onward, chanting and drumming became a feature of Wiccan rituals. Chants such as:

> Earth my body, Water my blood,
> Air my breath and Fire my spirit

encourage participants to identify with the natural world. Nature can also be an extension of self; healing the Earth and healing self are intertwined. Songs such as Charlie Murphy's modern folk song "The Burning Times" have been sung frequently at Wiccan gatherings and reinforce the idea of a link between healing of self, healing the Earth and the Earth as healer of self.

> Now the Earth is a Witch and the men still burn her,
> stripping her down with mining and the poisons of their
> wars;
> yet to us the Earth is a healer, a teacher, a mother,
> she's the weaver of a web of life which keeps us all alive.

Beginning in the 1980s, Earth healing became a major activity within Wicca. In 1989, Europe's Pagan Federation established its first mass public activity—an annual Earth Healing Day. Members alone or in groups are encouraged to conduct an outdoor rite for healing the Earth at a certain time GMT on a certain day. In Britain, the Dragon environmental group conducts magical healing rites at threatened natural sites. Druids orders are also frequently called upon by environmental organizations to perform rites at environmental protests. In the United States, the Gaia Group based on Staten Island is a network of covens whose main *raison d'être* is Earth healing and ecological magic. In North America, the large summer gatherings that are a feature of the continent's Wiccan life also encourage the development of an environmental awareness. In seeking acceptable magical foci for large groups of people who do not know one another, wider social issues such as threats to the environment are natural candidates for action. They concern all and they provide a legitimate outlet for magical activity that can at the same time be sufficiently emotionally involving to create bonds between a diverse group of people. Earth healing rituals raise awareness of environmental issues and those who take part in them are generally encouraged to take action on the material as well as on the magical plane to further their ends. Regardless of their magical efficacy, the rituals encourage environmental activism and an identification with the natural world. They heal the breach between humankind and Nature and, by creating social cohesion in the Wiccan community, they heal the breach between self and other.

CONCLUSION

Healing is an important part of Wiccan practice and belief. If Wicca is meeting needs for healing, it is likely to thrive as a movement insofar as there are people and things to be healed. Healing others is an age-old need that will continue; healing the earth will be a long-term task. If, however, healing of others and earth healing are by-products of and metaphors for a need for self-healing, then participants can be expected to exit Wicca when their healing is complete. Wicca will be for them a therapeutic process that serves similar needs to many New Age therapies and practices: Once the object is successfully achieved participants can be expected to move on.

However, healing in its literal and metaphorical sense is not the only need served by Wicca. The overt rationale of Wiccan practice is not to heal and to be healed. Wicca's aims are broader and address wider needs, such as worship of Deity, honoring the feminine, veneration of Nature, and the use of paranormal energies and powers. Abraham Maslow's (1943, 1970) Hierarchy of Needs divides human needs into five levels: physiological, safety, belongingness, self-esteem and self-actualization. The first four levels are "deficiency" needs: They can be satiated. The final level—self actualization—is a "being" need. It has no satiation point. Puttick (1997b) has made an interesting attempt to categorize new religious movements according to the needs they most satisfy in Maslow's hierarchy. Wicca is ascribed to "belongingness." This is problematic. While to an outsider the social cohesion of Wicca might be its most distinctive feature, this is rarely the conscious motive for people to join Wiccan covens. Typical reasons for joining (see for instance Adler 1986; Orion 1995; Puttick 1996) include developing magical powers (self-esteem), finding a system of belief which honors the Divine Feminine (for women, belongingness and self-esteem) and a desire for spiritual experience (self-actualization).

It could be argued, however, that while "belongingness" may not be a conscious motive for joining, it may be one of a number of powerful reasons for staying. An important aspect, and a healing aspect, of Wiccan groups is the social cohesion provided by the quasi-family bonds between group members. Belongingness may encourage participants to remain in Wicca once any self-healing they are seeking has worked its course.

Participants can also be expected to remain within Wicca to the extent that self-actualization is being achieved, in Maslow's terms a "non-satiable" need. Carpenter's (1994) work suggests that Wicca is providing participants with mystical experiences that lead to self-actualization. Ultimately, despite Orion's (1995) claim that the healing motif predominates in Wicca, it may be post-healing aspirations towards self-actualization, a process that goes beyond a healed "normality" that enables people to adapt successfully to the everyday world to a "super-normality," a realization of individuals' full potential, that encourages people to stay on the Wiccan path.

Notes

[1] Farrar and Farrar (1984:135–44), among others, give a good exposition of Witchcraft ethics.

[2] Luhrmann (1989:106f) incorrectly inflates this to 16 percent.

[3] Data collected by Vivianne Crowley from entrants to the U.K.-based Wicca Study Group.

[4] Created by Will Shepardson and the women of Greenham Common Peace Camp, England.

[5] See Crowley (1996:115).

[6] I have followed the Wiccan practice of capitalizing "Nature," which is frequently used interchangeably with Divinity.

[7] R.W. Hood (1975) reports mean scores of 109.3 (S.D. 22.6) for males and 119.4 (S.D. 18.8) for females in a group of 300 college students with nominal, mainly fundamentalist Protestant, religious affiliation; 132.2 (S.D. 23.4) for 65 students in a private Protestant college in the southern United States; 114.9 (S.D. 25.5) for 52 fundamentalist Protestant students; 110.2 (S.D. 26.9) for 83 undergraduate psychology students with mainstream Protes-

tant affiliations. Carpenter (1994:216) reports a mean score of 141.15 (S.D. 14.62) for his Pagan Spirit Gathering group.
    [8] Crowley (1996:41–89 and 171–92) gives an account of Wiccan ritual practices.
    [9] Batson et al. (1993:262–85) give a long review of studies.
    [10] See Bradburn (1969).
    [11] Gardnerian Wiccan material, quoted in Vivianne Crowley (1996:191).

Works Cited

Adler, Margot. 1986. *Drawing Down the Moon: The Resurgence of Paganism in America*. Boston: Beacon Press (originally 1979).
Batson, C.D., P. Schoenrade, and W.L. Ventis. 1993. *Religion and the Individual: A Social Psychology of Religion*. Oxford: Oxford University Press.
Benor, D.J. 1990. Survey on spiritual healing research, *Complem. Med. Res.* 4,3: 9–33.
Bradburn, Norman M. 1969. *The Structure of Psychological Well-Being*. Chicago: Adline.
Carpenter, D.D. 1994. Spiritual experiences, life changes, and ecological viewpoints of contemporary Pagans. Unpublished Ph.D. thesis, Saybrook Institute.
Crowley, Vivianne. 1996. *Wicca: The Old Religion in the New Millennium*. London: Thorsons/HarperCollins.
———. 1997. *Principles of Wicca*. London: Thorsons/HarperCollins.
Ellwood, Robert S. and Partin, Harry B. 1988. *Religious and Spiritual Groups in Modern America*. 2nd ed., Englewood Cliffs, NJ: Prentice-Hall.
Faber, M.D. 1993. *Modern Witchcraft and Psychoanalysis*. Cranbury, NJ, and London: Associated University Presses.
Farrar, Janet, and Stewart Farrar. 1984.*The Witches' Way*. London: Hale.
Gardner, Gerald B. 1954. *Witchcraft Today*. London: Rider & Co.
Greeley, A.M. 1975. The sociology of the paranormal: A reconnaissance. *Research Papers in the Social Sciences*, Vol. 3, series no. 90-023. London: Sage.
Hood, R.W. 1975. The construction and preliminary validations of a measure of reported mystical experience. *Journal for the Scientific Study of Religion*, 14. Pages 29–41.
———. 1977. Different triggering of mystical experience as a function of self actualization, *Review of Religious Research*, 18, Pages 264–70.
Luhrmann, Tanya. 1989. *Persuasions of the Witch's Craft: Ritual Magic and Witchcraft in Present-day England*. Oxford: Basil Blackwell.
Maslow, Abraham. 1943. A theory of human motivation. *Psychological Review*, 50.
———. 1970. *Motivation and Personality*. 2nd ed. NY: Harper & Row. Pages 370–96.

Orion, Loretta. 1995. *Never Again the Burning Times: Paganism Revived*. Prospect Heights, IL: Waveland Press.

Puttick, Elizabeth. 1997a. *Women in New Religions: In Search of Community, Sexuality and Spiritual Power*. London: Macmillan.

———. 1997b. A new typology of religion based on needs and values, *Journal of Beliefs and Values: Studies in Religion and Education*, 18 (2): 133–45.

Starhawk. 1982. *Dreaming the Dark: Magic, Sex and Politics*. Boston: Beacon Press.

Valiente, Doreen. 1964. *Pentagram*, no. 2.

———. 1973. *An ABC of Witchcraft Past and Present*. London: Hale.

১০ 10 ১০

The Goddess Dances

Spirituality and American Women's Interpretations of Middle Eastern Dance

by Janice Crosby

A woman stands within a patch of full moonlight, surrounded by candles lit for each of the sacred directions and elements. Garbed in a flowing white skirt, she begins her dance of invocation to the Great Mother. In the east she twirls, chiffon floating as she calls on the powers of air; in the south sensual heat is reflected as she tosses her hair, hips circling. With water in the west she is rippling hand motions, eternal circles of birth, while hip drops and foot stamping celebrate the earthiness of the north. Circle cast, she dances her prayer, drawing energy from sky and moon, earth and fire, as she gives glad thanks for what has been given, and speaks through her body of her heart's desire. With the last pulse of energy she sends all back to the cosmos, and drops to the floor, drained yet complete.

This scene may not be what one thinks of when one thinks of Middle Eastern dance, or bellydance,[1] but it can be found in a dancer's private ritual or a women's circle. A significant proportion[2] of Middle Eastern dancers go beyond espousing the art as a sensuous expression of female grace and power; they see it as charged with spiritual signification, most often in the form of association with Goddess imagery.

INTRODUCTION

My research springs from a desire to understand and articulate why bellydancers, most of whom characterize themselves as feminist,[3] would select a dance form that has historically been presented in the United States as closer to burlesque than high art, replete with associations of female performance for the gratification of the male gaze. That a great number of dancers would additionally present the dance form as linked to, or a means of, spiritual expression grounded in images of the divine female/Goddess, is another indication that Middle Eastern dance has gone far beyond a 1970s national fad (Forner 1993). The area of "Goddess history" and issues such as body image, sexuality, and spiritual interconnection reveal connections to the Goddess movement which have allowed women to shape this dance tradition in a way generally prohibited for women in its countries of origin.

BELLYDANCE AND REVISIONIST HISTORY

Turning to the issue of the Goddess in Middle Eastern dance, a topic which seems initially to be a *non sequitur* for a form which originates in predominantly Islamic countries,[4] one discovers that since bellydance gained its popularity in the United States along with other feminist activities in the 1970s, including the rise of Goddess spirituality in its many guises, it exhibits many of the same hallmarks of revisionist history, focus on the female body and its processes, and subversive potential in images or roles traditionally denigrated by patriarchal society.

Many feminists exploring Goddess spirituality employ revisionist history to speak of a time before patriarchal dominance, a history which feminists "return to . . . in art and imagination, seeking inspiration and sustenance, learning the taste and feel of being human on earth when civilization and nature were in synergy, not competition" (Eller 1993:151). While interpretations of the evidence Goddess feminists offer to support their assertions vary and are hotly disputed,[5] Eller is correct in pointing to alternative *herstory* as "a religiously and politically useful myth" (1993:157), or, as Gloria Orenstein refers to these alternative narratives, "medicine stories" (1990:3). In order to discuss what they find appealing in a dance both celebrated and looked down on in Arabic/Islamic culture, some western dancers have posited the origins of the dance in a prehistory which bypasses the problem of patriarchal Islam altogether. Typical of such revisionist historical approaches is Daniela Gioseffi's *Earth Dancing: Mother Nature's Oldest Rite*, which argues for the origins of bellydance in ancient women's culture as a "dance of life and birth" (1980:72) which originated as "a worship to the ancient Earth Mother Goddess" (9). Michelle Forner describes this approach as the "Spiritual Orientation"

> . . . which broaches an attitudinal dimension usually concerned with mystical belief systems, personal empowerment, and ritual. These practitioners often believe the origins of Oriental dance predate Arab cultures and associate them with pre-patriarchal, ancient times. The origins are linked to birthing rituals and fertility rites, and the dance is thought to celebrate the feminine principle rather than express an ethnic identity or an entertaining performance. (Forner 1993:18)

Dancers such as Morocco, one of the primary cultivators of Middle Eastern dance in this country, have noted connections between bellydance movements and LaMaze, a connection which was furthered by her participation in a Moroccan woman's birthing ritual (1997). Morocco was one of the first to publish an article commenting on Middle Eastern dance's origin as "the oldest form of natural childbirth instruction" (1964—on-line).

THE BODY OF THE GODDESS

Envisioning the dance as an ancient female tradition which celebrates the Mother Goddess and women as celebrants/teachers allows many dancers to see themselves as embodying the divine female, while at the same time this position puts women in a superior stance to those who would like to see the dance as something which "naughty" women do to titillate men. Judith Hanna in *Dance, Sex, and Gender*, a text which focuses mainly on ballet and modern dance, acknowledges that these mindsets may collide: "Artist and audience may hold different views—the dancer seeing performance as artistic skill and work, the audience, the titillation of an erotic fantasy figure and femme fatale" (1988:64). Most dancers are willing to educate audiences as much as possible as to the performer's view of the dance in the hopes of changing such perceptions.

References to goddesses have been included in the nomenclature of groups and dancers in the United States for several decades.

Jamila Salimpour, arguably one of the most influential proponents of bellydancing in this country in the 1960s and 1970s, headed the troupe named Bal Anat (Dance of the Mother Goddess). The troupe's style, which Michelle Forner refers to as "ethnic fantasy" (1993:18), is also the progenitor of the current "California Tribal," a style increasingly popular among young women just coming into the dance, many of whom are familiar with alternative spiritualities. Indicating further spiritual connection, dancers occasionally name themselves after goddesses such as Sakti, Artemis, Ishtar, or Inanna. A glance through a major Middle Eastern dance publication such as *Habibi* reveals troupe names with connections to either goddesses or goddess symbols: Simone's Seventh Veil Dance Company, The Goddess Dancing, The Hand Maidens of Isis, and Dancers of the Crescent Moon. Additionally, event and video titles evoke or promote the divine feminine: Dhyanis' "The Call of the Goddess," "A Sacred Temple Tribal and Ritual Bellydance Retreat—Awaken the God Goddess Within," *The Veil of Isis*, and *Dance to the Great Mother*. In this art form, the Goddess is an enduring presence.

The general focus on the dance as one suited to the female body because of its circular and flowing movements is very strong. If one looks at the Goddess in an archetypal rather than historical sense, bellydance's emphasis on the art form as embodying female attributes such as creation and sensuality also links it to Goddess spirituality's idea of all women as goddesses. As Carol Christ observes in *The Laughter of Aphrodite*, "The symbol of the Goddess aids the process of naming and reclaiming the female body and its cycles and processes" (Christ 1987:125). Although there are men involved in Middle Eastern dance as performers in the United States, the primary performers of Middle Eastern dance are women. While some feminists object to Goddess spirituality for what they see as a biologically reductionist viewpoint, there is little doubt that when women see their bodies as divine, they get a taste of the power which has been the traditional province of men for millennia. Additionally, they reclaim their bodies from male profanation. As Melissa Raphael puts it in *Thealogy and Embodiment*, "Because the Goddess is eternally immanent and 'female,' spiritual feminism makes the body a powerful site of resistance to its own desacralization and the energetic source of its own resacralization" (1996:82). Bellydancers in general share a more positive view of their bodies than women in mainstream culture are encouraged to hold, and bellydancers who see the dance in the context of Goddess spirituality dance not only to celebrate the female body, but also to use the medium as an embodiment for an archetypal feminine power which is strong, graceful, playful, seductive, transcendent, and joyous.

Like Goddess feminists, bellydancers can also enjoy subverting traditional female images and roles. Salome is a prime example in this regard. She is to bellydance what Lilith, Adam's rebellious first wife, is to women's spirituality. Her presence in the dance world has always proven disruptive to mainstream ideas of female decorum. Hanna reports that a "Salome Craze" in 1908, inspired by Maud Allen's *Dance of Salome*, had New York theater managers "'guarding against outbreaks of Salomania'" on the parts of other female dancers (1998:183). Although a number of Middle Eastern dancers have taken the name Salome, it is Salome as an icon that captures the imagination of dancers and their public. The dancer's Salome is not a king's puppet, nor a tramp who serves Satan, nor a mother's dutiful daughter. Rather, she is the dancer whose dance is *so* powerful that it is stronger than prophets, kings, or empires. When an audience member tells a dancer, "Salome must have danced so," the dancer knows this latter meaning is what is intended. In further tribute to Salome, contemporary author/dancer Wendy Buonaventura even produced a dance drama, "Revelations: the Testament of Salome." Clearly, the powerful Salome is far more popular than the stereotypical image of harem slaves awaiting their master's pleasure.

METHODOLOGY

The research for this chapter involved multiple methods of data gathering as an attempt to check the consistency of observed patterns of behavior within the Middle Eastern dance community. This included distribution of a written survey, review of literature on Middle Eastern dance and spirituality, review of postings to the Med-dance internet listserve, and participant observation. The initial run of the survey in December 1996 resulted in 38 respondents from a target group of approximately 250 to 300. The survey was posted on the Med-dance internet listserve, and after eliminating responses from male dancers and dancers in other countries, the number of responses was 35, or about 12 percent. Three out of four students in my fall dance class returned the survey. Seventy-five copies of the survey were also distributed at a dance seminar in Dallas in February 1997, with seven persons responding, resulting in a group of 45. The low return rate (12.7 percent) may be due to the length of the questions, as well as reflective of the fairly unexplored field of internet surveying. A recent survey of this same listserve (Sherezzah 1997) yielded less than 10 percent return, so my rate appears typical for this list. Unless otherwise indicated, all non-published quotations included within this essay are taken from survey materials.[6] In addition my insights are drawn from eight years of participant observation as a student, teacher, troupe member, solo performer, and paid performer.

THE DANCERS

Who are the women pursuing bellydance? Interestingly, several of the demographic factors revealed in my survey of Middle Eastern dancers as a group correlate with Cynthia Eller's description of American women involved with Goddess spirituality (1993:18–23). Both groups tend to be in their thirties and forties, overwhelmingly white, and highly educated, with 37 percent of my respondents having Bachelor's degrees, and 26 percent with graduate degrees. Wendy Griffin (1995) notes that one of the Goddess spirituality groups she studied was characterized by college education and professional occupations. I did not include a question on sexual orientation, so the proportion of lesbians in the bellydance community is an unknown quantity; although there are no doubt lesbians involved in the dance, very little mention is made of this subject in any discussion venue. In terms of participation levels in Middle Eastern dance, 71 percent had been dancing five years or more, often going on to become performers in various situations (recitals, parties, restaurants, bellygrams, stage, etc.) and even bellydance teachers, while usually pursuing primary careers outside of the field of dance. As with any interest area, some people investigate it for a while and then leave, but the ongoing involvement of the survey respondents suggests that bellydance has a transformative action that causes it to become an integral part of the dancer's life in a way unusual for an exercise activity. In fact, some personal accounts of dancers' first exposure to the dance read like conversion narratives, or "love at first sight" anecdotes.

Although the general public, particularly in smaller cities and towns where the populace may have had little exposure to Middle Eastern dance, may hold a stereotypical image of a bellydancer as a type of harem girl "bimbo" reminiscent of the 70s television sitcom "I Dream of Jeannie," the dancers who responded to my survey, as well as other dancers from across the country and the world, make it clear in their written and verbal comments that they are strong, intelligent, independent women who dance in order to enrich their own lives. Although from New Zealand, Kashmir's experience of a workshop organized with a drama teacher strikes a note of familiarity with American practitioners of the dance who encounter stereotypes:

> She was totally thrown when she discovered rather than a gaggle of silly young things she was dealing with an engineer, a ferry boat pilot, a fixed wing pilot, science graduates, a vet, a lawyer. . . . All these women had confidence in their own intellectual abilities and also were at ease with their physical and sensual selves. (3/24/98)

While certainly bellydancers may perform for significant males in their lives, over and over one hears that the dance is something that women do for themselves, not for men. As Morocco so succinctly puts it, "'Honey, I can think of a lot easier ways to attract a man; I do this dance for me'" (in Angelique 1996:28). In fact, sometimes men are threatened by a woman's pursuit of the dance. Kashmir's partner made her life miserable until she decided "After trying to talk him through it there was only one other solution—I left him. One has to get one's priorities right" (3/19/98). James Janner, who is a devoted observer of the Los Angeles dance scene, warned of such responses in a recent posting: "You should be emotionally prepared for the likelihood that the number of guys who will accept you will decrease significantly as you grow as a dancer" (3/12/98). Apparently, the ways in which the dance increases women's sense of power and self prove unacceptable to men who prefer their women to be less than they can be.

The negative connotations and misconceptions associated with the dance, about which many articles in Middle Eastern dance magazines are written, only pose an additional challenge for these women's many abilities, while the dance offers them benefits which make any necessary public (or private) education worthwhile. These benefits vary for each woman, but include positive body image, an opportunity to play with traditionally feminine attributes, the creation of an alternative female persona, sensual exploration, and a chance to work creatively in one of the few artistic fields dominated by women. The majority of teachers, vendors, and seminar producers/directors are female, thus making bellydance in the United States a uniquely female-controlled dance form. Having seen how bellydance shares territory held by Goddess spirituality in general, survey responses and anecdotes as well as the more traditional print sources will further illustrate its healing potential in the crucial areas of body image, sexuality, and spiritual interconnection in the dance.

BODY IMAGE AND SELF-EXPRESSION

Raphael's cogent discussion of the religious and philosophical implications of western culture's obsession with female dieting, which she views as "one of the most recent attacks on female sacral embodiment," reveals that Goddess imagery has immense liberating potential in regard to the way women view their bodies (1996:83). Just as the Venus of Willendorf expands women's images of what the female body divine can look like, so too does Middle Eastern dance. One proponent, Karen Andes (1998), observes that:

> Myths and stories about goddesses do not preach formulas for health and happiness, mention optimal daily intake of calories and fat, numbers of reps or workouts to do each week or revere one body type above all others and therefore feed a sense of hopelessness and inadequacy. (168)

In this spirit Aisha Maya of Baton Rouge's Middle Eastern Dance Artists, a non-profit dance organization, did a dance demonstration for her Women of Size support group. She reported that they were amazed by two things: the agility of movement that she possessed, and the wonderful costume she wore. The women had been conditioned to think of themselves not only as graceless exercisers, but also as having bodies unworthy of ornamentation. They have welcomed her back several more times. Aisha's experience points to one of the most frequently praised aspects of this dance: its open-ness to women of all body types. Bellydance is often contrasted with ballet, a dance form incompatible with most women's mature bod-ies, which "is dedicated to woman as an ethereal being rather than a creature of flesh and blood" (Buonaventura 1989:200). In this re-gard bellydance continues a Middle Eastern tradition. Journalist Geraldine Brooks writes of seeing one of Egypt's premier dancers, Souhair Zaki, for the first time:

> [she] was the most celebrated dancer in Cairo, but she hadn't seen thirty in a while. Flesh clung heavily to her hips. Her abdomen bulged like a ripe pear. I had never seen traditional oriental dance before, but I recognized every movement. What she was doing . . . was what a woman's body *did*—the natural movements of sex and childbirth. The dance drew the eye to the hips and abdomen, the very center of the fe-male body's womanliness. (Brooks 1996:216–17)

Here one sees the immediate recognition factor which bellydance has for so many women. Women sense the veneration for the female body which, unlike so many bodies on display (especially in the West), does not have to be thin or absurdly youthful. The focus on the hips, an area "frozen [as] . . . the area of our bodies we most dislike" allows women to reclaim and accept the site of that which marks us as female (Andes 1998:51).

Not surprisingly then, when the survey respondents answered the question, "How does studying/performing Middle Eastern dance make you feel about yourself as a woman?," the most fre-quently used terms were "powerful," "sexy," "creative," "beauti-ful," "confident," "stronger," "more accepting of physique," and "more feminine/female." Margaret notes that bellydance gives her "the opportunity to enjoy *looking* at [herself]." How rare it is for women to enjoy that process, when so many of us are trained to enact the self–critical gaze! For Basheera, the dance helps her to feel "beautiful, sexy, and desirable as [she is] now. It makes [her] feel comfortable with [herself] and her body." Notice that sexiness is *now*, not if some condition is met to make one "desirable." Most bellydance teachers help to foster the sense of desirability among their students, encouraging them to leave shyness behind and "work what they've got." Several women used the words "in tune" to describe the relationship bellydance fosters with their bodies and even with the planet, indicating a sense of oneness and interconnection which goes beyond the ordinary bounds of body image.

Ayla, another listserve respondent, brings up an additional feminist issue when she writes of seeing herself as "more *female*—quite a contrast to daily corporate life." Over the past several decades of feminist change, women have found that standards of conformity often necessary to compete in traditionally male fields have limited the ways in which women may choose to express themselves through dress or ornamentation. In addition, the idea of a feminist litmus test based on how thoroughly one eschews such traditionally feminine markers as makeup has become increasingly passé. For a woman who plays hardball on the job and meets other increasing demands elsewhere in her life, the chance to go dance in class or at home, listen to rhythmic music, perhaps twirling a silken veil while she undulates and twists her hips, is an opportunity to let her body, rather than society's expectations, do the talking. Women add balance to their lives in this way.

Bellydance provides transformative opportunities for self-expression and play. Andrea Deagon, professor of Classics and Women's Studies at the University of North Carolina, Wilmington, as well as a performer and instructor, writes of the power of seeing herself in her first bellydance costume: ". . . I recognized a part of myself I had seldom seen before. . . . *she* was made to dance—to whirl and shimmy and express her love of life and take her audience along for the ride" (1996:28). Sometimes Deagon helps other women to glimpse this transformation: "I love to see women who may be caught in bad body images recognize their beauty in the universal attraction of a dance costume, which has the potential to compliment and beautify any body type" (1996:29). Referring to bellydance's costuming components as "goddess wear" (1998:92), Andes argues that ". . . if there were more places where women . . . could tie beads, tassels and chiffon around our hips, shake, shimmy, swivel and grind without fear of judgment . . . we'd storm the doors to this experience" (1998:56–57). Diane Wakoski presents this idea well in her poem "Belly Dancer," when the speaker says of her silks, "Surely any woman wearing such fabrics/would move her body just to feel them touching every part of her" (1996:4–5).

Goddesses come in every shape and form; sometimes, they come wearing silk and beads.

SEXUALITY

Body image and sexuality are closely linked ideas in Goddess spirituality, as women in the movement celebrate visions of the Goddess which include sensuality and sexual expression; a goddess like Inanna, for example, is seductress, fertility goddess, queen, and she who faces death to claim her full power (Kinsley 1989:126). In reflecting on such multidimensional attributes, I am reminded of my first bellydance teacher, Khawliya, a rape survivor and Wiccan; her dancing was a source of healing and empowerment for herself and her students. When I saw her perform, I saw a woman proud to be in her body and in command of her sensuality. She could move effortlessly from a gypsy pose on a chair, scissor kicking her legs in a flirtatious way, to a leap and a toss of her long red hair which said "You can't touch this!" When Khawliya danced, she reclaimed her power. Here was no victim. And though her story might not be a common one, it typifies the healing potential of the dance for some women.[7] In *Jareeda*, a west coast bellydance magazine, Angelique writes of a similar effect she has observed as an instructor: "Most women victims who learn to belly dance, stop acting like victims, stop walking like victims and stop being victims. This is one of my favorite things about the dance" (1996:29). On her website, Mésmera echoes this in her experience as a teacher: "The greatest pleasure is seeking the awakening, empowerment, and transformation that continually develops."

Many dancers are sometimes hindered from recognizing the sexual, healing power of the dance because of the perceived need in the dance community to defend the art against the preconceptions of a misinformed public. To draw a clear line between bellydancing and stripping, for instance, dancers emphasize the training and education most performers receive, and downplay the sexual aspects. Some even mince words, dividing the sensual from the sexual, a division ultimately as useful/less as the distinctions between erotica and pornography—highly personal, debatable, and confusing for many people. If sexuality only referred to "bumping and grinding," the difference would be clear, but of course sexuality is a far broader complex of ideas and behaviors. Barbara Sellers-Young, professor and dance researcher at the University of California at Davis, comments that "the diversity of performing environments and styles reflects the consistent search by women to understand their sensuality" (1992:148). Most dancers are aware of the erotic potential of the dance, especially in a Western context, and consciously choose how much of the erotic element to channel into the dance at any given time.

Dancers such as Alia Thabit also remind us that "Women's sexual power is something that terrifies people (and a lot of feminists) because it has been demonized . . . called manipulative, something women use to control men." Valuing her sexuality, she declares, "I will not sacrifice any part of me any longer for anyone" (4/2/98). Her posting was greeted with a number of affirmations of this stance as inherently feminist. Raphael argues that Goddess spirituality "is an ancient pagan worldview and one which would regard modern patriarchy's quasi-aesthetic refusal of female bodily maturity, sexuality and fertility as ingratitude to the Goddess" (1996:95). Acceptance of female sexuality becomes an act of sacred celebration. Going further, some dancers find that performing turns *them* on. One instructor, who sometimes encouraged her students to engage in rather lusty creative visualization in order to understand their moves, once remarked that dancing made her physically aroused. Her arousal did not center around an audience, but instead on the fact that when dancing she felt truly free in her female body. For her and others, the expression of joy in the movements of her female body was ultimately a sexual expression, one Inanna herself would approve of. Sherry Reardon speaks for many on this continuum when she observes that, ". . . most people interpret 'sexual' as meaning you're trying to seduce someone in the audience, and that isn't it at all. It's saying 'I am a human being, and sexuality is part of my being human'" (4/5/98).

THE GODDESS

Finally, women write and speak very eloquently of the sense of connection with and embodiment of the Goddess they feel when dancing. Athena's remarks invoke a sense of sisterhood as well; she feels the connection

. . . intensely. . . . this dance is so old that for me, there is a kind of mystical connection with every woman who has danced this dance throughout Time, right back to that first camel-walk round the camp-fire. Sometimes, in the midst of a good chiftitelli [drum rhythm], I can almost feel them!

Karen adds that "The dance comes from deep within me. . . . It puts me in touch with my creative force. It is beyond words. I enjoy my own femininity and have respect and admiration for all women. I feel a connection with other dancers because they understand the joy of the dance." Raphael points out that a tenet of Goddess spirituality is that "female spiritual agency and creativity has never been finally destroyed and is now resurgent . . ." (1996:82) and these remarks attest to that spirit of connection and rebirth.

Baraka's statement reflects a sense of the Goddess' power in a beneficent cosmos. She writes, "For me, dance is prayer—prayer for greater understanding, for compassion, for gentleness and humility, for growth, for fellowship, for a better world. When I dance, I touch the face of the Goddess." With Mésmera, one of the most ancient goddess symbols stands out: "For me, it's been the Serpent, the ancient symbol of the Goddess, that's brought me [my] inspiration . . ." Margaret, who is both a feminist artist and therapist, had this to say: "The movement, the attitude, the costume of Bellydancing *exude* the powerful erotic sensual feminine—aware of her power and charms. When we dance, we enliven the Goddess Herself." For Ayla, this exhibition of the Goddess' charms and power has an effect on the audience as well. She summarizes the thoughts of many dancers when she observes that "those who dance from the spirit are goddesses—we are directly connected with the Goddess energy, we become our other, higher selves when in the 'dance trance.' Observers feel the power and are transfixed, in awe." Survey respondent Sharon Andrews, an ordained Methodist minister whose spiritual journey has led her to Goddess spirituality and Middle Eastern dance, wrote that "there is an almost sacramental aspect to this self-celebration. Joyous, ecstatic, passionate, and sensual, the dance says that bodies created in the image of the Divine are worth loving, physically, spiritually, and erotically." These comments point to a powerful mystical aspect achieved through the dance, which dancers claim as part of their female birthright, where "cosmogonic meanings of the female body are being newly and transgressively written and danced as the abundance of the immanent sacred . . ." (Raphael 1996:123).

My involvement in Goddess spirituality predates my study of Middle Eastern dance. Upon finding out how the ancient origins of the dance dovetailed with what I had been discovering about ancient Goddess worship, I became excited by the spiritual and artistic possibilities of this dance. Now, as a teacher of bellydance, I have great feminist rewards: I see women standing straighter, prouder, starting to value their neglected sensual sides. I see them start to realize that they can create and express themselves, tell their stories in new ways. I see them begin to see the Goddess within. As Sarah-Jewel of the Nile puts it in her poem "The Belly Dancer in All of Us,"

> I believe
> That in every woman
> A bellydancer is hidden,
> Longing to escape.
> To feel the music
> And move with passion.
> To mesmerize men
> And enchant women. (1996)

With each class and with each dance, I hope that our work in front of the dance studio mirrors will help each woman see a reflection of the Goddess.

CONCLUSION

Goddess spirituality in bellydance takes the art beyond a dance form and beyond a mode of artistic and erotic expression into a statement about sensuality and play as meaningful attributes of a comprehensively female divine power. Ironically, the Goddess spirituality movement in the west has allowed this to take place in such countries as the United States, not in the countries of the dance's origin. In general, feminists in those countries are still fighting for their rights within Islam (or Judaism), not in postpatriarchal spiritual movements. Many bellydance commentators like Morocco and Eva Cernik have noted how religious extremism in these countries threatens the dance, putting American dancers in the unlooked-for role of cultural preservationists.

However, dancers face misunderstanding from some American feminists who don't understand that "Patriarchal rule thrives on women being disconnected from their bodies" (Kahena 3/25/98). When Aiphecca posted about receiving "Feminist Family Fallout" from women in her family who, though academically trained feminists, could not understand her motivation to dance, she generated a long-running thread in which many dancers articulated their perception of the dance as absolutely feminist. Several with graduate degrees (some in Women's Studies) offered to correspond with the errant family members. In venues like this essay, those of us trained in the academy and in the dance hope to foster dialogue within the feminist family. And by re-linking Middle Eastern dance to its Goddess ancestry, bellydancers look to a future where all women may dance divinely.

Notes

[1] Much debate exists within the community as to which terminology most accurately names the dance as it is performed by American dancers. Many prefer the term Middle Eastern dance because it carries fewer negative connotations, but use bellydance since it has a higher recognition factor. Others feel bellydance is more appropriate for the dance Americans perform. Still others (or even some of the same people) use the terms "Oriental Dance" or "Raks Sharki," among others. Following common practice, I use the terms interchangeably in this essay.

[2] I would estimate one-third or more dancers associate the idea of a Goddess with Middle Eastern dance in some way. However, it should be noted that some women see the dance as simply another dance form, or associate another form of spirituality, such as Sufism, with the dance.

[3] As Naomi Wolf's *Fire with Fire* so eloquently points out, some women have become hesitant to claim the "f" word, since the conservative media have been so successful with portraying feminists as male-bashing (1993:58–59); nonetheless, such women also claim themselves to be in favor of goals or ideals traditionally considered feminist: equal opportunity, sexual self-determination, actualization, and so forth.

[4] Of course, there is a Hebrew tradition of bellydancing, as well as non-Arabic traditions such as Persian classical dance. Still, the majority of performers and music are Arabic in influence or origin. For an interesting

article on how Jewish women are seeking their ancient roots, see Cia (Sautter, Cynthia). "Searching for Biblical Roots of Belly Dance." *Habibi* 16.1 (1997): 8–9 ff.

[5] Carol Christ gives a good discussion of the debate in "Resistance to Goddess History," the fourth chapter in her latest book, *Rebirth of the Goddess: Finding Meaning in Feminist Spirituality*, Reading, MA: Addison-Wesley, 1997.

[6] Listserve postings will be indicated by a date in parentheses.

[7] Of course, dance alone is not sufficient to heal the scars of rape— support groups, counseling, and other forms of support are necessary.

Works Cited

Andes, Karen. 1998. *A Woman's Book of Power: Using Dance to Cultivate Energy and Health in Mind, Body, and Spirit.* New York: Perigee.

Andrews, Sharon. 1997. Letter to the author. March 20.

Angelique. 1996. Belly Dance: What it is, what it isn't. *Jareeda Middle Eastern Dance Magazine.* Nov-Dec. Pages 28–29.

Brooks, Geraldine. 1996. *Nine Parts of Desire: the Hidden World of Islamic Women.* (1995.) New York: Anchor.

Buonaventura, Wendy. 1989. *Serpent of the Nile: Women and Dance in the Arab World.* London: Saqi Books.

Christ, Carol. 1987. *The Laughter of Aphrodite.* San Francisco: Harper & Row.

Deagon, Andrea. 1996. Costumes: Magic, identity and power. *Jareeda Middle Eastern Dance Magazine.* March. Pages 28–29.

Eller, Cynthia. 1993. *Living in the Lap of the Goddess: The Feminist Spirituality Movement in America.* New York: Crossroad.

Forner, Michelle. 1993. The transmission of oriental dance in the United States: From *raqs Sharqi* to belly dance. Master's Thesis. UCLA.

Gioseffi, Daniela. 1991. *Earth Dancing: Mother Nature's Oldest Rite.* 1980. Pacific Grove, CA: Artemis Imports.

Griffin, Wendy. 1995. The embodied Goddess: Feminist Witchcraft and female divinity. *Sociology of Religion* 56.1. Pages 35–49. Online. July 1, 1998. Http://www.csulb.edu/~wgriffin/publications/embodied.html

Hanna, Judith Lynne. 1988. *Dance, Sex, and Gender: Signs of Identity, Dominance, Defiance, and Desire.* Chicago: Chicago University Press.

Janner, James. 1998. Re: PERF Others' reactions . . ." March 12. Online posting. Med-dance listserve. med-dance@world.std.com. Used with permission.

Kahena. 1998. Re:OTH Feminist family fallout. March 25. Online posting. Med-dance listserve. Med-dance@world.std.com.

Kashmir (jvarga). 1998. OTH: Feminist fallout." March 24. Online posting. Med-dance listserve. Med-dance@world.std.com.

———. 1998. Re: PERF: Men reactions. March 19. Online posting. Med-dance listserve. Med-dance@world.std.com.

Kinsley, David. 1989. *The Goddesses' Mirror*. Albany, NY: SUNY.

Mésmera. 1998. Home page." Online. April 22. Http://www.mesmera.com.

Morocco [Carolina Dinicu]. 1964. 'Belly dancing' and childbirth. *Sexology*. Online. Internet. November 28, 1997. Available www.tiac.net/users/morocco.

———. 1997. Roots. *Habibi* 5.12. Online. Internet. November 28, 1997. Available www.tiac.net/users/morocco.

Orenstein, Gloria. 1990. *The Reflowering of the Goddess*. New York: Pergamon.

Raphael, Melissa. 1996. *Thealogy and Embodiment*. Sheffield: Sheffield Academic Press.

Sarah-Jewel of the Nile. 1996. The belly dancer in all of us. *Jareeda Middle Eastern Dance Magazine*. April. Page 30.

Sellers-Young, Barbara. 1992. Raks el Sharki: Transculturation of a folk form. *Journal of Popular Culture* 26.2. Pages 141–52.

Sherezzah [Reardon, Sherry]. 1998. Re: PERF Men's attitudes, FFF. April 5. Online posting. Med-dance listserve. Med-dance@world.std.com.

Thabit, Alia. 1998. Re: PERF Men's attitudes, FFF. April 2. Online posting. Med-dance listserve. Med-dance@world.std.com.

Wakoski, Diane. 1985. Belly dancer. (1966.) *The Norton Anthology of Literature by Women*. Sandra Gilbert and Susan Gubar, eds. New York: Norton. Page 2270.

Wolf, Naomi. 1993. *Fire with Fire*. New York: Random.

PART TWO – THE TEACHINGS

⚭ 11 ⚭

The Power of Ritual

by Ruth Rhiannon Barrett

Kay enters the room dressed in colorful robes and followed by a procession of singing women praising the Crone, the elder woman who bleeds no more and whose sacred river now flows underground. Her ancestors are invoked and she calls the spirits who have guided her in her life as a woman and musician. A priestess explains to the guests how, in women's rituals, every age is honored and each transition marked as one passes into another stage of being. This ritual tonight honors Kay as an elder, who enters a new stage of life as a wise woman. She lights seven symbolic candles, speaking of a memory, image or some wisdom from every stage of her life. Her daughter presents her with a symbol of her motherline. Kay plays her flute, improvising from Spirit, letting divine inspiration come through into her music. She speaks aloud her visions and wishes for the future and makes a commitment to her elderhood. Lifting a full chalice to her lips, Kay drinks in her visions, making the magic a part of her body and psyche. She then punctuates the magic externally by lighting an eighth candle, symbolizing the manifestation of creativity in her next stage of life.[1]

Ritual practices are at the heart of the women's spirituality movement. Creating and participating in ritual brings value to life's passages, whether they be physical crossroads or emotional transitions. It is often through women's rites that women connect to and honor the deepest parts of themselves, bringing their inner knowledge to conscious awareness. It is also within ritual that women witness and support one another in their path of healing and diverse celebrations of the rites of life.

185

WOMEN'S MYSTERIES

The heart of the feminist Goddess-focused spiritual practice focuses on Women's Mysteries, the ritualized celebrations honoring the rites of passage of women's lives. Women's Mysteries are the essential physical, emotional, and psychic rites of passage women experience by having been born into a female body. These include the five blood mysteries of birth, menstruation, birth/lactation, menopause, and death, which are women's ability to create life, sustain life, and return our bodies to the Source in death. Women's Mysteries celebrate the Earth's seasonal cycles of birth, death and regeneration, and women's likewise cyclical nature.

As women, we embody Goddess as Creatrix. Our female bodies reflect the power of the Goddess in her capacity to create and sustain life. Our wombs become the metaphor and are experienced as the very source of our creative power, the cauldron of our potential and ability to manifest. Even if a woman has had a hysterectomy, she has had a womb at one time, known its power, and will continue to carry within her that creative womb space. She has also been raised as female in this culture, and to greater or lesser degrees has experienced oppression and cultural attitudes toward the female gender. These degrees of oppression vary depending on a woman's color, class, ability, sexual orientation, and body size. These experiences together inform women's lives, enable women to identify with each other, and thus provide the basis for the majority of rituals women are celebrating together. It is for these reasons that most feminist Goddess rituals are celebrated in women-only space.

Females are naturally born into the mysteries of womanhood at birth, and through ritual we are initiated into the circle of women. The circle of women is the very circle of life itself, for it is upon our sacred womb blood, the gift that is passed from mother to daughter, that human life depends. This is a mystery that we can fully experience and celebrate, though we stand humbled by the enormity of it. As women, we can initiate ourselves and assist others in accessing the knowledge and innate power of creation that is our birthright.

> Initiation does not necessarily confer great powers or show how knowledge is to be used: it is merely the implantation of a seed which life's experiences will help germinate, de-

pending on the resources of the initiate. It stimulates the latent potential of the candidate, enabling her to share in the patterns of life at deeper levels than that of surface awareness. (Matthews and Matthews 1986:37)

When we take our power as women to initiate ourselves into the Mysteries, we are taking the initiative to consciously evolve ourselves.

To celebrate women's mysteries is to reclaim what is naturally our own as women. Although the blood mysteries are physiological and natural occurrences, these passages become tainted even to us by being ignored, discounted, or invalidated through male-dominated religions and a cultural denial of women's blood. Women don't even realize that they are being robbed of the opportunity for profound spiritual connection through the reverent celebration of their bodies. Under patriarchy the natural cycles of womb blood are defined as unclean, polluting, and shameful, when recognized at all. Young girls are taught to hide the "evidence" of their monthly cycle, and most menopausal women experience this passage in silence and isolation. By looking through the layers of lies with eyes open, women are returning to celebrate those passages that are uniquely female. For women reclaiming our ancient Goddess heritage and birthright, these transitions become the most sacred and spiritual part of their lives.

By celebrating women-oriented ritual, women have the opportunity to discover their true selves, apart from the messages of patriarchal culture. Inspired by ancient mythic cosmology of the Goddess where she draws herself out of herself in the original act of creation, many women embrace the metaphor of spiritually giving birth to themselves and each other. Within feminist Goddess rituals, the focus is on each woman's own experience, opinions, and ideas.

Common to women's rituals is the experience of immanence and transcendence. Women's spirituality rituals seek to allow women an experience of connection to the life force within all living things (Christ 1987). Through this experience, many women feel that their rituals set a standard of how life should feel outside of the ritual circle. When a woman has an experience of connection to the Divine, unconditional love, trust, empowerment, or sense of true sisterhood, however briefly, she is less likely to tolerate the lack of connection in her life outside of the ritual circle. Often these experiences empower her to make more positive choices in behavior toward herself and others. "Having experienced something during ritual in the framework of religious meaning, we are changed when we return to the common sense world, and so is that world " (Geertz 1983:122). Although aspects of women's ritual can be experienced as therapeutic, its general purpose is to empower women to participate in their lives at a deeper, fuller level. I have seen women inclined to exercise the power of choice with greater clarity and to take greater responsibility for their lives and their extended communities after participating in women's rituals.

RITUAL AND WOMEN'S LIVES

Ritual provides a form to convey meaning through the manipulation of symbolic objects, specific activities or actions. When consciously chosen, the medium carries purposeful symbolic meaning that has the power to speak to the conscious and unconscious mind. When ritual is consciously understood and performed, the consciousness of the participant is changed and carries the potential to link the past, present and future into a continuum that can be observed, felt, and from which we can learn. When life passages are clearly marked through ritual we can connect the dots of our lives to see the pattern in what may have previously felt like a random series of events that affected our lives. We can observe, understand, and integrate the events that have shaped our attitudes about womanhood, sexuality, love, and life.

Sadly, many women describe previous experience of religious ritual as meaningless. This response is mostly derived from experiences of religious traditions that are male-focused, with little or no attention to the realities of women's lives and experiences. When women are empowered to ritualize passages that *they* deem significant and ascribe their own meaning to them, they participate more consciously in their own lives. To create and participate in life cycle rituals is saying that their lives are important, that their stories matter, and that every human life is a gift to the present and future generations.

From any life passage or transition we experience, we internalize attitudes or beliefs about ourselves, our bodies, our sexuality, and life in general based on that experience and how we and others responded to it. In the aftermath of a significant transition, we often formulate life decisions, consciously or unconsciously, and we act on, and are influenced by, these decisions through behaviors and future choices. One example of this would be a girl's first menstruation. Often, the first experience was met with secrecy, embarrassment, or shame, or somewhat more positively but less frequently, the girl's parents did their best to not make it a "big deal." Internally, the girl develops an attitude that either being a woman is dirty or shameful, or that becoming a woman is "no big deal." Either decision follows her into womanhood, affecting her relationship with her body, her sexuality, and the physical symptoms of her monthly cycle. In other words, what we do or don't do in treating or responding to a significant passage or transition has an enormous effect.

The present impact upon our lives from past passages that were unmarked by ritual is impossible to say. To help heal and change an attitude or belief that impacts the present, many women are creating rituals that revisit past experiences and milestones not recognized as significant at the time. Significant passages not usually considered for ritual include: weaning a baby, following a miscarriage or abortion, becoming a grandmother, choosing not to become a biological mother, the birth of a sibling, starting a new career, a house blessing, becoming an adoptive parent (or for the adopted adult or birth mother), before making love, becoming clean and sober, one's children leaving home (the empty nest), forgiving oneself for past behavior, coming out, divorce or separation, quitting a job one hates, finding that first gray hair, and healing from childhood abuse.

Within ritual, it is through the vehicle of symbols that we give our psyches the messages we choose to internalize. One of the most significant traits that distinguishes humans from other animals is the mental ability to manipulate symbols. Symbols in and of themselves are not magical, except by what significance and power we give them. They are a vehicle for human awareness. As human beings, we externalize beliefs and personal processes through symbols, and then through these symbols, give the awareness the symbol signifies back to ourselves in a deeper way.

The aspect of human consciousness reached through meaningful symbols and ritual is sometimes called the psyche. The psyche is the part of our awareness, our being, that resonates with symbols, myths, and stores. It, in turn, is connected to a larger consciousness that Jung called the "collective unconsciousness." In effective ritual, both the right and left hemispheres of the brain are involved through the simultaneous use of visual symbols, spoken words, movement, and/or rhythm. The whole person is addressed and engaged. There is the potential for the rhythms of the two brain hemispheres to synchronize on the alpha level of consciousness, creating feelings of euphoria, expanded mental powers, and intense creativity. This "hemispheric synchronization" may be the neurological basis for a higher state of consciousness (Redmond 1997:173).

In order to become transformed by ritual you must be willing to be fully present in your consciousness. Participating in ritual is unlike a movie where you pay for your ticket and simply observe the action without becoming involved. Thus, rituals in which participants ingest quantities of "recreational" drugs or alcohol are usually ineffective in terms of transformation, with only a few rare exceptions such as the peyote rituals of the native peoples of Mexico and Central America where there is a cultural context for the use of psychoactive plants. Beginning very early in mainstream American culture, we are trained to more or less disassociate or check out, rather than "tune in." A good example is the problem of chronic television watching. But if you are not present in ritual, both in mind and heart, it rarely works.

CREATING WOMEN'S RITUAL

The Women's Spirituality movement is just over a quarter of a century old. Although there are greater numbers of women practicing Goddess-centered ritual now, there has been little guidance in the actual creation of personal or group ritual other than books of the "cookbook" variety used primarily for seasonal celebrations of the Solstices, Equinoxes and cross-quarter holy days. Ritual cookbooks that tell you what to do, say, and wear can be beneficial when read for inspiration, not as Gospel. Within the feminist-oriented Goddess spirituality, neopagan movements, and many more traditional Wiccan groups, there is limited liturgy and few truly authentic ancient ceremonies to draw upon. Contemporary Goddess rituals are, for the most part, inspired and drawn from fragments of folk custom, oral tradition, conjecture, personal creativity, and other religious influences. Although there are most often an understood purpose, a basic outline, and agreed-upon enactments, feminist Goddess rituals tend to be improvised from spirited inspiration.

I have been teaching ritual skills and have facilitated small and large rituals for the Los Angeles women's community for almost twenty years. As religious director of Circle of Aradia, the largest and oldest feminist Goddess community in the United States, I have been privileged to participate in, teach, and work with thousands of women interested in developing their skills as ritualists. From small-group rituals of six women to 175 at community seasonal gatherings, my students and co-facilitators have been learning about the care and feeding of any given ritual: how to clarify the purpose, develop the theme, understand the sometimes subtle nuances of working with group energy, and appropriate ritual structure. Larger seasonal gatherings have often been described by participants as life-enhancing or transforming. This is primarily due to the consciousness of the ritual facilitators in careful, purposeful development of the ritual, their own preparation to facilitate, and the mindfulness they have learned to hold while being in service to others. Another reason for the power of my community's rituals is that many women attending come with the expectation to be emotionally or psychically moved.

In my many travels to teach away from my own spiritual community, I've too often attended rituals which are disappointing for me, falling short in the ability to truly transform the group or individual. I have observed that women generally didn't understand how to approach the creation of a ritual or how to purposefully guide the energy flow. Without this understanding, the intention of the ritual cannot be fully realized no matter how urgent the need or how inspired to do it. I have also observed that women are often hesitant to take on leadership or facilitator roles within a ritual. Patriarchal cultural role models for spiritual leadership, and leadership in general, have been part of promoting hierarchy based on domination and control. Although many women are exploring more egalitarian models of leadership for spiritual service, others resist the idea of taking on any aspect of leadership. For many women, previous religious ritual experience was limited to observing rituals done by others, and most often done only by men. Only fairly recently, in a few Christian and Jewish denominations, have women been empowered to fully participate in their faith. Thus the process of ritual-making and facilitation has been for many entirely an experimental and organic process with varying results ranging from poor to ecstatic.

I began to more closely examine what makes women's ritual so healing and transformational in my community, and I became passionate to develop and share my step by step process of ritual-making that could empower women living in other parts of the country. I learned to articulate the components that make women's ritual so powerful and effective in personal transformation, and how to pass on ways for women to meet their own ritual needs from a woman-identified perspective. Enthusiastic inspiration is necessary for good ritual, but without skills to support the inspiration, it is like an aspiring artist who loves art and is drawn to the creation of art, but hasn't the actual physical skills and mental ability to manifest what she envisions from her heart and soul. Over the past decades, my priestess work has primarily focused on teaching women how to *think* like a ritualist and develop the skills to create meaningful experiences for themselves and others.

Developing the Purpose

The first step in the creation process is to reflect upon and list occasions for ritual that the student would find personally meaningful to experience. Included in this list may be events from the past which, in retrospect, she now understands would have benefited from having a ritual. Occasions for ritual range from life cycle events, emotional or physical transitions, and changes in one's mental outlook, to seasonal or lunar rituals.

The next part of this process is to develop the purpose or intention of a specific ritual, and whether it is to be done solo or with a group. The student must clearly be able to answer and write down what will sound quite obvious, but is easier said then done: What is the reason for the ritual? What is its purpose? Having a clear purpose is the foundation for the process of creating a ritual. The second round of questions includes: How does she want to feel in the ritual? What does she want the ritual to accomplish for her? Where in her body does she feel the experience is located? What are her feelings surrounding this passage, and which feeling(s) does she wish to honor in the ritual? How much participation does she wish from others? After writing about the experience, a clear, concise purpose must be articulated that she resonates with as complete.

For example, Bonnie wants to celebrate her 50th birthday. She sees it as a time of new beginnings in her life as she starts a new career. She is feeling appreciation for the skills that she has developed that have not been seen by others. The ritual purpose would be to celebrate Bonnie's 50th birthday, and to honor the new beginnings in her life. She wants to share with her invited guests the aspects of herself and her talents that she has developed over the years. A second example would be Carrie, who has just weaned the last of her three children and does not plan on having any more. She doesn't know what it will feel like to return her body back to herself, as it has been in service to others so intensely. In this case, the ritual purpose would be for Carrie to honor the power of her body that has created and sustained the lives of her children, and celebrate the return of her body to herself. She also wants to hear from other mothers invited to the ritual about their similar experiences.

Developing the Theme

Step two in the process is the development of the ritual's theme. I provide guidelines and meditations to access usable associations from both the body and mind of the student. She intuitively selects visual images, kinesthetic sensory information, and auditory messages that are meaningful to her. I also teach about the purpose of altar making and how visual symbols are used to enhance the experience. We then explore various categories of ritual and ideas for types of symbolic physical enactments to stimulate the student's own creativity in finding what will fit her own connections. Categories of ritual include:

Creation Rituals are about bringing something into manifestation. Examples are fertility rites, starting a new project, or beginning a relationship. Ritual activities might include making something or enacting a symbolic birthing scene, weaving yarn into a new pattern, or dancing a new attitude into yourself.

Release/Transformation Rituals are about letting go of old ways of being in behavior or consciousness, such as healing from sexual abuse,

194 / Ruth Rhiannon Barrett

illness, shedding limiting habits or attitudes. Sometimes these rituals involve a conscious act of forgiveness of oneself and others. Ritual enactments might include dissolving earth or salt in water, burning an image representing what is being let go of, throwing a rock that symbolically contains the negativity into a deep body of water and not looking back.

Honoring Rituals acknowledge an accomplishment or having arrived at a new station in one's life. Examples are a girl's first menses, Croning ritual, graduation, or a birthday. Enactments might include receiving formal blessings from loved ones, passing over a symbolic threshold, or being presented with a symbolic gift of this new station in life.

Celebration Rituals emphasize the transition to a new cycle of life, focusing on bringing what is occurring outside in the natural world into self-awareness. Celebration rituals may also commemorate historical events that continue to have meaning in the present and may be linked to time-honored traditions such as seasonal and lunar holy days. Enactments might include invoking the ancestors, dressing in clothing to reflect the colors or mood of the season, or eating special seasonal or symbolic foods.

Energetics

Determining a clear purpose is like deciding on the destination for your ritual journey. Developing the ritual theme is like deciding what vehicle will get yourself there, what to bring with you. The third step of the creation process is knowing what kind of "fuel" or energy will move you and others through to the destination. Depending on the type of vehicle, you need specific fuel, or the vehicle will either not move at all or simply chug along, clearly in distress. The *energetics* of a ritual is where you consciously look at the quality of energy you will need to move yourself and others through the ritual.

Energetics is the conscious working of energy that directly expresses the ritual theme, personally and/or with a group. You must learn and understand what it means to be in an energetic alignment with the ritual theme, how to embody and express it. It is this area of ritual which, in my experience, is the most neglected and ironically the most important aspect of any ritual if it is to be trans-forming to the participants. In my classes I present such categories of elemental energy as Air, Fire, Water, and Earth, which express specific qualities of energy, and teach how our connection to these forces and purposeful alignment with these energies enhance ritual workings. My students learn how to physically and psychically generate specific energy in preparation for a ritual. They learn how to align a group of women together so that the group can better work together for the success of the ritual.

A simple example to begin creating an energetic is by making time in advance of a ritual to think or meditate about the occasion personally. Once connected to the ritual's theme, one then expands one's understanding more broadly to include the more universal symbolism that the ritual occasion represents. This helps to inter-nalize the purpose which generates a mental, emotional, and physi-cal mood or energetic that can be felt by others. One, in effect, embodies the *feel* of the ritual. Other ways to create an energetic might be to take a pre-ritual bath with the intention to immerse oneself into the ritual theme, or take a walk or a hike, using move-ment to awaken, energize, and sensitize the mind and body together to the ritual focus.

Ritual Structure

The forth step in the process is the creation of an appropriate ritual structure to contain the energy of the ritual. All rituals must have a beginning, middle, and end, but depending on the type of ritual, the structure will vary with each ritual. Instead of teaching a fixed ritual structure at the beginning, I teach the *concept* of it last. This allows for optimum creativity in designing the ritual, rather than fitting the contents into a pre-conceived form. I clarify the purpose of "casting" a ritual circle, which is an enacted meditation often used in women's rituals to enclose the dimensions of the ritual space, contain the energy that is raised, focus and protect the participants if needed. This circle is perceived as an energetic boundary for the ritual and visualized in the shape of a large sphere that encloses the individual or group. Students also learn practices of purification, consecration, and self-blessing, the purpose of which is to alter everyday consciousness and access the magical mind in preparation for ritual work.

Evaluation

Developing oneself as a ritualist necessitates the ability to evaluate one's experience. Since women's rituals are so original and subjective in how they are experienced, on what basis can one critique a ritual? In order to develop as a ritualist with or without a ritual group, one must be able to evaluate one's experience to gain useful information for future ritual application. A loving, critical, and open look at one's experience enriches the ritualist in ways that are invaluable. I provide helpful questions that help students evaluate their experience of ritual. A few of these questions are: Did the ritual accomplish what it set out to do? Did the ritual flow well from beginning to end as it was structured to do? Was there enough time to do it, or was it too long/short? What parts of the ritual felt more/less focused, and what may have been the contributing factors?

RITUAL FOR A RAPE SURVIVOR

In closing, I share a brief description of a ritual that was created by a group of 18 women in a ritual-making workshop I taught several years ago. The women created and participated in eight rituals over a five-day period covering a variety of themes. The level of experience within the group varied from complete newcomers to feminist Goddess rituals to women who had several years of experience. The following is a ritual created for a rape survivor. I chose this example because of the emotional intensity of its content and the profound power of the experience for everyone who created and participated in it. This is a good example of the kind of ritual that women can create out of a need to heal and return to fuller participation in life. Because of my experience with this kind of intense ritual, I facilitated the more difficult parts, allowing Susan, the survivor, and the group to feel more relaxed. This experience illustrated the potential of ritual to empower women in their lives.

Preparation

Background: Susan is a rape survivor. She wants to heal from the emotional and psychic effects of rape. She feels that she has worked through the worst of it, and feels the need to help others now who have survived.

Ritual Purpose: Susan's words, "I want to honor my feelings of anger and sadness from rape and share my relief in moving through it." *Theme:* In order to make her internal connections with the ritual, Susan meditates on the ritual purpose while considering the five sensual correspondences of sight, sound, smell, taste, and touch. Susan shares with her ritual group that she sees colors of purple, black, and green. She is at the ocean at sunset. The sounds of dolphins can be heard. There is chanting, drumming, and a fire. She smells lemon grass; she wants to drink something sweet during the ritual. There is a circle of women holding hands.

The rest of the ritual is created by the group with Susan's full participation and final approval. The group discusses personal preparation for this ritual where group members will be Susan's support, witnesses, and energetic container. We also discuss what we will do as our own emotions are brought to the surface, especially other rape survivors. Two women volunteer to be available for others in crisis. We discuss and agree that it is important for the group to be especially present in their feelings for the duration of the ritual, and that showing feelings doesn't mean automatically that one is in crisis or in need of intervention. We also agreed that if it looked like someone was in actual crisis, that she would be asked up to three times if she needed anything.

Prior to gathering, we take a couple of hours for our own preparation so that we can really be present emotionally for Susan. We agree to observe a 45-minute silent period prior to the beginning of the ritual.

The Ritual

Location: By the shore of a lake. There is complete privacy. A short distance from the lakeshore is a fire circle. It is evening, and the sun is going down.

The Altar: We gather early to help build the altar. Susan is meditating elsewhere and preparing for the ritual with a support person with her. She has given some altar items to others so they can be on the altar when she arrives. Susan's chalice, healing crystals, fresh lavender, a dolphin image, a candle which was brought back from

Kildare, Ireland, and containing in its wick the flame of Brigid, a goddess of healing; a bowl of water, and other objects of healing were brought by others.

The ritual space is purified with incense and water. Most of the group lines up at the entrance of the ritual space with Susan at the end of the line. There are some women drumming a steady and meditative rhythm, as one by one all approach the threshold of the ritual space and are asked, "How do you enter the circle?" They each answer the question with, "I enter in perfect love and perfect trust." By saying this, each woman is making a personal commitment to creating a space of love and safety for Susan and with each other.

The group makes a circle and begins to chant the sound, "MA" (the universal sound for Mother), creating with our voices a sound vibration which will raise personal and group energy for the casting of the circle. It has been agreed in advance that the ritual circle will be extended to include the beach and the lakeside. Invocations are spoken to the elemental powers, asking for healing and blessings for this work. An invocation is similar to speaking a prayer and meant to issue an invitation to the elemental powers to become more consciously present in the ritual space. The Goddess of Healing is also invoked, and the purpose for the ritual is stated within the circle.

We escort Susan down to the beach to the water's edge. I give her a few rocks to begin throwing into the water, asking her to breathe gently, and to keep breathing as she lets out a sound with each throw of a rock. Susan appears a little reluctant or emotionally "stuck," so I ask her to get into a physical posture designed to bring emotions to the surface by making the body physically uncomfortable. As she bends over with me, I instruct her to stand on one bent leg, lifting the other leg high behind her. The only support is the one bent leg, using just one finger on each hand to lightly touch on the sand below her. With our heads also bowed low, we begin to make sounds as the posture becomes more tiring and difficult to hold. After a while I suggest that she switch legs, which she does. Women by the water near us are making sounds with us, encouraging Susan's anger to emerge.

Susan turns again to the river and begins to throw rocks, this time with vocal sounds authentically from her pain. Rock after rock is passed to her, and she seems entranced with her process of throwing and vocalizing her anger and grief. When she finishes, she spontaneously undresses and jumps into the cold lake water with a vocal elation of joy. After swimming for a couple of minutes, she returns to the shore where she is dried off by the waiting women.

Susan is escorted back to the ritual area where her body is blessed with sacred water. This is to re-consecrate Susan's body as her temple. The group begins to chant words praising the Goddess who brings healing and change. Spontaneously, women enclose Susan in a group hug, a final envelopment of love and support. The circle is "opened," releasing the energy that has set the energetic container, with grateful thanks to the elemental forces and the Goddess who was invoked.

In the days that followed the ritual, women processed their experiences. Susan shared that she could feel that the ritual helped her to move into a new perspective with her life that she had not previously been able to access. She felt relieved of the burden she was carrying and felt that she could now go on with her life. Others felt that, by supporting Susan, they had healed a part of themselves that had been victimized. Many of the women stated that, although some of the ritual experience was emotionally intense and painful, preparing well prior to the ritual, both psychologically and energetically, enabled them to be present and able to spiritually serve Susan. I felt that the group did a beautiful job of creating and facilitating this ritual experience. It was one of the more emotionally moving experiences I have had because the group worked and focused together so beautifully and selflessly in service to Susan. The group recognized the importance of the ritual the members had created and how powerful their organized intention was. They were able to experience their ability to make a difference in the life of another and how their own lives were touched in turn.

It is rituals like this and others that are drawing women to women's spirituality and to ritual-making. Women's ritual is about women's lives, experiences, joys, and sorrows, whether done alone or within a group. To learn how to create ritual is to learn how to heal ourselves and others, joyfully participating in life's blessings, and feeling spiritually connected to themselves, others, and the Source of life. When done with care and consciousness, ritual is a powerful tool for personal and social transformation.

Notes

[1] Adapted from a Croning ritual created by Kay Gardner and Ruth Barrett, December 1996.

Works Cited

Christ, Carol. 1987. *Laughter of Aphrodite*. San Francisco: Harper & Row.
Geertz, Clifford. 1983. *The Interpretation of Symbols*. New York: Basic Books.
Matthews, Caitlin and John. 1986. *The Western Way*. New York: Routledge & Kegan Paul.
Redmond, Layne. 1997. *When the Drummers Were Women*. New York: Three Rivers Press.

ꙴ **12** ꙴ

Woman Mysteries of the Ancient Future Sisterhood

by Vajra Ma

I believe global transformation hangs upon the empowerment of women. "Woman is the creator of the Universe. The Universe is her form." So says a sacred Hindu text, the Shaktisangama Tantra (in Mookerjee 1988:6). Woman, with her capacity to conceive, gestate, birth, and sustain life from her physical form, embodies the generative power of the Universe in a direct and complete way. These female creative powers called "women's mysteries" were integral to much of humanity's earliest religious experiences, which included body-based, sexually ecstatic communion with each other and the cosmos. Today we are walking a razor's edge, ensconced in a cultural trance of arrogance based on spiritual ignorance; we flirt with self-destruction and the devastation of Earth. The illusory schism between spirit and matter fosters sexual repression and violence. I believe the most potent antidote to patriarchal alienation and violence is to re-turn (religion means to re-link) to women's mysteries, to once again recognize woman's body as holy and deeply intelligent, to recognize and embrace sexuality as an essentially spiritual power, and to revivify women's mysteries. This is the aim of my work with women that I call *Woman Mysteries of the Ancient Future Sisterhood*.

THE MYSTERY SCHOOL

The *Woman Mysteries* work was "impulsed" from my desire to bring together four strands of study in my life: (1) Tantric Dance, a moving meditation using sexual energy, (2) Continuum[1], subtle, " internal" free-form movement, (3) the study of ancient goddesses, and (4) feminist spirituality. I wanted to "cross-pollinate" some of the unique qualities, skills and "treasures" of each, to develop and share with others the synergistic feedback loop between body and information that was happening spontaneously in my own experience. For instance, when studying about a particular goddess or her animal power (such as lion or serpent), I found during my movement explorations that I would have a spontaneous sensate experience of that goddess or her animal power. This was a *direct knowing* unmediated by word or concept—what I call "BodyKnowing." I wanted to share such epiphanies with other women to whom the Goddess was numinous, knowing that by sharing, the experiences would be amplified for all of us.

From this original impulse, *Woman Mysteries of the Ancient Future Sisterhood* has developed over the years into a Mystery School and a Priestess Tradition. A Mystery School is a course of study that enables one to progress in her capacity to live in conscious participation with the forces of nature and the cosmos. We do this through sacred dance, movement and sounding classes, and rituals that are both informational and experiential.

I teach body-based skills that enable women to empower themselves. These skills increase women's capacity to "hold power," which I define as the mental and physical capacity to sustain condensed concentrations of energy in the body. Women also learn from each other, not only through observation, verbal sharing, and processing, but by subtle energetic transmission, body to body. We co-generate a resonant energetic field, and thus create the potent synergy of the female shamanic group which is central to women's mysteries. Women ordained as priestesses in the *Woman Mysteries* tradition are trained to intensify this force field. We seek to utilize this power with integrity, skill, and compassion in service to the resurgence of the Great Goddess and for the benefit of all. Some feminist scholars argue, and I concur, that women's mysteries, particularly menses, have been a pivotal catalyzing factor in the evolution of human consciousness and civilization.[2] At *Woman Mysteries* we envision our personal growth in the context of the evolution of human consciousness and global transformation.

I have been teaching classes and facilitating ritual on the Goddess path since 1989. I have taught at women's conferences and programs across the country, but most of my teaching takes place in the greater Los Angeles area. I estimate about 700 women, about 250 on an ongoing basis, have participated in my Los Angeles-based classes, workshops, and rituals, ranging from corporate women (a small percentage) to healers, bodyworkers, and artists, (a larger percentage than in the population at large). Ages range from 16 to 60, with most in their 30s and 40s. About 25 percent in both the classes and the Priestesshood are women of color. We find the ritual and dance work unifies us as women, both beyond and encompassing of our occupation, social-economic status, race, nationality, and sexual preference.

Many women starting my classes know nothing about the Goddess; they come saying, "I need to connect more to my body." They learn about the Goddess through their bodies. Many stay with the work for several consecutive months, some come and go over a period of a few years, and a handful stay consistently with the work for several years.

I myself came to the Goddess path in 1986 at age 36 by studying the Tantric Dance with its originator Gena Reno. I have been teaching my own form of Tantric Dance since 1992. I teach the Dance in five-week series of weekly three-hour classes. The work is in-depth and requires individual attention, so class size is small, ranging from six to twenty women. Having an ongoing group provides follow-up, integration time and a sense of safety and trust which is necessary in such intensely transformative work. However, I also teach weekend and one-day Tantric Dance intensives and it is always amazing to me how profound a one-class experience can be for a woman. I teach other series and one-day workshops on Goddess studies and feminist spirituality, always grounding it in movement and sounding work. Currently I am developing movement classes that can be taught in larger groups, thus creating an entry point for more women.

For women who desire more comprehensive training, particularly women who feel called to become priestesses in the *Ancient Future Sisterhood*, I provide a year-long program which consists of two three-hour sessions per week, four (quarterly) private sessions, and a reading list of required books. Upon successful completion, a woman receives ceremonial initiation into the *Ancient Future Sisterhood*. Ordination as a priestess requires further studies, usually an additional one or two years.

As my work developed over the years, a series of synchronicities seemed to call for a Priestesshood, a female shamanic group of women thoroughly schooled in the unique *Woman Mysteries* synthesis. Two women, Tecia Layson and Xia, and myself, in a witnessed ceremony of thirteen women, established this Priestesshood in October of 1994. At the time of this writing we have six ordained Priestesses and ten more studying for ordination. Priestesshood is about service to the Goddess and community.

WOMEN'S MYSTERIES AND THE FEMALE SHAMANIC GROUP

Before describing the various elements that comprise this synthesis and sharing examples of how this work affects women's lives, I would like to delineate what I mean by women's mysteries. These mysteries are based in the female blood cycle of birth, menses, lactation ("converting" blood into milk), menopause, and death (cessation of blood circulation). It is my experience that women's mysteries arise not only out of the blood cycle, but also out of the particular capacity women have to function collectively. A female shamanic group has the potential to generate a power vortex that enables a woman to access deeper levels of what I call feminine knowledge (holistic ways of functioning and perceiving) than she might alone. In the collective force field of the circle, a woman strengthens her courage to break patriarchal taboos against female power.

Patriarchal monotheism having created a broken spiritual lineage for women, we are essentially without elders. The elders we turn to at *Woman Mysteries* are those who gather around our circles from the spirit plane. Their presence is palpable to me and to many of the women who participate in our ritual circles. They are the Grandmothers, Shamanesses, tribal women, and Dakinis[3]—spirit women in the other dimensions who are worthy to be trusted as guides in our spiritual development, worthy to be called Ancestors. They need us to create the future; we need them to awaken our ancient knowledge and power. Together we make the eternal round, an "ouroborous of knowledge," the snake swallowing its own tail, linking a past so distant it is the future, a future so evolved it is unified with the most ancient past—Source. Together we create the *Ancient Future Sisterhood.*

BODYKNOWING

For women's empowerment to be full it must activate and integrate all aspects of self: physical, emotional, mental, and spiritual. The matrix of Goddess studies, feminist spirituality and BodyKnowing accomplish this. BodyKnowing is the conscious awareness and participation with subtle body energetics, an attunement to the body's language that gives a direct experience of Spirit. The body speaks through subtle sensation, breath, sound, trance, movement, and e-motion. At *Woman Mysteries* we directly "source" ancient knowledge which cannot be found in books. We awaken it neurologically, genetically, cellularly, atomically—in the body. The work takes on elements and powers of shamanism and Tantra, for these spiritual practices are originally body-based.

Spiritual embodiment, working spiritually through the body, is the most rapid route to spiritual knowledge. The body is *direct*; it bypasses mental and psychological defenses and obfuscations. Quite simply, it does not lie. What's more, the body is a microcosmic enfoldment of the macrocosm—the Universe—and as such contains the knowledge of the whole cosmos. As the ancient Hindu sacred text the *Chandogya Upanishad* puts it, "As large and potent as the universe outside, even so large and potent is the universe within our being. . . . Everything in the macrocosm is in this our micro-cosm" (in Douglas 1997:2). Quantum physicists, explaining the holographic universe concept, remind us that each fragment of the hologram contains the image of the whole (Talbot 1991). The God-dess as channeled through a modern writer says simply, ". . . if that which you seek, you find not within yourself, you will never find it without."[4] When cosmic knowledge is released from the neural matrix, cells, atoms, and dark matter of our body, it imprints and integrates into our conscious mind in an indelible way. This is *direct* knowledge, transmitted from Source, without the intermediary of words or techniques. Working spiritually through the body indeed puts you on the spiritual fast track.

The BodyKnowing work at *Woman Mysteries* affects women on three levels: (1) stimulating personal healing and emotional clearing (to a large degree our body is our personal subconscious), (2) awakening ancestral-cellular-genetic memory, and (3) increasing our body's vibratory frequency which links us to divine, cosmic levels. Of course, these levels interweave and interplay—the work is indeed inter/intradimensional.

GODDESS STUDIES AND FEMINIST SPIRITUALITY

The conceptual context of Goddess studies and feminist consciousness sparks women's awakening from the cultural trance and internalized patriarchal conditioning that has kept us afraid, ignorant, repressed, and asleep. Feminist spirituality combines feminist consciousness with the ritual and magical skills that enable women to effectively change their lives. Magic and ritual are powerful agents of personal growth, for they engage the limbic portion of the brain, that part of the brain which relays signals from the "lower" brain of instincts, biological drives, and involuntary body processes to the "higher" brain of reasoning and cognitive powers. The limbic brain is ". . . a kind of crossroads where visceral feelings, cognition, and memory meet . . . [and thus] *helps shape the basic motivations and emotions of our lives"* (Guinness, 1990:84; italics mine).

Integrating BodyKnowing skills into this ritual equation magnifies the potential for personal transformation and the ability "to change consciousness at will" (Dion Fortune's definition of *magic*). When a woman dares to break patriarchal taboos against being powerful and autonomous, she empowers herself to make self-loving choices in work, relationships, creative expression, and sexuality.

Feminist spirituality is Earth-based, celebrating the cyclic nature of life, particularly in the Earth seasons and the moon and menstrual cycles. Death is not demonized, but rather honored as a natural part of the cycle. Feminist spirituality is grounded in the recognition that all things, even so-called inanimate objects, are alive and inherently sacred. Thus, the elements of earth, air, fire, and water are sacred, living forces whose inherent powers can be communed with and utilized in ritual and magic. This spirituality recognizes women's unique needs, contributions, and capacities as we emerge from oppression into economic-social-political and emotional-mental-sexual empowerment.

Goddess studies—archeological, anthropological, and mythological evidence of civilization's pre-patriarchal roots—provide the conceptual framework in which we dismantle patriarchal distortions concerning the nature of civilization and humanity. It is potent spiritual medicine for a woman to discover that humanity revered female images of spiritual power for 30,000 years, or to learn of civilizations where "Goddess-centered art with its striking absence of images of warfare and male domination, reflects a social order in which women as heads of clans or queen-priestesses played a central part" (Gimbutas 1989:xix–xx).

GODDESS CIRCLES AND SACRED DANCE CIRCLES

One way in which I integrate Goddess studies, feminist spirituality and BodyKnowing is through what I call a "Goddess Circle" where we explore the energetic of a particular goddess. First, I take the women on a guided journey. This conveys factual information about the selected goddess—her mythology, powers, iconography, and animal associations—in a way that *engages the emotions*. When the emotions are activated, knowledge "sticks." It is one thing to hear that the swan and honey are associated with Aphrodite. It is quite another to "feel" yourself riding on the back of a swan that flies over difficult scenes from your life, dropping honey to sweeten those situations, helping you to visualize and feel your power to change them. In the guided journey I also include time for a personal internal encounter with the Goddess in which a woman may pour out need, supplications, and questions from the heart and receive comfort and guidance in return. Where appropriate, I highlight the distinction between early versions and the later patriarchal distortions of her mythology.

Next we explore the particular goddess' energetic through a Sacred Dance Circle, a spontaneous, yet highly focused body-sourced ritual. A woman begins in stillness in the center of the circle. This stillness is crucial, for it helps her drop below fear and mental interference, into the receptivity and authenticity of BodyKnowing. We do not give her music or a beat to dance to, but rather we attune to the instinctual intelligence of her body and breath, amplifying *her* process with our voices, drums, and rattles. Working spontaneously and intuitively frees the vast intelligence of the Deeper Collective Mind. The work becomes potent, transformative, shamanic. As women surrender to their BodyKnowing, they behave, move, and sound in ways they never imagined they could.

Such circles attract the presence of the spirit women of the *Ancient Future Sisterhood*. Many times I have "heard" tribes of women chanting around us. When we let these spirit women vocalize through us, the sound electrifies the dancer into an intensified freedom of movement; everyone present is catapulted into a new level of power. One such Goddess Circle can dramatically catalyze a woman's personal healing and growth. Over months of such work a woman builds a profound respect and trust in her innate shamanic powers.

SUBTLE MOVEMENT ENERGETICS

We can read all we want about the goddesses while never coming to know them. Yet, in one intense moment of spiritual embodiment, we can experience volumes come alive in the body. This is true of both broad-stroked movement and of subtler, internal movement. However, subtle work opens dimensional realms that broader movement cannot. Exploring consciousness through subtle sensation opens a whole new world, awesomely rich, varied and far more vast than the meager spectrum of our day-to-day sensate awareness. We have little facility in our language to express it.

I begin my Tantric Dance classes with what I call the Breath-Stretch Meditation. This guided meditation serves as a warm-up and stretch-out but, unlike a mechanical warm-up, it engages our consciousness. We begin in stillness, standing, sitting, or lying down. We focus on the breath which is the fundamental wave pattern of the body, swelling and ebbing in continuous cycle, as do the waves of the ocean. We hold awareness of the breath throughout, letting breath affect movement, movement affect breath. We set intention by "dropping the question into the body," and ask the body, "What do you want to do to shed tensions, to be fluid and free again?" or words to that effect. The body answers in sensation and movement impulse. The more acutely we focus our attention, the more creative the body will be in finding subtle moves and positions to release deep, habitual tensions—moves and positions we could never discover through a technical warm-up.

Impeccable attention to sensation opens us to altered states of being. After achieving a certain level of relaxation and inner focus, we bring attention to a specific part or dynamic of the body. I have focused on such things as: the push-pull force of muscles with gravity; the two orbs of consciousness, skull/brain and pelvis/womb and their energetic spinal link; lion-cat movements; exploring the spine as a "living serpent." The possibilities are endless. Deceptively simple, but surprisingly challenging, is just to be in continual awareness of pleasure as we move. Pleasure is a great teacher. Sometimes I prepare a focus ahead of time, but most often I listen/channel in the moment, discovering new dynamics myself as I guide the women.

THE TANTRIC DANCE OF FEMININE POWER

There are two primary ways in which I work with women in movement: (1) free-form, including both broad and subtle movement, and (2) the Tantric Dance of Feminine Power. Both types of trance dancing are, or can be, shamanic—that is, they bridge the ordinary world with the non-ordinary world, generate healing, and develop relationship with spirit beings, earth elements, and animal powers. However, the Tantric Dance is the core of the *Woman Mysteries* work, for it is by far the most powerful BodyKnowing modality I have discovered.

Tantra is the ancient art of realizing divine essence through bodily experience, particularly the creative force of sexuality. The Sanskrit word "Tantra" comes from the root "tan," which means "to extend, stretch, weave." Tantra is the art of weaving worlds: spirit and matter, macrocosm and microcosm, past and present, non-ordinary powers into our ordinary world. We extend our conscious mind to include cosmic awareness.

The sacred, sensual moving meditation that I teach does this; therefore I call it Tantric Dance. In fact, it does it par excellence. Upon experiencing the Dance, one student, a therapist in her professional life, recognized it as " . . . the woman's way of meditation. On a par with Tai Chi and Yoga." The refinement of sensate awareness and movement articulation, the circulation, refinement, and integration of sexual energy throughout the body and psyche, and the intense mental concentration and the condensation of physical energy that the Dance requires catalyze transformation that is both rapid and profound. It touches and awakens a woman at both the personal and transpersonal levels.

It is a dance of knowledge. We "track" the intelligent flow of cosmic energies within, enjoying a direct sensate experience of goddess archetypes, animal powers, and forces of nature. It is difficult for the Western mind to grasp how innately intelligent the human body is. Medical doctor Deepak Chopra "languages" the wisdom of the 6,000-year-old medical-philosophical system of Ayurveda in Western scientific terms when he says, "Our thoughts, feelings, emotions, desires, concepts, ideas, notions literally translate into a shower of chemicals in our brain called the neuropeptides. And these chemicals are not confined to the brain. Chopra reminds us they are in every cell of our body" (in Toms 1990:7). These showers of chemicals create subtle sensations in the body. Thus we may begin to understand how the Tantric Dance, in which we commune intimately with subtle sensation, can be an (al)chemical dance which affects us not only physically, but emotionally, mentally, and spiritually and thus has the potential to transform our lives.

The Tantric Dance is a direct "bust" of patriarchal taboos. We embrace pleasure rather than pain as our teacher. We awaken the female power center—the Yoni (womb and vulva). We dance our deep sexual feelings and circulate this creative energy throughout the chakras, refining and integrating it as it passes through these energetic power centers of the body. We dare to be powerful, sensual, sexual, and autonomous. We restore our natural wildness. We enjoy the deeply relational communication that is uniquely satisfied through Sisterhood. We extend our awareness to encompass and integrate the innate divinity of our female bodies.

Kundalini, the Hindu Serpent Goddess, is fundamental to the Dance (and to Tantra). She sleeps coiled at the base of the spine or root chakra. When this Life Force awakens, she rises through the chakras, profoundly transforming consciousness. Chakras receive, integrate, and transmit life-force energies. They are doorways to other dimensions. Kundalini opens these doorways by increasing the vibratory rate of the chakras' spinning pattern. Like attracts like. The higher the frequency in a chakra, the higher, more refined dimension with which we will align. We can receive and transmit energies to and from these other dimensions.[5] Kundalini-Serpent moves in the wave pattern that is a fundamental pattern of the Universe. Light and sound travel in wave patterns. The ocean, womb of biological life, undulates with waves and tides. As we undulate our spine, our heartbeat, brain waves, and breath harmonize and stimulate various areas in the brain (Judith 1992). When Kundalini has traveled through all the chakras, the individual has achieved "enlightenment." Truly, Serpent is the great teacher.

One of my students described her profound Kundalini dance experience that awakened her ancestral-cellular-genetic memory:

> You can feel the trembling in the walls of your vagina and uterus . . . the snake coiled within awakens sleepily. Drinking in the universe through the root, the snake rises slowly, from the root to the womb and up. The serpent makes love to each chakra, spinning the energy through you. At the throat, energy builds up, and an energy cobra hood extends . . . a wall of energy to undulate and move against. Then a woman becomes the snake, undulating with the energy of the core of all things. One opens to her vast universe connections through time and space when her own identity melts away. Inside her comes the energy of all her bloodlines. She communes with and connects with her other selves, melding in a point with no time or all times. It is now that she can truly incorporate the vast knowledge of her ancestors, descendants, and other lives. She holds the knowledge.

The Tantric Dance is a spontaneous moving meditation, yet it is a dance form, governed by a few simple but powerful guidelines that create its power and uniqueness. Two of these guidelines are refinement of movement and "holding the energy." Refinement of movement is the result of exquisite attention, receptivity, and sensitivity to subtle sensation and emotions. "Holding the energy" means that as the energy intensifies through our inner attention, we do not let the energy leak or explode out through movements that break the essential underlying wave pattern. We condense high-voltage energy into subtle, refined movement. Holding the energy as it intensifies increases the frequency. The potential for higher

frequencies is increased by the phenomenon of "witnessing." As a woman dances in class, the other women witness—that is, observe with receptive full-body attention. This collective force field creates a kind of magnetic polarity that oscillates between dancer and witness, "sparking" expanded awareness in both.

Ultimately the Dance cannot be comprehended through words, but only through BodyKnowing. However, a conceptual frame of reference can be helpful. According to Ayurveda, the entire Universe, from galaxies to the sub-atomic level and including the "Void" from which it all arises, consists of two components—energy and information. Everything, even a thought, has the energy and information (in-form-ation) to be what it is. (Chopra in Toms 1990) We are all familiar with electricity traveling through a power line into a computer where it is translated into sound, word, and picture. These sounds, words, and pictures are encoded in the programs and files held in the computer. So it is with the Dance. Our body (the computer) translates the electromagnetic wave currents (the "power lines" of divine consciousness) into sensations and into "pictures of feminine knowledge." The challenge of the Dance is to hold higher and higher frequencies, and thus more power (energy) and knowledge (information).

In class, women talk and write about their Dance experience. "Bringing it down" into words helps us understand and integrate what is energetically encoded in the dance. One woman writes, "Electrical currents buzz along the pathways of my inner meridians—the same pathways used in Chinese acupuncture." The information encoded in those electrical currents made her ". . . feel intimately loved. . . . I am being danced by the ancient, sacred spirits of time. They energetically caress me, love me and nurture the beauty of my soul." Experiencing divine love can increase a woman's self-esteem, which in turn empowers her to make more empowering choices and actions in her life.

One dancer shares her perceptions of dimensional doorways and her process of "changing consciousness at will" through interaction with the energy and information found beyond those doorways.

> The Dance opens doorways to the physical, spiritual and emotional transformation process on a molecular level. . . .
> I am drenched in pleasure and excruciatingly aware of my body's relationship and interactions with space. The space

around me vibrates with energy, information and dimensions layered on top of each other, vibrating at different levels. It is extremely sensual and empowering to find the core of energy within myself that creates who I am. . . . I feel my cells changing in the Dance, metamorphosing me into my future, connecting me to the truth of my Past and bringing me more conscious in my Present. . . . the Dance is the doorway to true magic. . . . it is the conscious skill to slip in between the worlds, explore the energy lines, find the one you need and work with that.

We source the Dance from our female power center—the Yoni. The Yoni, which gives physical birth, is the ultimate weaver of spirit and matter. The womb is so deeply affected by the Dance that some post-menopausal women have reported bleeding again after experiencing the Dance! In the Dance the feelings of the heart are anchored and amplified by the power of the womb. This heart-womb connection helps heal the "Madonna-Whore split" that originates from patriarchy's fundamental schism between spirit and matter. The heart-womb connection *weaves* the love and compassion of the heart (Madonna) with the power and erotic pleasure of the Yoni (Whore). This mystical blend of mother love and erotic love is called Karuna. It is the essence of Tantra.

One woman came to me saying she had closed her heart after her brother's death, but now desired to open it again. I helped her feel how the arms and hands are an energetic extension of the heart; how they have an intelligence of their own which can both express and affect the feelings of the heart. But it was not until she connected with her *womb* that she began to transform. After she danced awhile, I told her to "drop her consciousness into her womb" and let the movement originate from there. "I felt it!" she later shared. "A warm channel opened between my womb and heart. I got glimpses into a whole other world. . . . Even the word 'compassion' isn't adequate for the love I sense coming from that world!" The Dance facilitated the healing she sought. As one woman puts it, "The Dance is prayer. And the answer to the prayer."

Women often receive direct transmissions of knowledge and power from the dancer. One woman writes,

It starts with JOY spiraling up my legs and nestling in my pelvis. It ripples up my torso, a lover's touch. As JOY breathes throughout my body, the OPENING begins. My rib cage is being sprung open, peeled back like a ripe fig, my pelvis bursting forth, a red rose unfolding. Ah! Now the KNOW-ING opens the gates. *Waves of information undulate into my body.* This is not knowing like "Oh, I know about that." This is KNOWING that pushes through, *must be transmitted,* flowing out in every gesture and movement of my body, *directly from my body to those that witness it.* And we are changed. [Italics mine]

Sometimes I deliberately teach the Dance this way. A woman writes, "Working with Vajra, I find that because her body resonates so powerfully I can 'find the pathway' in the Dance in a very sensate way, by attuning to her energetic field." Another woman tells me, "You transferred the Dance from your belly to mine."

A woman may receive transmissions from a particular goddess as she dances. One dancer began to weep when she perceived the Hindu goddess Sarasvati standing in front of her, transmitting energy into her womb, heart, and third eye, unifying these power centers. All who witnessed this agreed that the room felt holy. She said this transmission helped her resolve an internal conflict between her intellectual and artistic pursuits. Significantly, Sarasvati rules both science and art and thus holds the integration of *intellectual* left-brain and *artistic* right-brain functions.

The energy circulated during the Dance stimulates creativity. One woman says the Dance has taught her "the skill of surrender," changing her relationship to her creativity from ". . . anxiously grasping at it, to opening and letting it fill and move me. . . . On a concrete level, my process as a writer-composer has been profoundly affected by this work." Another woman, after her first Tantric Dance workshop, was up into the wee hours painting in watercolors, a medium new to her. The paints were "teaching me how to use them, telling me where to place them, how much to use, how to stroke them onto the canvas." Then, still creatively "high," she shared an especially powerful and sacred sexual experience with her lover. Another woman said, "Never having had children, this is the closest thing to giving birth." On a more mundane level: "The dance changes the way I move in the world, the way I turn my head, pick up a glass, the grace in which I hold myself." After only three classes one woman's friends commented on how differently she moved.

The Dance affords opportunity to transform negative life patterns. A woman reported that her first dance initiated a profound healing process that lasted several weeks, catalyzing her to understand the dysfunctional dynamic between herself and her mother and even how this dynamic had repeated in her relationship with her first boyfriend.

The Dance is sexually healing. As we dance, we resacralize our woman bodies. We cellularly and energetically purify our physical and emotional bodies from the denigrating thought-forms and psychic invasions of sexual abuse and disrespect, which is so prevalent in our modern lives. All women in patriarchal society experience this onslaught, deriving from the modern schism between spirituality and sexuality, whether we have been overtly abused or not. Another woman describes the Dance as an ongoing spiritual practice.

> The Tantric Dance is the most life-changing thing I have done besides giving birth to my son. When I first experienced the dance I described it as my prayer. To this day, it is still my prayer, but it has also become my therapy, my expression of self, my connection, my creativity, and my place of power. Ultimately, the Dance informs everything, all aspects of my life.

As we integrate the information of Goddess studies and feminist spirituality with our body's energetic intelligence, we become Women of Power, better able to midwife the resurgence of the Divine Feminine. As we serve the Great Goddess, reclaiming and revivifying women's mysteries, we help heal the fundamental wound and ignorance of patriarchy—the illusory schism between spirit and matter, between spirituality and sexuality. Healing this fundamental schism will transform civilization.

Notes

[1] Founded by Emilie Conrad and developed with close associate Susan Harper.

[2] See Judy Grahn, *Blood, Bread and Roses: How Menstruation Created the World* (Boston: Beacon Press, 1993) and Monica Sjöö & Barbara Mor, *The Great Cosmic Mother: Rediscovering the Religion of the Earth* (San Francisco: Harper & Row, 1987).

[3] Dakinis (Sanskrit for "sky dancer") are the female enlighteners/tantric initiators of the Hindu and Buddhist pantheons.
[4] From "The Charge of the Star Goddess," which has been attributed to Doreen Valiente.
[5] This is one definition of an altered state or trance.

Works Cited

Ajit Mookerjee, Kali. 1988. *The Feminine Force.* New York: Destiny Books.
Chopra, Deepak. 1996. *Journey to the Boundless.* Audio Cassette Program, Tape One. Niles, IL: Nightingale-Conant.
Douglas, Nik. 1997. *Spiritual Secrets of Tantra from the New Age to the New Millennium.* New York: Pocket Books.
Gimbutas, Marija. 1989. *The Language of the Goddess.* San Francisco: Harper & Row.
Guinness, Alma E, editor. 1990. *ABC's of the Human Mind.* New York: The Reader's Digest Association, Inc.
Judith, Anodea. 1992. *Wheels of Life: A User's Guide to the Chakra System.* St. Paul: Llewellyn Publications.
Talbot, Michael. 1980. *Mysticism and the New Physics.* New York: Bantam Books.
———. 1991 *The Holographic Universe.* New York: HarperCollins Publishers.
Toms, Michael. 1990. "The unity of mind and body." *New Dimensions Magazine.* September-October. Pages 6–8.

ೞ 13 ೞ

Technicians of the Sacred[1]

by Layne Redmond

Eighteen years ago, I first began to learn to play the frame drum. This is a wheel-shaped drum whose diameter is greater than the depth of its shell, much like a grain sieve. The rituals of the earliest known religions evolved around the beat of this drum, in part because their rhythms helped shamans and seers attain the sacred trance state necessary for healing and prophecy. Although I began to learn to play almost on a whim, the drum was to take me on a journey that spanned thousands of years and several continents, and changed my life irrevocably.

As I studied various styles of frame drumming, I learned something of their history and began to look at images of frame drummers from the ancient Mediterranean world. I was surprised to see that almost all of them were female. Some of them clearly represented goddesses, and so I began to read the large, new body of scholarship about ancient religions stretching back to the Paleolithic.

My life became more focused as I realized I needed to know why goddesses had been associated with the frame drum and why we don't know anything about this now. I had to find out who the female drummers were, when they stopped drumming, and why. Over the next decade, my search for answers to questions like these led me to museums and temple ruins throughout the ancient Mediterranean world. The evidence showed me plainly that for a period of almost 3,000 years, the drummers were women and the barring of women's drumming from religious life was central to the disempowerment of women in Western culture.

ANCIENT RHYTHMS

Some of the earliest religions were founded on the worship of female deities—Mother Goddesses who evolved into the many goddesses of Mediterranean cultures in classical times. In every one of these that I studied, it was a goddess who transmitted to humans the gift of making music and, in some cases, the drum itself. In Sumer it was Inanna; in Egypt, Hathor; in Greece, the nine-fold goddess called the Muses. Musical, artistic, and poetic inspiration was always thought to spring from the Divine Feminine. One of the main techniques for connecting to this power of inspiration was drumming.

The drum was a sacred tool, the means our ancestors used to summon the Goddess and also the instrument through which she spoke. The drumming priestess was a technician of the sacred, an intermediary between divine and human realms. She acted as summoner and transformer, invoking divine energy and transmitting it to the community. The drum was the primary trance-inducing instrument in rites of passage, signaling the release of outmoded behavior patterns and the transition to a new status in life. Death and rebirth rituals were often symbolic reenactments of the death and resurrection myths found in many ancient mythologies. Inanna, Osiris, Persephone, Adonis, and Dionysos were among many deities recalled from the underworld to renewed life by the power of the drum. Funeral rites took their shape from these metaphorical resurrections. Throughout the Mediterranean world, the beat of a drum guided the passage of ordinary mortals through the realms of the afterlife and was believed to hasten their rebirth. In many areas, the dead were buried with figurines of female drummers.

Invoking the elemental powers of the deities, the voice of the drum called forth the cyclical rebirth of nature. Its vibrational force was believed to wake the sleeping life within the earth. Women drummers played over freshly sown seeds to quicken their ripening, and later over the burgeoning vegetation to protect and enhance its growth. The drum's association with fertility encompassed human sexuality, especially feminine sexual energy. As instigator of creation, the Goddess manifested in sexual desire and union. The drum she held identified her with the primal rhythms of life apparent in the sexual act. Sacred sexual priestesses of Inanna, Hathor,

Aphrodite, and Cybele all played the frame drum to increase the energy of sexual attraction and the powers of femininity. In menstruation and birthing rites, certain drum rhythms caused the womb to contract, aiding the flow of menstrual blood or facilitating labor in childbirth.

The forceful beat of the drum was believed to drive away evil spirits that spread confusion and disease and create a purified space where health and well-being could flourish. Priestesses drummed during the eclipse of the moon, drawing the community together and protecting both it and the moon from the dangers hidden in the threatening darkness.

The rhythms of the drum evoked the rhythmic web from which human, plant, and animal life evolved. Human communities survived by understanding the natural rhythms of their environment. The daily cycles of the sun initiated the primary rhythms of activity and rest. Its seasonal cycles governed growth and decay. The need to predict rhythmic patterns—the ebb and flow of tides, the growth and fruiting of plants, the migration and mating patterns of animals—gave rise to the earliest time-keeping systems. Sacred drumming probably began as an echo of the human pulse. The pulse of our mother's blood was our first continuous experience as we quickened in the womb. Our physical being formed in response to the rhythms of her body. No other sensation is so basic. The beat of the priestesses' frame drums articulated this process of creation, bonding the individual with the rhythms of the community, the environment, and the cosmos.

THE RHYTHMS OF SCIENCE

Scientific research from astrophysics to biology tends to support the idea that rhythm is a fundamental force. One of our most popular origin myths is the Big Bang theory of modern astrophysics. According to this theory, all the material of the universe was once compacted into a hot, dense ball. About 15 to 20 billion years ago, there was a tremendous explosion. The shock waves of this primordial sound flung matter across space, where it eventually coalesced into the galaxies, solar systems, and individual planets. Scientists still have no better way to describe this moment than as the "instant the universe was born."

A related concept in physics today is the Superstring Theory, which uses the metaphor of loops of vibrating strings made up of subatomic particles. The frequency at which these strings vibrate and the rhythmic patterns generated by their interplay determine how they manifest. The idea that the universe is in essence a symphony of vibrations emanating out of an enormous first beat suggests the science of music, and many scientists use musical analogies to describe their theories. Princeton physicist Edward Witten says, "In the case of the superstring, the different harmonics correspond to different elementary particles—electron, graviton, proton, neutrino and all the others, are different harmonics of a fundamental string, just as the different overtones of a violin string are different harmonics of one string" (in Davies and Brown 1988:93).

Experiments performed by Hans Jenny, founder of cymatics, the study of waveforms, lends support to the theory that vibrations give form to the material world. Jenny found that when sound waves were introduced to various material substances—water, alcohol, pastes, oils, and so forth—they created symmetrical patterns with uniform characteristics (Jenny 1974). Put very simply, Jenny's research shows that rhythm shapes matter.

To approach creation from another perspective, let's move from astrophysics to biology, from the birth of the cosmos to the birth of a single human being. It is often said that the first sound we hear in the womb is our mother's heartbeat. Actually, the first sound to vibrate our newly developed hearing apparatus is the pulse of our mother's blood through her veins and arteries. We vibrate to that primordial rhythm even before we have ears to hear. Before we were conceived, we existed in part as an egg in our mother's ovary. All the eggs a woman will ever carry form in her ovaries while she is a four-month-old fetus in the womb of *her* mother. This means our cellular life as an egg begins in the womb of our grandmother. Each of us spent five months in our grandmother's womb and she, in turn, formed within the womb of her grandmother. We vibrate to the rhythms of our mother's blood before she herself is born. And this pulse is the thread of blood that runs all the way back through the grandmothers to the first mother.

As a tiny, pulsing egg we experienced the birth of our mother, the growth of her body, her joys, her fears, her triumphs. For years, sometimes decades, we rocked as an egg to the rhythms of her body.

Men cannot convey this continuity of cellular energy to their sperm. The father imparts not the imprint of a lifetime but only the fleeting energy of a few weeks. Man's nature is in many metaphorical ways a quick rise and fall—the vanishing and resurrecting energy reflected in so many of the ancient male gods.

Our auditory nerve begins to pick up vibrations from our environment about six months after conception. We begin to synchronize our movements not only to physical sounds but to the rhythms of voices, the vibrations of thoughts. Our mother's emotions create complex chemical interactions in her body, and their particular energies permeate the womb. Her dream cycles affect our sleep patterns. By the time we are born, we are already imprinted with the rhythms of the language, emotions, feelings, and interactions around us. These rhythms will always seem the most familiar and natural to us no matter how beneficial or detrimental they actually are.

THE SCIENCE OF RHYTHMS

Consciousness itself is rhythmic and can be detected as brain waves— rhythmic vibrations emanating from the brain and nervous system. All through our lives, our state of consciousness is governed by the rate of these vibrations. Using electroencephalographs, scientists can measure the number of energy waves per second pulsing through the brain. They have developed a system of classification differentiating states of consciousness.

As you read these words your brain is probably vibrating between 14 and 21 cycles per second. These are called beta waves and dominate in most humans past puberty. This state of awareness is associated with active, waking attention, focused on everyday external activities. Beta waves are also in evidence during states of anxiety, tension, and fear. Alpha waves vibrate at 7 to 14 waves per second. They indicate a relaxed internal focus and a sense of well-being. Theta waves vibrate at about 4 to 7 cycles per second and indicate the drowsy, semiconscious state usually experienced at the threshold of sleep. The slowest frequency, from 1 to 4 cycles per second, is the delta level, the state of unconsciousness or deep sleep.

Neurological studies indicate that the brain is divided into two hemispheres that share control of mental activity. In very young children these develop as one, but at about five years of age each hemisphere begins to specialize. The right brain functions as the creative center. It is the seat of visual, aural, and emotional memory, and processes information in holistic, intuitive terms, relying on pattern recognition. The left brain is the administrator, what we sometimes call the rational mind. It proceeds in logical, analytical, verbal, and sequential fashion. Incoming information is identified, classified, and explained. If one hemisphere is damaged, the other one is able, within limits, to take over its functions. Normally, though, the memories, mental associations, ideas, and processes of each hemisphere are inaccessible to the other. In ordinary consciousness, either the left or the right brain dominates in cycles. We shift from one side to the other depending on which skills we require.

Not only do the two hemispheres of our brains operate in different modes, they also usually operate in different rhythms (Johari 1987). The right brain may be generating alpha waves while the left brain is in a beta state. Or both hemispheres can also be generating the same type of brain waves, but remain out of sync with each other. But in states of intense creativity, deep meditation, or under the influence of rhythmic sound, both hemispheres may begin operating in the same synchronized rhythm. This state of unified whole brain functioning is called hemispheric synchronization.

As the rhythms of the two hemispheres synchronize, there is a sense of clarity and heightened awareness. Feelings of self-consciousness and separation fall away. The individual is able to draw on both the left and the right hemispheres simultaneously. Hemispheric synchronization on the alpha level can create feelings of euphoria, expanded mental powers, and intense creativity. This may be the neurological basis of higher states of consciousness.

Many ancient religious practices seem to have originated in attempts to induce the transcendent experience of hemispheric synchronization. Chanting rhythmically while gazing at geometric figures like mandalas facilitates synchronization by simultaneously engaging the verbal skills of one hemisphere and the visual skills of the other. Because each hemisphere controls the motor skills of one-half of the body, rhythmic movement can also affect synchronization. Rhythmic dancing, accompanied by music and chanting, was an integral part of the pre-Christian religious experience, often bringing the dancer into a trance-like state of ecstasy.

Drumming is perhaps the most effective way to induce brain-wave synchronization. Musical comprehension has been found to be a joint function of left and right hemispheres. Andrew Neher conducted a series of well-known experiments showing that the rhythms of the drum act as an auditory driving mechanism. They could drive or entrain the subject's brain waves into alpha or theta patterns (Neher 1962). This ability of one rhythm to draw another into harmonic resonance with it is called entrainment, and has been called one of the great organizing principles of the world, as inescapable as gravity (in Chapple 1970).

Major events like birth, marriage, pregnancy, illness, separation, or death are stressful partly because they break familiar rhythms. People who are experiencing grief or depression seem to be painfully unable to create and maintain organized patterns of behavior. They have lost their personal rhythm. The need to replace broken rhythms often drives people unconsciously to try to recreate lost relationships.

In archaic communities, the shaman used the drum to entrain the consciousness of initiates with the divine rhythms of the earth. Hindu philosophy and science are based on the concept that vibration manifesting on the physical plane as sound creates the physical universe. Practitioners of Nada Yoga use the entraining capacities of music to align their minds with what they believe is the *unstruck sound* that vibrates the world into existence. In some ancient religions, oracular priestesses, temple priestesses, and maenads were skilled at drawing from the skin head of the drum rhythms that entrained the minds of worshippers, moving them inexorably toward a state of ecstatic union with the Divine. Drumming was a necessary and respected skill among these holy women. People knew then, as modern science is finally realizing today, that life is inexorably rhythmic. It drives the planets in their orbits and the fetus in its growth. Rhythm prompts the cycle of the earth as well as the cycles of our emotions.

OUT OF RHYTHM

Nevertheless, this hard-won knowledge seems to have little practical effect on our contemporary culture. It's becoming apparent that some of our major physiological and psychological ills may be a result of being out of sync with environmental time. Anthropologist Edward T. Hall argues that it is the tension between the internal clocks and the clock on the wall that causes so much of the stress in today's world. "We have now constructed an entire complex system of schedules, manners, and expectations to which we are trying to adjust ourselves, when, in reality, it should be the other way around" (Hall 1984:176).

Nestled between the hemispheres of the brain, in a spot directly behind the center of the forehead that mystics call the third eye, is a small organ called the pineal gland. Although its function was once a matter of scientific dispute, today we know that it is a kind of biological clock. The sun and, to a lesser extent, the moon pour energy into the biological environment in the form of light and affect our bodily rhythms through our nervous systems. Light enters our eyes and activates the pineal gland, which then transmits messages in the form of hormones to the body's master gland, the pituitary. The pituitary responds by releasing chemicals that affect all organ systems. Thus, the pineal gland is the jewel in our biological clockworks, keeping us in sync with environmental time and influencing the physiological and emotional rhythms of the body. The 24-hour solar cycle, called the circadian rhythm, appears to be the most basic of the natural cycles which affects us.

But by shutting ourselves off within our steel, concrete, and glass prisons, insulated from rhythmic fluctuations in light and temperature, we block ourselves off from seasonally appropriate changes in physiology and behavior. We run the risk of damaging our biological cycles. Laboratory experiments in which human beings are isolated from environmental energies produce symptoms of lethargy, fatigue, irritability, and boredom. The physical costs may be even more deadly. Some research suggests that our biological clocks affect the functioning of every cell in our bodies, and cancerous cells may be cells that have lost this vital rhythmic regulation (Chapple 1970).

In ancient cultures, the tempo of human life was synchronized with the rhythms of the earth. The priestess's frame drum was the thread that led back through countless millennia to that first beat that vibrated the world into being. People understood life as rhythm and woman's body as a reflection of that primordial truth. The readily observable correspondence between menstrual and lunar cycles would have made women particularly sensitive to their intimate connection with the natural, and may have been the basis for the earliest calendars.

Because of its easily visible cycles, the lunar calendar was used by ancient Mediterranean cultures, with the new moon heralding the start of a new month. As civilizations became larger and more complex, lunar time began to cause problems for the growing bureaucracies. First, the length of the lunar cycle is not constant. Second, the actual time of the rising of the new moon varied depending on the longitude and latitude of the observer. As early as 2500 B.C.E., the bureaucrats of Sumer came up with a new calendar in order to regulate tax collection. This change from calendars based on nature to calendars designed to serve the purposes of those in power was one of the earliest rejections of the truth of direct experience.

The ancients studied the stars and the earth with humility, motivated by a sense of awe and a desire to participate as fully as possible in the rhythms of the universe. Our division between objective and subjective truths—science and religion—didn't exist for them. Contemporary science, with its left-brain analytical bias, is skeptical of anything that smacks of the intuitive or the mystical. The only experiences worthy of its interest are those that can be measured or expressed as formulas.

Many modern scientific advances have greatly improved the lot of humankind, but when science attempts to define the nature of reality using only what are called objective criteria, it denies the validity of the sacred. Its scientists are the new priesthood; they minister to a religion devoid of the Divine. Judaism, Christianity, and Islam have stripped divinity of feminine qualities; science goes one step further, canceling the concept of divinity entirely. Religious experience is subjective; it is not rational. Therefore, it cannot be validated scientifically. In this new religion, nothing is sacred but the dry truths of statistics and objective rather than experienced truth. But those who separate themselves from the natural world in order to make a study of it lose the vital connection that makes sense of the whole. They have forgotten that consciousness itself is subjective. When a human being subtracts herself from the equation of the universe, her results are doomed to be incomplete and out of rhythm.

We need to find effective ways of reconnecting with the rhythms of our environment, our bodies, and our deepest selves. For a growing number of women, drumming is once again becoming a sacred technology capable of restoring those patterns.

RECLAIMING OUR RHYTHMS

In the late 1980s, I began speaking about the frame drum's incredible history after my performances. The response was overwhelming. After each concert, women would approach me to ask if I would teach them to drum. Although most of them had never seen a frame drum before, they felt an overwhelming urge to learn its rhythms. I soon found myself conducting five classes a week, teaching more than 50 women. The majority of them had never played any musical instrument before, but they shared a conviction that drumming could lead them back to something essential within themselves. As one student expressed it, "When I heard you play, I realized I was thirsty for something I didn't even know existed." Another woman said, "It took me back into my mother, into her womb, where I floated to the beat of the drum."

I discovered I had a knack for teaching people who weren't musicians. Professional musicians spend hours alone in a room with their instrument, doing the same things over and over again. I found a way to teach non-musicians how to practice the same strokes and rhythms repeatedly without becoming bored. I taught them to listen deeply and with concentration by synchronizing their breathing and walking to the rhythms they were playing.

Teaching women to play, I felt I was really listened to for the first time in my life. I was honored for who I was and what I had accomplished. Throughout my life, I have been searching for something I felt was missing. I practiced Yoga, studied Tibetan Buddhism and the Japanese Tea Ceremony with traditional teachers from those cultures. I studied Ericksonian hypnosis and the early teachings of Gnostic Christianity. As a multimedia artist, I explored mythological iconography. I studied drumming with both contemporary master drummers in the West and traditional teachers from the Middle East and Brazil. My teaching women to drum provided a context for all of these practices to coalesce into something that specifically addressed my needs as an American woman of the late twentieth century. I began the process of reclaiming the authority of my own rhythm.

With my students I formed a group called the Mob of Angels. We set out to revive the ancient Mediterranean tradition of women's ceremonial drumming. Although I have studied and listened to many contemporary traditions of frame drumming, I neither copied those traditions nor tried to recreate what I thought women might have played. My aim was and is always to create a contemporary new music that is non-traditional but pulses with the rhythms of an archaic language. The music in turn inspires rituals that celebrate the feminine.

Drawing on images from Paleolithic times to the present, we studied and absorbed the goddesses, priestesses, and laywomen who played the frame drum (for these stories, see Redmond 1997). We grounded ourselves in the energy of the earth and focused on the relationship of the different strokes to the elements of air, fire, water, and earth. We learned the ancient technology for synchronizing our minds and bodies to gain access to other levels of awareness. Our goal was to release the primordial archetype of feminine energy. This allowed our primal mind to emerge, whispering of the eternally flowing presence of the Divine Feminine—the raw force of nature, the Earth herself.

The rituals the Mob and I created almost always included processions of drummers. Ancient processions toward a shrine or holy place mirrored the archetypal journey to the center of the self. In our rituals, the audience often entered between two lines of tambourine players, while sage, cedar, and frankincense—ancient purifiers—smoked in censors. Though the Mob's ritual practices seemed to be developing naturally out of our drumming, my research into the history of Goddess worship turned up astonishing parallels, like the images of processions of drumming priestesses parading across the walls in Hathor's temple at Dendera, Egypt.

We did our public rituals at seasonally important times of the year, such as the summer and winter solstices and the spring and fall equinoxes. We also gave some traditional American holidays a new focus. On Mother's Day, we acknowledged and honored the ancient Great Mother as well as our own mothers. On Valentine's Day, in recognition of the sacredness of sexuality, we read the sexually joyful texts of "The Courtship of Inanna and Dumuzi" from ancient Sumer. Halloween became our Day of the Dead, a ritual remembrance of those loved ones who have died and a reminder of the cyclical nature of life and death.

Our Rattlesnake Ritual used the ancient archetype of the snake, a symbol associated with the Goddess in most ancient cultures. The music I composed for it invokes the rattlesnake, who rises up and, with a great rattle, warns that any intruder who violates her space is at great peril. The snake symbolizes the transformational energy of the earth. The shedding of skin is a beautiful act, a purification and cleansing. It is a necessary stage in the passage to a new self. It also can be painful and frightening. The snake constantly sheds her skin. Her message is that we, too, must constantly shed our old skin, even though it is familiar, and stand naked and exposed to accept whatever our lives offer next. The ritual celebrated the shedding of outgrown selves, of outmoded and dysfunctional family and social structures, and of outworn religious thinking that devalues women.

These rituals are also an opportunity for those of us who have been studying the frame drum to explore the reality of trance-revelation. Continuous drumming and dancing expands the parameters of our habitual mind-sets, releasing the experience of undistracted awareness. It's as if a gateway, an "in-trance-way" between the conscious and unconscious minds was gradually and imperceptibly opening. Across this threshold flow new visions and heightened creativity. The rhythms of our drums have the power to draw listeners away from the constraints of clock time back to the cyclical time of mythology. There, habitual patterns of thought are revealed for what they are and begin melting away. Blocks of information surface in the form of powerful archetypes. Drummers and dancers are fused in a place beyond conceptualization and conditioned patterns of behavior, entrained in a deeper awareness.

Recently I have created an intensive frame drum and ritual retreat for women drummers called Giving Birth to Ourselves. In these retreats we explore the history of the drum's use in initiations, blood mysteries, purifications, and ritual death-and-rebirth ceremonies. Participants have already studied the frame drum prior to the retreat, and we are able to create very powerful rituals. The retreat climaxes with each participant's symbolic death and release of her past life. We found that the sure knowledge that we will die can be a source of strength. It is like a wind that burns one clean. Everything pales in the face of our death. Our misunderstandings and confusions seem trivial. Habitual worries and anxieties evaporate, leaving each of us energized and inspired to proceed with the precious time we do have left to live. We feel that we understand the rites of the ancient mystery schools, in which each initiate became the Mother of God, giving birth to the divinity within themselves. Often after these retreats the women go on to make major changes in their lives.

THE EARTH AS GODDESS

If there was a fall from grace, it was a fall out of rhythm. The order of the universe is rhythmic, and we have a psychic and physiological need to be in sync with the Earth's cycles. By divorcing ourselves from the natural world, we are doing violence to ourselves and to the planet. I am convinced that the role of women's sacred drumming in the past served to heal and transform, and to place the self and the community in the context of nature. The frame drum has historically been a vehicle for expressing female energy, and I remain dedicated to helping women rediscover that heritage and become whole. Ritual drumming enables women to reclaim our ancient role as transmitters of the sacred. It returns us to who we were before we learned the patterns of self-destruction. This is why I believe that the ancient path of the Goddess is still valid—in fact, essential—today. Women need the archetypal image of a Divine Female. We need to reconnect with the inherent sacredness of woman as creator and nourisher, rather than accept a vision of ourselves as less-than-divine inferiors. Women need to reconnect with the archetype of feminine energy—the raw force of nature, the earth herself, so that, freed from suffocating bondage to violent gods, she may once again be remembered and revered as the power of birth, life, death, and resurrection. As we do this, ancient emotions, thoughts, and revelations pour across the barriers of time, and forgotten rites of celebration, healing, and purification can be remembered.

As much as we need feminine energy to right the balance of our culture, I know that the divine energy behind creation cannot be contained in any human-made image or mental concept. Ultimate reality—the force within the atoms of earth, air, water, and fire, the force that pulses through our veins—is far beyond the attributes we ascribe to femaleness or maleness. I teach women how to connect with that pulse through the frame drum, how to tap into the rhythms of being. We remember who we were and see what we can become, as we explore ways to give divinity fuller expression.

Notes

[1] This chapter has been adapted from the book *When the Drummers Were Women: A Spiritual History of Rhythm*, by Layne Redmond (NY: Three Rivers Press, 1997).

Works Cited

Chapple, Eliot D. 1970. *Culture and Biological Man*. NY: Holt, Rinehart & Winston.

Davies, P.C.W., and J. Brown. 1988 *Superstrings: A Theory of Everything?* Cambridge: Cambridge University Press.

Hall, Edward T. 1984. *The Dance of Life: The Other Dimensions of Time*. NY: Anchor Books.

Jenny, Hans. 1974. *Cymatics*. Basil, Switzerland: Basilius Presse AG.

Johari. Harish. 1987. *Chakras: Energy Centers of Transformation*. Rochester, VT: Destiny Books.

Neher, Andrew. 1962. A physiological explanation of unusual behavior in ceremonies involving drums. *Human Biology* 34. Pages 151–60.

Redmond, Layne. 1997. *When the Drummers Were Women: A Spiritual History of Rhythm*. New York: Three Rivers Press.

ᴔᴔ Index ᴔᴔ